B+ 4.76

D1094362

DECADE OF FEAR

SENATOR THOMAS C. HENNINGS, JR.

DECADE

OF

FEAR

SENATOR HENNINGS
AND CIVIL LIBERTIES

BY

Donald J. Kemper

UNIVERSITY OF MISSOURI PRESS

COLUMBIA • MISSOURI

Acknowledgments

THE AUTHOR wishes to express his gratitude to the many persons whose help made the preparation of this manuscript both possible and pleasant. The Most Reverend Joseph M. Marling, the Bishop of Jefferson City Diocese and the author's superior, provided the opportunity for research and composition; Mrs. Thomas C. Hennings, Jr., widow of Senator Hennings, kindly consented to open her husband's papers in the interest of scholarship; Professor James L. Bugg, Jr., Dean of Faculty, University of Missouri at St. Louis, suggested the topic initially and guided its development; Professors Richard S. Kirkendall, Frederick C. Spiegel, Lewis E. Atherton, and Walter V. Scholes counseled and encouraged the author both by word and example; relatives and former associates of Senator Hennings graciously gave their time for interviews.

A special note of thanks is due to Mrs. Nancy Prewitt, Director of the Western Historical Manuscripts Collection at the University of Missouri, Mrs. Leon T. Dickinson, and Mrs. Shirley Meyer, whose assistance in the painstaking task of research and typing was invaluable.

D. J. K.

Columbia, Missouri
April, 1965

v

Contents

Introduction

Every DEMOCRATIC GOVERNMENT must continually cope with the problem of balancing freedom and order in its national life. Individual citizens demand liberty to think, act, and communicate with their fellows, yet they wish this liberty to prevail under orderly conditions. Their government undertakes to provide these orderly conditions, but in doing so must at times limit the freedom of individual citizens to act and to communicate their thoughts to other citizens.

This continuing problem of providing the conditions for both order and freedom becomes more acute when complicated by an international crisis that threatens not only the national order but the nation's very existence. Open warfare creates the problem of calculating the extent to which individual freedom must be limited in the interests of national security. Open warfare is temporary, however, and the limitations it imposes on freedom are transitory and terminate with the cessation of hostilities. It is otherwise during an international crisis, aptly termed a "cold war," whose end is discernible only with difficulty, if at all. Indeed, in the modern nuclear world, characterized by the continuing political hostility between communism and democracy, cold war is endemic, and the tension between order and freedom becomes a constant problem for a democratic government.

The persisting cold war underlay the conflicts between the

demands of order and of freedom that recurred during the 1950's. In this decade, which coincided with the senatorial career of Thomas C. Hennings, Jr., the late Senator Joseph R. McCarthy of Wisconsin reached the peak of his power, encountered the censure of his colleagues, and passed from the national scene. In the same period, congressional investigations of Communist activity in the United States reached their zenith and, also, declined. In the middle years of the decade the loyalty-security programs of the executive branch of the government expanded to record scope and contracted to something less than that. Finally, during the latter half of the decade, the Supreme Court of the United States came under severe attack for overturning loyalty-security procedures that it judged were in conflict with the demands of individual freedom, and the attack called forth a spirited defense.

In the midst of such conflicts, American statesmen differed basically over the relative importance they attached to order or to freedom. Generally speaking, those who tended to emphasize order were labeled conservatives; those who ranked freedom in the first place were labeled liberals. Senator Hennings was in this sense a liberal, yet he rationalized his position with an appeal to order, asserting that unless a wide range of freedom to think and act were allowed Americans, national order and security would perish.

But the conservative-liberal or order-freedom dichotomies leave untouched much of the story of the 1950's. A third element, frequently the crux of the problem and often the decisive factor, entered these conflicts. Most often labeled justice or fairness, it embraced such values as the right of an individual to seek employment on his merits and his right to an unsullied reputation. Concern for justice is not identical with the values of the liberal, though it is, usually, one of them. It antedates the rationale of democratic government and individual freedoms. It is the simple, ethical value of decency to which generous men are spontaneously attached. One can prefer order to freedom, yet favor justice over either; on the other hand, there are professed liberals who violate justice in their dealings with their opponents. The genius of Thomas Hennings lay in his fundamental attachment to justice, his constant emphasis on the widest limits for individual freedom, and withal his realistic approach to the need for order in American society. For the most part, he fulfilled the definition of a civil libertarian as given by Charles Slayman, chief counsel and staff director of the Hennings Subcommittee on Constitutional Rights:

[One who believes] that organized society should punish an individual for overt acts only, [that it] owes the highest standards of civilized conduct in its operations against an individual whether he is guilty or innocent of any wrongdoing, [and that it] should not interfere with, or inquire into, his religious or political beliefs, his associations with other human beings, or the books and other papers he wants to read.

In a time when emotion was overruling reason in the nation's Senate, Hennings was able to remain sufficiently pragmatic and undoctrinaire to examine each situation individually and to attend wholly to the demands of justice, freedom, and order. Because of the sustained objectivity he brought to public questions, his influence was felt widely in the United States throughout a decade of controversies over civil liberties; a study of his career in the Senate can provide important insights into the nature and significance of these controversies.

The limits of this study preclude more than passing consideration of other significant aspects of Hennings' public life, even of his important contributions to the advancement of civil rights and racial equality. Although the phrase "civil rights" at times has been taken to include "civil liberties," in this work it seems preferable, for the sake of clarity, to restrict it to "equality among citizens." "Civil liberties," then, will refer only to an individual's right to freedom and justice as guaranteed by the Bill of Rights. Since Hennings made no significant contribution to the cause of civil liberties prior to his service in the Senate, this work will focus on Hennings the senator.

I

Thomas Carey Hennings, Jr.

THE DAY AFTER he defeated Forrest C. Donnell in the 1950 general election, Senator-elect Thomas C. Hennings, Jr., held a press conference in his St. Louis home. Inevitably, the newsmen questioned the forty-seven-year-old lawyer about the vigorous criticism he had directed during the campaign toward the controversial senator from Wisconsin, Joseph R. McCarthy, and toward McCarthy's anti-Communist crusade. Hennings responded that he felt no hesitation in condemning McCarthyism: "It is automatic with me to be in sympathy with the rights of the individual."[1]

According to Senator Hennings' own estimate, the single most influential source of his sympathy for the rights of the individual was his father, Judge Thomas C. Hennings, Sr., an eminent lawyer and for six years a judge of the circuit court in St. Louis. Judge Hennings, who outlived his famous son by nearly two years, enjoyed a distinguished career that extended from the beginning of the twentieth century to his death in 1962. Born in St. Louis on September 11, 1874, he received his law degree from Washington University and was admitted to the bar of his native state in 1899. Soon after entering private practice, he joined the Jefferson Club, a reform group of the Democratic party in St. Louis. Initially established by Senator Harry B. Hawes in 1892 to oppose bossism in the city's regular Democratic organization, the Jefferson Club

---

[1] John R. Hahn, *St. Louis Globe-Democrat*, March 15, 1956.

1

reached the height of its power at the turn of the century and then gradually declined. The young lawyer entered the 1912 primary as a candidate for judge in Missouri's Eighth Circuit Court, which embraced the city of St. Louis. After success in the primary, he won a six-year term in the general election and began his career as a trial judge at the relatively early age of thirty-eight.[2]

Judge Hennings declined to run for re-election in 1918; instead, he embarked on a second career by joining the Mercantile Commerce Trust Company of St. Louis, and he thus became a pioneer in the legal phase of the rising trust business. During the next twenty years he built a national reputation as an authority on trusts, which he once eulogized as "the greatest father in the world." On his resignation in 1939 from an active role in the bank, Hennings entered private practice with a prominent St. Louis law firm, which then became Hennings, Green, Henry and Hennings. Although the partnership was dissolved a year later, when the younger Hennings was elected circuit attorney in St. Louis, Judge Hennings continued in private practice until his death.[3]

A variety of legal and civic activities spiced the long career of the elder Hennings. In the mid-1920's he headed a survey made by the Missouri Association for Criminal Justice, of which he was a founder. From the results of this survey, the association urged reform in the state's criminal procedure in order to reduce Missouri's rising crime rate. In Missouri's 1943–1944 constitutional convention, Judge Hennings played an active role within a small coterie of elderly delegates who, surprisingly, supplied the convention's progressive and enlightened leadership. In addi-

[2] Hennings Papers, Box 48, letter from Hennings to Richard Cohen, January 17, 1957. Thomas C. Hennings, Sr., Papers, autobiographical account, July 2, 1940, Missouri Historical Society, St. Louis. *Who's Who in America,* 21, 1226. John W. Leonard, ed., *The Book of St. Louisans,* 272. On the Jefferson Club: William Hyde and Howard L. Conard, *Encyclopedia of the History of St. Louis,* 1123; *The Mirror,* 10 (February 7, 1901), 4 ff.; Louis G. Geiger, *Joseph W. Folk of Missouri,* 14 ff. *Official Manual of the State of Missouri, 1913–1914,* 738, 1126. Thomas C. Hennings, Sr., died on April 9, 1962.

[3] On Hennings' career in the trust business: Gilbert T. Stephenson, "The Story of a Trust Man," *Trusts and Estates,* 68 (April, 1939), 459. On Hennings' reference to trusts: Thomas C. Hennings, Sr., "The Greatest Father in the World," *Trust Companies,* 53 (October, 1924), 449.

tion to his public activities, he maintained a constant interest in private groups that grappled with the problem of juvenile delinquency, especially the Big Brothers organization.[4]

Although the younger Hennings felt no direct pressure from his father in choosing a career, the Judge's pattern of law and politics—but not the banking—reappeared in his handsome and talented son. Born in St. Louis on June 25, 1903, Thomas Carey Hennings, Jr., had a sister two years younger than he and no brothers. As an only son he felt the full force of his father's influence, an impact that was heightened by the unusually close association of the intelligent youngster with the vigorous and strong-willed father whose own intellectual qualities had enabled him to move easily from the bench to the countinghouse. A suggestion of the direction of that influence appeared in the Senator's recollection that throughout his boyhood replicas of the Magna Carta and the Bill of Rights hung on the wall of his room, indicating the Judge's regard for individual liberty and his desire to inspire this same spirit in his gifted son. The elder Hennings' penchant for politics also touched the youngster. Through his father's intercession, the future senator was introduced to political life when, as a youth of thirteen, he served as a page during the convention of the Democratic party, at St. Louis, that nominated Woodrow Wilson.[5]

But in these early years neither the Bill of Rights nor politics dominated the activities of Tom Hennings. No musty relics of American history or party politics, but the cinder path of the stadium attracted Hennings in high school, college, and even in law school. At Soldan High School in St. Louis he developed his abilities for distance running more effectively than his grade point. This interest in track directed him to Cornell University, where

[4] Missouri Association for Criminal Justice, *The Missouri Crime Survey,* 7 ff. Henry J. Schmandt, "The Personnel of the 1943–1944 Missouri Constitutional Convention," *Missouri Historical Review,* 45 (April, 1951), 235 ff. *St. Louis Globe-Democrat,* August 16, 1959.

[5] Judge Hennings Papers, autobiographical account, July 2, 1940. Hennings Papers, Box 3, Speech to the National Society of Magna Charta Dames, April 19, 1951; Box 1, biographical sketch in 1950 campaign. *St. Louis Globe-Democrat,* March 2 and April 14, 1927, and April 13, 1928; *St. Louis Post-Dispatch,* April 12, 1927.

his favorite coach taught him the fine points of the 440-yard dash and the demanding mile run. Despite his below-average grades at Cornell, Hennings decided to make the law his profession, and he combined his first year of law with the final year of the Bachelor of Arts program. Athletics continued as an interest, however, for in addition to doubling as an instructor in English, he coached the track team at Washington University in St. Louis while completing his last three years of law.[6]

As soon as he received his law degree and passed the examinations for the Missouri bar, Hennings obtained his first taste of practical politics by engaging in the senatorial campaign of Missouri Democrat Harry B. Hawes and by participating in a revival of the defunct Jefferson Club. Re-established in 1927 by Hennings and a small group of friends brought together by Hawes, the new Jefferson Club was organized differently from its predecessor. While the original organization began as a reform movement made up of "young men of some intellectual aspiration and social position," its 1927 version had no such pretensions. Essentially, it was a group of young Democrats who were eager to assist the City Committee in electing all Democratic candidates but who promised explicitly to remain aloof from the primary struggles. Characteristic also of the new Jefferson Club was a noticeable devotion, on the surface at least, to the philosophy of the group's patron, as interpreted in the writings of Claude Bowers.[7]

After serving two years as the first treasurer of the revived Jefferson Club, Hennings was appointed assistant circuit attorney and assigned to prosecuting felony cases in the circuit court of St. Louis. In the next six years, from 1928 to 1934, Hennings established an enviable record as a vigorous and talented prosecutor in a large city well supplied with equally talented criminals. Because of the city's peculiar position outside any of the state's counties, the circuit attorney and his assistants served as state prosecutors. Undertaking his share of the burden, Hennings prosecuted, during his term, nearly a third of the felony cases—2,548

[6] Interview with Mrs. Thomas C. Hennings, Sr., June, 1963.

[7] On the later Jefferson Club: *St. Louis Globe-Democrat,* March 2 and April 14, 1927, and April 13, 1928. On the earlier Jefferson Club: *The Mirror, op. cit.* For Bowers' viewpoint, compare the speeches reported in these newspapers with Claude G. Bowers, *Jefferson and Hamilton: The Struggle for Democracy in America.*

in all—and won convictions in 2,340. As a result of this experience and of his close contact with Circuit Attorney Franklin Miller, who took a fatherly interest in his assistant's career, the youthful attorney gained an intimate understanding of criminal law. He also earned the favor of the Democratic party for his next step forward in public life, to the United States Congress.[8]

In 1934 Hennings ran unopposed in the Democratic primary as nominee for Missouri's newly created Eleventh Congressional District. His Republican opponent in the general election, Leonidas C. Dyer, had served for twenty-two years as representative of the old Twelfth District, which embraced a large part of central St. Louis now included in the new Eleventh District. Relying on the attractive platform of the New Deal for all and civil rights for the district's large Negro population, Hennings won an easy victory over Dyer, and he now traveled east for his first taste of life in the nation's capital.[9]

Once established in Washington, the handsome and debonair congressman set about fulfilling his campaign promises by supporting the Administration's recovery program and by actively serving the interests of his Negro constituents. He voted with New Dealers on most economic issues and promoted equality for Negroes by appointing members of that race to his staff, by introducing civil rights legislation, and by encouraging the Administration to advance equality for Negroes in Missouri through its relief and recovery programs. Hennings won re-election in 1936 and again in 1938 simply by pointing to his own voting record and the Roosevelt Administration's accomplishments in domestic legislation.[10]

[8] On crime in St. Louis: *The Missouri Crime Survey*. On Hennings' record as Assistant Circuit Attorney: *St. Louis Globe-Democrat*, October 23, 1934.

[9] *St. Louis Post-Dispatch*, April 12, 1934. *Official Manual of the State of Missouri, 1933–1934*. Hennings had 59,119 votes to Dyer's 44,693.

[10] On Hennings' New Deal voting record: Hennings Papers, Box 9, congressional voting record, January 3, 1935, to January 3, 1941. For his civil rights record: *St. Louis American*, October 8, 1936; *St. Louis Argus*, October 28, 1938; St. Louis *Call*, September 13, 1940. On Hennings' 1936 campaign: Hennings Papers, Box 20, Speech at Sokol Hall, October 17, 1936; Speech to Affiliated Democratic Clubs, 1936; Speech to Fifth Ward, August 3, 1936. On his 1938 campaign: *St. Louis Star-Times*, August 12, 1938; *St. Louis Argus*, October 28, 1938; *St. Louis Globe-Democrat*, November 2, 1938.

Only in the closing days of his final term in the House did Hennings express concern for individual rights. Beginning on June 6, 1940, he spoke on three occasions in defense of the freedom of thought and expression guaranteed by the First Amendment and now threatened, he believed, by the widespread fear generated by Nazi aggression. Prior to 1940, he had ignored several opportunities for professing his faith in civil liberties when the issue confronted him in the House.[11]

One of the earliest controversies over individual rights during Hennings' congressional career concerned a "red rider" the House attached to its 1935 appropriation for the District of Columbia. According to this provision, no part of the funds appropriated for the District's public schools could be paid to persons professing Communist views. The following year liberals in the House attempted to repeal the red rider, but not until 1937 were they successful. To the debates that arose in each of these three years, Hennings contributed nothing, though he sided with the majority that eventually voted for repeal in 1937.[12]

A second measure bearing on civil liberties that arose during Hennings' congressional career was the Alien Registration Act of 1940, better known as the Smith Act. Introduced by Representative Howard W. Smith of Virginia in March of 1939, the bill aimed primarily at preventing subversive activities by aliens. One section of the act, however, referred to citizens; it prohibited them from teaching or advocating the overthrow of the government by force and from conspiring or organizing for such teaching or advocacy. Hennings offered no objections to the bill and was absent in July of 1939 when the House, after rejecting a motion to return the measure to committee, passed it. Later, when he was serving in the Senate, Hennings condemned this same provision of the Smith Act as a violation of the First Amendment's guarantee of freedom of speech.[13]

[11] *St. Louis Globe-Democrat,* June 5, 1940.
[12] U. S., *Congressional Record,* 74th Cong., 1st Sess., 1935, 79, Part 8, 8808; 75th Cong., 1st Sess., 1937, 81, Part 1, 1002; August Raymond Ogden, *The Dies Committee,* 39–40.
[13] This provision of the Smith Act had a very confusing origin, which is described in: *Congressional Record,* 76th Cong., 1st Sess., 1939, 84, Part 10, 10451–52. For its passage in the House, see: *ibid.,* 10455–56. For an analysis and critique of all provisions of the Smith Act: Zechariah Chafee, Jr., *Free Speech in the United States,* 439 ff.

The most intense controversy over individual rights during Hennings' three terms in the House erupted, not over the Smith Act, but over the controversial Dies Committee, forerunner of the postwar House Committee on Un-American Activities. After several years of bitter debate, the Lower Chamber established in May of 1938 a special committee to investigate subversive activity and named Representative Martin Dies of Texas as chairman. The fears that liberals held concerning the dangers involved in authorizing a committee to seek out subversives proved to be well founded, for the special committee and its chairman immediately began to use unfair methods in exposing "Communists." Reactions to Dies were like those that were to be aroused by Senator McCarthy in the 1950's. The man on the street supported him, believing he was accomplishing a necessary task, while liberals condemned him, charging that his methods of exposure constituted an abuse of congressional investigative powers and a violation of individual rights.[14]

When Dies, in February of 1939, sought approval to continue his special committee, only a small group of congressmen, which did not include Hennings, opposed him. The following year, when Dies received his second vote of confidence, Hennings was again absent from the dissenters, who now numbered only twenty-one. While this failure on Hennings' part to oppose Dies was deplorable, it did not mean that he approved the unfair methods employed by the committee; during his terms in the Senate he regularly approved appropriations for Senator McCarthy's committee while simultaneously condemning the group's unfair methods. When questioned about this apparent contradiction, Hennings answered that the abuses of a congressional committee did not justify withholding operating funds, since each committee served a useful purpose in the conduct of congressional affairs. Seemingly, then, this attitude was the basis for his earlier decisions concerning the Dies Committee.[15]

Unmistakable proof that Hennings felt deep concern over the methods of the Dies Committee began to appear with his eulogy

[14] Ogden, *The Dies Committee*, 38–46, 101–13.
[15] *Congressional Record*, 75th Cong., 3d Sess., 1938, 83, Part 7, 7586; 76th Cong., 1st Sess., 1939, 84, Part 1, 1127–28; 76th Cong., 3d Sess., 1940, 86, Part 1, 604–5. The votes recorded against the Dies Committee were 41 in 1938 and 35 in 1939.

on the Bill of Rights, delivered in June of 1940. He began this long speech with a history of the emergence of the principle of free thought and expression and its inclusion in the Bill of Rights. After voicing deep concern over the contemporary status of this principle, Hennings observed that social unrest and economic dislocations in the nation had created grave threats to its continuance: "The reactions of the general public to so much that is being said and printed in these days of turmoil and unrest would almost lead one to believe that there is a large group of people who do not want free speech and press, but who are actually afraid of it." He admitted the right of Congress to take measures designed to protect the nation from subversive acts, but he insisted that there was a line of demarcation beyond which Congress could not legislate: "The line must be drawn somewhere, and it would seem, rather than to install some new and wholly untried theory, to be in the best interests of the American public for us to see to it that our Bill of Rights is preserved intact for our posterity." The obligation of enforcing this line belonged to the courts, but even they had been "more than reasonably responsive to changing public opinion in such matters." In times of stress, Hennings concluded, the nation must resist the natural inclination to refuse freedom of expression to those who criticize or condemn our form of government.[16]

Pervading Hennings' Bill of Rights speech was a plea for curbing intolerance toward aliens. Although the red rider, the Smith Act, and the actions of the Dies Committee held latent threats to the rights of citizens, the preponderance of the antisubversive legislation in this period affected only aliens. Most of the Smith Act's provisions, for example, concerned foreigners rather than citizens. Since the Bill of Rights did not apply to aliens, they felt the full force of the antisubversive actions of Congress.[17]

The most severe action directed against an alien by Congress occurred seven days after Hennings' speech of June 6 and drew

[16] *Congressional Record,* 76th Cong., 3d Sess., 1940, 86, Part 7, 7698–701.
[17] Ogden, *The Dies Committee, passim;* Chafee, *Free Speech in the United States,* 196 ff., 439 ff.; Milton R. Konvitz, *Civil Rights in Immigration, passim.*

a stiff condemnation from the Democrat from Missouri. This action singled out for deportation, on the ground that he was a Communist, Australian-born labor leader Harry R. Bridges. If Bridges had been a citizen the measure would have been an obvious "bill of pains and penalties," which it was in spirit. The case was anything but simple; it involved highly complex labor issues in addition to the more patent questions. Briefly stated, the move to deport the Australian stemmed not only from the intensifying search for Communist subversives by the Dies Committee but also from the pressure by some employers to stifle the growing labor movement. When legal efforts to deport Bridges, in accord with existing statutes prohibiting aliens from membership in the Communist party, proved ineffective, Representative A. Leonard Allen of Louisiana introduced the bill to authorize the Secretary of Labor to deport Bridges. Affected by the surge of fear and alarm that followed the successful Nazi offensive of June, 1940, in France and the Low Countries, a decisive majority in the House approved Allen's bill. The vote was 330 to 42; Hennings stood with the liberal minority. Four days later, while inserting the press's criticism of the Bridges bill in the *Congressional Record,* Hennings offered his own condemnation of the measure and concluded with his hope that passage of the bill would not "mark the beginning of a stampede born of hysteria and unreasoning fear and prejudice, to emulate the tactics of the totalitarian governments, in derogation of principles so fundamental in our democracy, and as inimical to the spirit, if not the letter, of our Bill of Rights."[18]

Through most of his service in the House, however, Hennings had paid little attention to the problems of civil liberties. Other more pressing matters held the center of his attention and of the

[18] The most complete study of the Bridges case up to 1950 is Charles A. Madison, *American Labor Leaders,* 404-33 and 459-60 (Bibliography). Also, see: Konvitz, *Civil Rights in Immigration,* 114 ff.; Bridges v. United States, 346 U. S. 209 (1953). For an anti-Bridges viewpoint, in contrast to that of Madison, see the relevant issues of *Business Week.* On the relationship between the Bridges bill and the Dies Committee: Ogden, *The Dies Committee,* 110. On the passage of the Bridges bill: *Congressional Record,* 76th Cong., 3d Sess., 1940, 86, Part 8, 8215. For Hennings' speech: *ibid.,* Part 16, A3933. The bill ultimately failed to pass the Senate.

nation's stage. On the domestic scene, recovery from the nation's worst depression occupied legislators throughout the 1930's. In the last years of the decade, foreign affairs became increasingly important, particularly to Hennings, who worked for six consecutive years on the House Foreign Affairs Committee. In addition to these preoccupations, prudence dictated proceeding gingerly in opposing the Dies Committee. Even the Roosevelt Administration, according to the press, withheld its opposition to Dies because the Texan's national popularity made opposition both useless and dangerous. This fact of political life perhaps explains why Hennings' first public denunciation of violations of individual rights came only after he had decided against returning to the House.[19]

Hennings' decision not to seek re-election in 1940 seemed the result of his fitting into party regularity rather than of personal choice. He had already filed for the congressional primary when the Democratic Committee in St. Louis suggested that he run for city prosecutor. The party had appointed a special committee of lawyers to select Democratic nominees for the offices of circuit judge and circuit attorney, and this advisory group had concluded that the incumbent congressman would make the best candidate for circuit attorney. Following agreement by the Eleventh District Democratic Committee to support an alternate candidate for Congress, Hennings withdrew his name from the congressional race and filed for the city office.[20]

From the close of the 1940 session of Congress until his campaign in 1950 for a seat in the Senate, Hennings focused his attention on local affairs in St. Louis. He plunged into the campaign for the office of circuit attorney and won an easy victory over an able opponent. His platform consisted of a promise to appeal to the state legislature to enact numerous reforms in the criminal procedure that were aimed at facilitating the prosecution of crime in St. Louis. Significantly, each of the reforms he proposed reduced the rights of the accused and strengthened the hand of the prosecutor.[21]

These reforms, proposed by Hennings while he was campaigning in 1940, developed from his conviction, shared generally by

[19] Ogden, *The Dies Committee,* 109.
[20] *St. Louis Globe-Democrat,* June 6, 1940.
[21] *St. Louis Post-Dispatch,* October 12, 1940; *St. Louis Globe-Democrat,* October 13 and 30, 1940.

St. Louisans, that the existing criminal procedure was antiquated and had made the state a haven for criminals. The candidate for circuit attorney proposed (1) that the state be given the same rights as the accused to challenge the selection of trial juries; (2) that the state be allowed to preserve the testimony of its witnesses by taking depositions valid for introduction as evidence if the witness should die prior to the trial; (3) that the state, at the court's discretion, be allowed to prosecute in a single proceeding persons accused of committing crimes as a group; (4) that the state be allowed to cross-examine the spouse of the accused as to facts within his or her knowledge, not merely on matters the spouse chose to volunteer; (5) that the defense be required to inform the state, sufficiently in advance of the trial for an investigation, concerning an intended plea of insanity; and (6) that the state prosecutor be allowed to inform the jury that a defendant who chose not to testify could have testified if he had wished.[22]

On the surface, Hennings' support of these reforms seems in opposition to the position he later took in the Senate as defender of civil liberties. During the attack on the Supreme Court in the years 1957–1960, for example, he opposed those who wished to overturn the McNabb Rule, which enabled the court to invalidate a criminal conviction if it could be shown that the arresting officer failed to arraign the accused within a reasonable time after the arrest. Similarly, he condemned efforts to legalize wire tapping as an investigative technique for federal or local law enforcement officers. An important difference existed, however, between the reforms Hennings supported in 1940 and those he opposed in the 1950's. The reforms proposed in 1940 pertained to courtroom procedures that legal groups in Missouri had for years contended were outmoded—a contention the regularly liberal *St. Louis Post-Dispatch* thoroughly accepted; the reforms proposed in the 1950's, however, concerned those rights that protected the accused from mistreatment by the police—an entirely different matter.[23]

[22] On the reforms urged by Hennings, see note 21. On the widespread agreement with these reforms: Hennings Papers, Box 56, Report of the Criminal Law Committee of the Missouri Bar Association, 1941; *St. Louis Post-Dispatch,* September 27, 1940.
[23] On Hennings' view of the McNabb rule, see p. 157 ff. The wire tapping issue is treated p. 199 ff. *St. Louis Post-Dispatch,* September 27, 1940.

During his term as circuit attorney in St. Louis Hennings, for the first time in public office, failed to distinguish himself in the eyes of the voters. The problem began while Hennings was on a twenty-month leave of absence for service in the Navy. In September of 1941, seven months after he had assumed office, he left St. Louis with the rank of lieutenant commander, assigned as naval aide to Governor Rexford Tugwell of Puerto Rico. With him was his wife of only a few days, a stunningly beautiful St. Louis radio commentator and divorced mother of two children, the former Mrs. Josephine Halpin. Their stay in Puerto Rico was brief. Hennings and Tugwell engaged in an imbroglio, the details of which remain undisclosed, that led eventually to Hennings' reassignment to Hawaii and his divorce from Mrs. Hennings. According to published rumors, Mrs. Hennings precipitated the clash between the Governor and his Naval Aide by openly criticizing Tugwell. Immediately after his arrival in Hawaii Hennings contracted tropical influenza, which brought about his medical discharge from the Navy and his return, in April of 1943, to the office of circuit attorney in St. Louis.[24]

On returning to St. Louis, the inactivated Lieutenant Commander entered a difficult situation not of his own making. In July of 1942, while Hennings was in Hawaii, Edward Melendes, a Mexican national working as a waiter in St. Louis, died in the police holdover three days after his arrest on a charge of larceny. Although the initial coroner's verdict held that Melendes died from natural causes, a subsequent autopsy indicated that death resulted from a severe beating. St. Louis newspapers, as well as the local branches of the American Civil Liberties Union and the National Association for the Advancement of Colored People, demanded an investigation by Acting Circuit Attorney Henry G. Morris into the possibility that Melendes died as a result of police brutality. The NAACP suggested that, while Morris was at it, he might investigate a number of other cases of alleged police brutality involving specifically named Negroes. Morris undertook

24 *St. Louis Post-Dispatch,* August 30, 1941. For the clash with Tugwell: *El Mundo* (San Juan, Puerto Rico), May 20, 21, and 29, 1942; *New York Times,* May 20, 1942; *St. Louis Star-Times,* June 23, 1942. For Hennings' return from Hawaii: *St. Louis Post-Dispatch,* April 5 and 6, 1943; *St. Louis Star-Times,* April 5 and 8, 1943; *St. Louis Globe-Democrat,* April 6, 1943.

the investigation, but after five sessions with grand juries the case was no nearer solution and the Acting Circuit Attorney had become involved in a series of bizarre side issues. Hennings returned from Hawaii to find the press thoroughly unhappy, Morris engaged in a feud with a judge whose sanity some doubted, a local reporter in jail on the charge of bribing a witness, and the public with no precise information on the cause of Melendes' death.[25]

After Hennings resumed office, he sent Morris on an extended vacation and began sorting the debris. He was reassured by the press's expressed confidence that the well-regarded Circuit Attorney would get the facts and prosecute the guilty party—the police. Hennings began well; he dismissed Morris' unwarranted indictments and initiated an exhaustive investigation in cooperation with the state's attorney general. After the initial investigation, Hennings made a thorough presentation to the grand jury, which, to the satisfaction of no one, concluded that no indictment should be brought against the police, since there was no corpus delicti. An essential element of the corpus delicti, the grand jury pointed out, is proof that the victim had not died from natural causes. The Circuit Attorney had received opinions from two pathologists that Melendes' death was, or could have been, due to natural causes, so there was no corpus delicti. Because this conclusion seemed suspiciously convenient for the Circuit Attorney—relieving him of the necessity of prosecuting the police—and because Hennings had hired the dissenting pathologists, the press in St. Louis and over the nation questioned his integrity. *Time* termed the incident "Whitewash in St. Louis."[26]

Hennings refused at first to defend himself, but when the Mexican Government asked the United States Department of State for an explanation, Missouri's Governor Forrest C. Donnell released the report Hennings had submitted to him. Since the

[25] On the Melendes case prior to Hennings' return: *St. Louis Star-Times,* April 27, 1943 (summary), and *St. Louis Post-Dispatch,* September 27, 1943 (charges of CLU and NAACP).

[26] On Hennings' actions, in series: *St. Louis Post-Dispatch,* May 22, 1943; *St. Louis Star-Times,* May 25, 1943; *St. Louis Post-Dispatch,* May 28, 1943; *St. Louis Star-Times,* June 5, 1943; *St. Louis Post-Dispatch,* June 24, 25, 27, and 29, and August 2, 3, 12, 13, and 14, 1943; *Time,* 42 (August 16, 1943), 22.

details of a grand jury decision must remain secret, the report merely sketched the outlines of the group's reasoning. Hennings explained in his report that in addition to its doubt over the precise cause of Melendes' death, the jury had found numerous contradictions in the testimony of witnesses against the police. The jurors had discovered that these witnesses—many of them fellow-prisoners of Melendes—gave testimony to the grand jury that differed from their unsworn statements on which the press was basing its attack on the police. Hennings asserted that if the press had access to the evidence given the grand jury, the criticism would cease; moreover, the press had no right to question the integrity of the ordinary citizen impaneled in a grand jury.[27]

Hennings' report to the Governor failed to stop the criticism in the press. More importantly, several respected pathologists joined the attack, charging that the Circuit Attorney had misrepresented the opinion of one of the two pathologists who were quoted as stating that Melendes died from natural causes. Hennings responded by recalling the grand jury and reviewing the medical testimony he had presented. The grand jury issued a second decision, in which it stated that the Circuit Attorney had not misled its members; it also reiterated its refusal to bring an indictment against the police. Though the press continued agitating for prosecution of the police, Hennings ignored its demands.[28]

The Melendes case affected Hennings in several ways. In the first place, it forced him to turn a searching look on the possibilities of police brutality. Additional cases of alleged mistreatment of prisoners by the police came to light during and after the Melendes episode, increasing the Circuit Attorney's awareness of the potential for police brutality. It seems reasonable, then, that recollections from his career as circuit attorney contributed to the vigor of the campaign Hennings later waged in defense of the McNabb Rule, which forced the police to arraign an arrested person promptly so that his constitutional rights could be protected.[29]

27 *St. Louis Post-Dispatch,* August 17 and 19, 1943.

28 *St. Louis Star-Times,* August 20, 23, 24, and 27, and September 3, 4, 7, and 11, 1943.

29 For examples see: *St. Louis Post-Dispatch,* September 27, 1942; *St. Louis Star-Times,* May 1, 1943, and January 21 and 27, 1944. For Hennings' reaction, see *St. Louis Star-Times,* January 29, 1944.

A further effect of the Melendes case was that Hennings' polit-ical career was damaged by the bitter criticism the press directed toward him. Because of this criticism, after his term as circuit attorney ended in January of 1945, he relinquished public office for the first time in sixteen years and returned to the private practice of law, taking an office with a law firm that included John Raeburn Green, a staunch protector of civil liberties who was later to cross swords with Senator McCarthy. Not since the brief period of 1926–1929 had Hennings devoted full time to the practice of law, but 1945 seemed like an opportune moment to resume it and to allow the Melendes case and the resultant criti-cisms to fade into the background.[30]

Hennings' retirement from public office was more apparent than real. That he looked toward a seat in the Senate had been evident in 1944 when the election of Missouri's senator, Harry S Truman, to the Vice-Presidency became assured. Two years of Truman's term as senator remained, and some of Hennings' friends in Washington pressed both Roosevelt and Truman to encourage Missouri's Governor Phil M. Donnelly to appoint the St. Louisan to the vacancy. Truman approved the idea, but refused to interfere —certainly not from principle, as later events were to show. Roosevelt cooperated, but to no avail, for Donnelly had already decided to appoint his close friend, Frank P. Briggs of Macon. Hennings had been hopeful, but not optimistic, during the maneu-vering, correctly reasoning that the appointment would go to Briggs, whom he described as "an unknown quantity, but I think a good man in every respect."[31]

[30] The effect of the Melendes case on Hennings' political career was illustrated when Hennings was suggested as a possible candidate for mayor of St. Louis (*St. Louis Globe-Democrat,* September 26, 1943). On Mc-Carthy's later attack on Green: see p. 43 ff.

[31] Interview with former staff member, June, 1962. On the attempt to appoint Hennings to Truman's seat in the Senate, see: Hennings Papers, Box 59, letter from Robert E. Hannegan to Eugene Schmick, January 5, 1945; letter from Hennings to Robert H. Hinckley, January 20, 1945; letters from Julius Edelstein to Hennings, June 10, 1945, undated (but probably May or June, 1945) and March 14, 1946; Drew Pearson, *St. Louis Post-Dispatch,* November 11, 1950; Harry B. Wilson, *St. Louis Globe-Democrat,* January 15, 1950. The quotation is from Hennings' letter to Robert H. Hinckley.

Further indication that Hennings was awaiting the opportune moment to run for the Senate appeared the year after Briggs's appointment. The Attorney General of the United States, Thomas C. Clark, offered the St. Louisan an appointment as a special assistant to investigate acts of collaboration in the Philippine Islands. Hennings declined the offer with the explanation that obligations toward clients on retainer prevented his leaving his law practice. The *St. Louis Post-Dispatch* gave a different reason for his refusal, however, asserting that Hennings passed up the assignment because he intended to run for the Senate in 1946.[32]

But in 1946 Hennings made no move to enter the race. Briggs won the primary, and Hennings continued his law practice. According to the *St. Louis Globe-Democrat*'s political analyst Harry B. Wilson, Hennings stayed out of the race only because President Truman sent a friend to tell him that if he waited until 1950, the President would support his candidacy for the Senate.[33]

Hennings continued to bide his time until early in 1949, when he quietly began his move for the Democratic nomination. While attending President Truman's inauguration in January, Hennings met with Missouri Democrats, and word leaked out of the meeting that they agreed on his candidacy. Two months later he confided to an intimate that he had approached no one for support as yet, but had already received such strong encouragement that, "unless something unforeseen intervenes or other controlling situations arise, I will probably announce sometime in the early summer, or at least begin some active canvassing in the state."[34]

Near the end of June, Hennings felt his candidacy was advancing as hoped. In a revealing note to a Washington friend, he described his political status:

I can tell you, however, confidentially, that virtually all of St. Louis and Kansas City are now firmly committed to my candidacy, together with full White House and Jefferson City clearance. By this I mean that the President has said that my candidacy is satisfactory to him and that he

[32] Hennings Papers, Box 59, letter from Hennings to Tom Clark, November 28, 1945; *St. Louis Post-Dispatch,* November 30, 1945.

[33] Harry B. Wilson, *St. Louis Globe-Democrat,* January 15, 1950.

[34] *St. Louis Star-Times,* January 24, 1949; Hennings Papers, Box 76, letter from Hennings to Thomas C. Gilstrap, March 22, 1949.

will not take part in the Missouri primary. This is very important, of course, as you know, as it obviates the danger of last minute pressure being brought upon the President to support any particular candidate, and leaves us free to say that we have the approval of the President and the Governor without either of them being a part of the campaign, which is really just what I had hoped for.[35]

Confirmation of Hennings' description of Truman's position came early in July. James M. Pendergast, nephew of Boss Tom Pendergast and leader of a Democratic faction in Kansas City, met with the President early in July and reported to the press that Truman would keep his hands off the Democratic primary in Missouri. A similar report came from John J. Nangle, the Democratic national committeeman from Missouri, who had also met with the President. Whether or not Truman actually intended at this time to remain aloof from the Missouri primary, he certainly led Hennings and other Missourians to think so.[36]

Several days after Truman's position became known, a large group of Democratic leaders in St. Louis, including some members of the City Committee, adopted a resolution urging Hennings to be a candidate for the Senate in 1950. At the same time, another leader of a Democratic faction in Kansas City, Charles Binaggio, indicated that he would throw his support behind Hennings in the primary. Word also came from Democratic politicians that Governor Forrest Smith pronounced the St. Louisan's candidacy "entirely O.K." with him.[37]

With his plans progressing smoothly, Hennings merely waited for an opportune moment to announce his candidacy. During this time, he married the former Mrs. Elizabeth Setz, a divorcee and the mother of two daughters.[38]

Several weeks after the wedding, the Republican favorite in

[35] Hennings Papers, Box 76, letter from Hennings to Thomas C. Gilstrap, June 30, 1949.

[36] Washington *Star, Jefferson City Post-Tribune, Washington Times,* July 6, 1949.

[37] *St. Louis Star-Times,* July 15, 1949; *St. Louis Star-Times,* July 1, 1949; *Kansas City Star,* July 6, 1949; *St. Louis Globe-Democrat,* July 7, 1949.

[38] *St. Louis Star-Times,* October 27, 1949. For a biographical sketch of Mrs. Hennings: *St. Louis Post-Dispatch,* November 9, 1950.

the 1950 race for the Senate became the first nominee to announce his candidacy. The incumbent senator, Forrest C. Donnell, returned to St. Louis on November 6 and immediately began his campaign to counteract efforts of the Truman Administration and of organized labor to unseat him. Donnell had spent one term as governor of Missouri and had followed this by winning a seat in the Senate in 1944. A conservative and a close friend of Senator Robert A. Taft, Donnell had proved his vote-getting ability, especially in Missouri's rural areas, by running ahead of the rest of the Republican ticket in each of his campaigns.[39]

With Donnell's campaign already under way, the interest of the politically aware public turned to the Democrats. Early in December Hennings sent a campaign biography to the local newspapers, but before he could follow it with an announcement of his candidacy his drive for the Senate received a severe jolt. President Truman renounced his decision to keep hands off the primary; he chose now to interfere openly and decisively.

While spending a Christmas holiday in Kansas City, Mr. Truman met with Governor Smith, Missouri's Attorney General J. E. Taylor, and John H. Hendren, chairman of the state Democratic party, in his penthouse at the Muehlebach Hotel. As a result of the meeting, Truman agreed to lead Missouri Democrats in supporting the candidacy of Emery W. Allison, state senator from Rolla, in the senatorial primary. On his return to Washington in early January, the President confirmed the week-old rumor about "the penthouse gathering" by announcing at his press conference that he would vote for Allison in the primary. Subsequently, Truman repeated his endorsement and used the considerable power at his command to induce high-ranking Democrats in Missouri to support Allison.[40]

Although aware of Truman's intentions prior to the press

[39] *St. Louis Post-Dispatch*, November 7 and 8, 1949; *St. Louis Globe-Democrat*, November 8, 1949.

[40] On Hennings' campaign biography: *St. Louis Post-Dispatch*, December 11, 1949. On the penthouse meeting, see: *Kansas City Star*, December 28, 1949; *St. Louis Star-Times* and *St. Louis Post-Dispatch*, December 29, 1949. On the press conference and after, see: *St. Louis Post-Dispatch*, January 5 and 19, 1950; *St. Louis Globe-Democrat*, January 22, 23, and 26 and February 16, 1950.

conference, Hennings was, nevertheless, shocked. He reacted quickly by announcing his intention to seek the nomination. What had been a smoothly developing primary campaign now became a savage conflict that split the Democratic party in Missouri—an overwhelming majority of the leaders on Allison's side and a slender majority of the voters on Hennings'.[41]

Political observers immediately sought an explanation for the President's decision to interfere in the Missouri primary. Since no antagonism between Truman and Hennings had been apparent and since few Democrats felt enthusiasm for Allison, two questions needed answering: Why did Truman interfere at all? Why did he choose Allison? Two hypotheses appeared in the press, the one reflecting more harshly on the President than the other. According to one theory, Truman's anxiety to defeat Donnell, an avid opponent of the Fair Deal, led him to attempt to unite Missouri Democrats around one man early in the campaign to assure Donnell's defeat. Since Donnell's greatest strength was in the rural areas, Truman and his penthouse guests chose Allison, who was the strongest of the five "receptive" Democrats in the rural areas. In addition, Allison was acceptable to labor, whose eagerness to defeat Donnell perhaps surpassed Truman's. The second explanation involved Truman's connection with "Pendergastism." In this view, the President backed Allison in partial payment of a political and personal debt he owed to James M. Pendergast, an old army comrade who introduced Truman to Boss Tom early in the President's political career. James Pendergast was allegedly attempting to rebuild his uncle's political machine, but had collided with a similar effort of another Kansas City Democrat, Charles Binaggio. Binaggio's alleged attempt to exploit Hennings as a vehicle to patronage and power encountered Pendergast's efforts with his own candidate, Emery Allison. According to this explanation, Truman was attempting to weight the scales in favor of Pendergast's candidate.[42]

Whatever Truman's motive and the bases for the complicated

---

[41] For Hennings' announcement: *St. Louis Star-Times* and *St. Louis Post-Dispatch,* December 31, 1949.

[42] For an early reaction of Democrats to Allison's candidacy: William

(Continued on next page)

infighting among Missouri Democrats during the primary, Hennings' candidacy suffered. According to one rumor, Truman tried to force Hennings to withdraw, but the St. Louisan refused because Governor Smith's delay in announcing his support for Allison left a slender hope of successfully opposing the party leaders. To undermine more critically Hennings' already sinking fortunes, the promise of support from Binaggio became a mockery long before the primary, when the Kansas Citian and his bodyguard died in a shooting that had all the earmarks of a gang assassination. Immediately following the slaying, Missouri's lone Republican congressman, Dewey Short, virtually accused Truman on the House floor—where congressional immunity protected him—of masterminding the killings to assure Pendergast's dominance in Kansas City. Few took Short's farfetched accusation seriously, but it added some strength to the campaign issue Hennings decided to exploit against Allison's candidacy—Pendergastism.[43]

M. Blair, *New York Times,* January 7, 1950. For an expression of the first theory: Marion R. Lynes, *St. Louis Globe-Democrat,* December 29, 1949. The five potential candidates were: Allison, Hennings, Attorney General J. E. Taylor, Franklin E. Reagan, St. Louis lawyer and former assistant attorney general, and Lt. Gov. James T. Blair, Jr. (*St. Louis Star-Times,* December 29, 1949). For the second theory, see: William M. Blair, *New York Times,* January 7, 1950; Harry B. Wilson, *St. Louis Globe-Democrat,* January 8, 11, and 15, 1950. For an explanation of Truman's earlier relationship to James Pendergast, see: Eugene F. Schmidtlein, "Truman the Senator," unpublished doctoral dissertation, University of Missouri, 26 ff. For a background sketch of Allison: Curtis A. Betts, *St. Louis Post-Dispatch,* February 19, 1950 (first of a series). For the same on Binaggio: Harry B. Wilson, *St. Louis Globe-Democrat,* March 12, 1950 (first of a series). A rumor persisted that Truman disclosed his reasons for not supporting Hennings in a secret letter to Allison, but the mystery was never solved (Jack Steele, *New York Herald-Tribune,* November 3, 1950; Truman Papers, 300 Missouri-B, letters from William H. Becker to Matthew J. Connelly, November 6 and 14, 1950). During an interview in October, 1963, I received no answer from Mr. Truman when I asked him to comment on the 1950 primary race.

43 On rumors of Hennings' withdrawal: Harry B. Wilson, *St. Louis Globe-Democrat,* February 26, 1950. On Binaggio's death, see: *Kansas City Star,* April 6, 1950; *Congressional Record,* 81st Cong., 2d Sess., 1950, 96, Part 4, 4938-39. On Pendergastism, see: William M. Reddig, *Tom's Town, passim.* For a vigorous attack on Short's implication that Hennings was in any way associated with Binaggio, see: *St. Joseph News-Press,* May 24, 1950.

On national issues there was little difference between the plat-
forms of Hennings and Allison; both supported the Fair Deal, and
both sided with labor. But as the campaign progressed, Hennings
played heavily on the theme that Allison's candidacy constituted
a return to Pendergastism. To exploit the resentment many Democrats felt toward Truman's interference, the St. Louisan, in his
campaign utterances, publicly assured the President that Missouri
Democrats were capable of selecting their own candidates in
accord with democratic processes. Hence, while Truman's support
forced most of the Democratic leaders into Allison's camp, the
help from on high had its drawbacks.[44]

In addition to exploiting the public's attitudes toward Pendergastism, Hennings had a more tangible asset—backing from a
solid bloc of Democratic ward leaders in St. Louis, held in line by
a local power, Sheriff Thomas F. Callanan. Despite strong pressure
from more powerful St. Louis Democrats who were supporting
Allison, Callanan held firm, enabling Hennings to concentrate
his campaign on the rural counties. But even the combination of
resentment against Truman, support from the Callanan bloc, and
strenuous campaigning in the rural areas would have been insufficient to win the primary for Hennings. Except for the apparently
accidental concurrence with the primary election of a bitter local
fight over a new St. Louis charter, he would have lost. Conflict
over the city charter more than doubled the number of St. Louis
Democrats who normally voted in an off-year primary and added
approximately 50,000 to their vote. Since his total margin of
victory over Allison was only 4,132 votes, the fight over the
charter was clearly the reason for Hennings' victory.[45]

[44] On Allison's platform, see: Curtis A. Betts, *St. Louis Post-Dispatch,*
May 20, 1950. For Hennings' platform, see: Hennings Papers, Box 1,
Address, Kiel Auditorium, June 19, 1950, St. Louis. For Hennings' use
of the Pendergastism theme: *St. Louis Globe-Democrat,* June 2, 1950;
Address of June 19, 1950; *Columbia Missourian,* May 26, 1950.

[45] On Callanan's background: Harry B. Wilson, *St. Louis Globe-
Democrat,* January 29, 1950. On Callanan's power and support for Hennings: Interview with former staff member, June, 1962; Harry B. Wilson,
St. Louis Globe-Democrat, March 1 and 14, 1950. On the St. Louis charter
and its effect on the primary: *St. Louis Post-Dispatch,* July 16 and August
2, 1950; *Hannibal Courier-Post,* July 20, 1950; *St. Louis Globe-Democrat,*

(Continued on next page)

Issues touching civil liberties were totally absent from the primary struggle, so Hennings' sharp attack on McCarthy and McCarthyism during the campaign preceding the general election came somewhat as a surprise. Nevertheless, this defense of individual rights was not a radical departure from his past. Underlying it was the respect for individual freedom, as enshrined in the Bill of Rights, that he had acquired from his father. His legal training, his contact with the life and thought of Thomas Jefferson as patron of the Jefferson Club, and, as he approached the close of his congressional career, the violations of individual freedom that resulted from the nation's reaction to the advance of European "isms" heightened that respect and stimulated his concern. When he returned to Congress as a senator, his concern over the Bill of Rights had mounted; the frantic reaction of Americans to revelations of subversion in Canada and the United States during the late 1940's had affected him. The Cold War was subtly transforming Hennings from a hesitant spokesman for civil liberties in the House to an aggressive defender of individual rights in the Senate. But this transformation became clear to the nation only gradually, as Hennings' Senate career unfolded.

July 21, 1950; *Kansas City Star,* July 23, 1950; *New York Times,* August 4, 1950. The official returns were: Hennings' total in state, 182,333; Allison's total in state, 178,201; Hennings' St. Louis vote, 84,329; Allison's St. Louis vote, 23,037; total vote in Democratic senatorial primary of 1950 in St. Louis, 114,228; total vote in 1946, 32,541; Democratic primary by counties: Hennings, 13 counties; Allison, 101 counties; tied, 1 *(Official Manual of the State of Missouri, 1947–1948; 1951–1952).* On the charter vote in St. Louis: 182,834 votes cast *(St. Louis Post-Dispatch,* August 2, 1950).

II

Mandate against Hysteria

O<small>N THE EVE</small> of his senatorial career Hennings' growing concern for individual rights received little notice. From his six years in the House, *Time* magazine could recall only that the dark-haired congressman had been a "two-fisted drinker" who supported President Roosevelt. Even his outspoken defense of the Bill of Rights during the closing days of his last term in the House assumed significance only in retrospect of his entire career. Nonetheless, Hennings was to emerge at the end of the decade as a dominant defender in the Senate of individual rights as they were threatened by Communist-aroused panic over national security.

In the early 1950's Hennings began, undramatically but persistently, to oppose Senator McCarthy. In sum, he contributed as much as any single public figure to McCarthy's decline in power. His opposition had personal as well as political basis, for to him McCarthy embodied much that was personally and politically distasteful. McCarthy's crude discourtesy, his practice of name-calling, his pursuit of personal vendettas, and his accusations based on flimsy evidence offended the Missourian's sense of decency, while the fever McCarthy fomented against the expression of any but the most orthodox and "patriotic" sentiments violated Hennings' commitment to the broadest liberty of thought and expression. Despite the very immediate danger of becoming involved in a personal feud with McCarthy, Hennings vigorously opposed him and, eventually, succeeded in lessening his impact on public life.

In the mid-1950's Hennings joined with those who objected to the loyalty-security measures employed by various departments within the Eisenhower Administration. The dilemma of order-and-security versus liberty-and-justice was seldom more clearly presented than in the efforts of the departments of Defense and Justice to safeguard the nation's security in a cold war of the nuclear age. To Hennings, the invasions of liberty and justice perpetrated in the name of security neither squared with the Bill of Rights nor promoted American security. Through the creation of a new subcommittee of the Judiciary Committee he publicly examined and criticized the loyalty-security program of the executive branch and pointed to the dangers of raising order and security above freedom and fairness. In the wake of this criticism a noticeable shift of emphasis appeared, and concern for liberty and justice once more came into closer balance with concern for order and security.

In the closing years of the decade, Hennings focused attention on another phase of the continuing liberty-order dilemma. When the Supreme Court, in a series of decisions in the late 1950's, ruled that Congress and the executive branch were violating individual rights in the interest of security, many in the nation followed the advice given publicly by the venerable legal scholar Edward S. Corwin to "tweak the nose" of the Supreme Court. Hennings immediately initiated a move to defend the Court from these attacks. Congressional defenders of the judiciary quickly formed ranks behind Hennings' able leadership, and the persuasive constitutional arguments of the Senator from Missouri contributed effectively to the eventual defeat of every anti-Court proposal.

But none of these future accomplishments appeared likely as Hennings inaugurated his 1950 senatorial campaign against Forrest C. Donnell. For the nation as well as for Hennings the congressional contests of that year were fateful; the American voter, for the first time since the beginning of the Cold War, was to pass judgment on the conflicting demands of internal security and individual freedom. Since 1945 this conflict had been intensifying, and the steadily increasing fear of Communist subversion was pro-

ducing a national mood that became progressively less sensitive
to individual rights. The smoldering issue had little effect in the
1946 and 1948 elections, but in 1950 the Republican party, in
attacking the Truman Administration, made Communist subversion at home a companion piece to Russian triumphs abroad. The
strategy succeeded, and Republican gains in 1950 showed that
communism at home had unexplored potential as a political issue.
▷To guardians of civil liberties the use of communism as a political
issue foreshadowed a steady shrinking of individual freedom.
In this atmosphere, Hennings emerged from the 1950 contest as
a defender of individual freedom, and Missouri, showing a liberal
spirit of its own, approved.[1]

The open clash that erupted in the 1950 campaign had its roots
in the Seventy-ninth Congress. In 1945, during the opening
minutes of that Congress, Representative John E. Rankin, Democrat from Mississippi, made a dramatic proposal to transform the
collapsing Dies Committee into a permanent investigating body.
Liberals had often criticized the procedures of this security-
conscious group and had rejoiced at the prospect of its dying
with the adjournment of the Seventy-eighth Congress. But their
happiness was squelched by Rankin's proposal. Their opposition to
continuing the committee proved futile, for they could neither
delay the vote on the measure nor muster enough ballots to prevent its passage. Helplessly, they witnessed the birth of the House
Committee on Un-American Activities.

The House Un-American Activities Committee, as it came to
be known, made headlines frequently two years later, when
J. Parnell Thomas became its chairman and the Republican party
organized the House. Under Thomas' leadership the committee
suddenly stepped up its activity, and by 1948 it was charging
members of the wartime Roosevelt Administration with Communist sympathies and activities. During 1949 and 1950 the
committee improved the fairness of its procedures as its personnel

[1] On the absence of issues related to civil liberties in the 1948 election:
U. S. News & World Report, 25 (November 12, 1948), 26; *Nation,* 167,
(November 13, 1948), 540; *New Republic,* 119 (November 15, 1948), 6.
On the growth of national concern over subversion: *Annual Report of the
American Civil Liberties Union, 1947-1948; 1948-1949; 1950-1951.*

changed: the committee's aggressive chairman exchanged his congressional seat for a jail cell after conviction of fraud for padding his congressional payroll; its original sponsor and most vocal Democratic member, Representative Rankin, was removed in accord with the Democrats' policy of barring from membership on the committee all chairmen of other House committees. Only the scene and the actors shifted, however, for in February of 1950, Senator Joseph McCarthy breathed new life into the antisubversive movement with his running assault on the State Department.[2]

Even before McCarthy's appearance, HUAC had stirred up an extraordinary amount of criticism. The committee's opponents objected to its methods and even questioned the congressional prerogatives that underlay them. Criticism centered on two points: congressional immunity from prosecution for libel and the investigative power of Congress. The former enabled committee members and witnesses to indulge in public accusations without showing proof, while the latter permitted the committee to engage in the dangerous practice of "exposure for the sake of exposure," The call for reform of the committee's methods received little popular response, however, and in Congress the opponents of HUAC decreased from the 186 who voted against the original charter in 1945 to 12 dissenters in 1950.[3]

[2] For this development of the House Un-American Activities Committee (henceforth HUAC): *Congressional Quarterly*, 1, 79; 3, 85; 4, 274; 5, 34; Robert K. Carr, *The House Committee on Un-American Activities, 1945–1950, passim;* William F. Buckley and the editors of *National Review, The Committee and Its Critics; A Calm Review of the House Committee on Un-American Activities, passim.* (Carr opposes and Buckley *et al.* defend HUAC.) Apparently Rankin's sudden move resulted from his fear that the files of the Dies Committee would be destroyed unless it became a permanent committee (Buckley *et al., The Committee and Its Critics,* 105). The literature on McCarthy is as partisan as that on HUAC: Jack Anderson and Ronald W. May, *McCarthy, the Man, the Senator, the "Ism";* Richard H. Rovere, *Senator Joe McCarthy;* Herbert Agar, *The Price of Power; America since 1945, passim;* William F. Buckley and Brent Bozell, *McCarthy and his Enemies.* The first three volumes are unfriendly to McCarthy, while the fourth is pro-McCarthy. After McCarthy's death, his papers were deposited at Marquette University, but at this writing they were not yet open for research.

[3] For criticism of HUAC: Carr, *The House Committee on Un-American Activities, 1945–1950,* 284 ff., 422 ff., 449 ff.; Buckley *et al., The Committee and Its Critics,* 13 ff., 34 ff., 219 ff.; Alan Barth, *Government by Investi-*

The Administration and the Supreme Court reflected the new antisubversive spirit also. Under pressure from HUAC, Truman initiated in August of 1947 a loyalty program for employees of the executive branch. The following summer, a special grand jury in New York indicted twelve leaders of the Communist party for violating a Smith Act prohibition against teaching or advocating the violent overthrow of the government. When they appealed, the Supreme Court, in *Dennis v. United States,* sustained the convictions by concluding that the Smith Act did not violate freedom of speech. Nonetheless, neither the Administration nor the Court rivaled Congress in stimulating national concern over internal security. In fact, the Truman loyalty program, besides being relatively mild, probably lessened the vehemence of the antisubversive spirit, since Congress might have proposed a harsher program if the President had not acted promptly in 1947.[4]

The search for Communists inevitably became a weapon for partisan politics. In the 1950 congressional campaign, the Republican party consciously exploited the nation's fear of subversion by charging that the Administration was "soft on Communists." Though the President's vigorous reaction to the Korean crisis should have made this charge ridiculous, the strategy worked. Leonard W. Hall, chairman of the Republicans' Congressional Campaign Committee, bluntly attributed the party's 1950 gains to "resentment against the Administration's coddling of Communists at home and the appeasement of Russia and Communist China abroad." Much of this resentment was generated by Senator McCarthy, the new leader of the "fight against communism." During the campaign, the Senator from Wisconsin received over two

gation, passim; Telford Taylor, *Grand Inquest, passim; New Republic,* 117 (August 11, 1947), 10; 121 (August 1, 1949), 8; (November 11, 1949), 9; Scott W. Lucas, "Congressional Hearings: A Plea for Reform," *New York Times Magazine* (March 19, 1950), 13; *New Republic,* 122 (April 3, 1950), 12; *Congressional Digest,* 29 (April, 1950), 97; Richard H. Rovere, "Letter From Washington," *New Yorker,* 26 (May 13, 1950), 96.

[4] *Congressional Quarterly,* 3, 479. On the Truman loyalty program: Eleanor Bontecou, *The Federal Loyalty-Security Program,* Chap. 1, 21–34. In Dennis v. United States, 341 U.S. 494 (1951), the Supreme Court, by a vote of 6 to 2, held that Sections 2 and 3 of the Smith Act (54 Stat. 671) violated neither the First nor the Fifth Amendment to the Constitution.

thousand invitations—more than all other Republican senators combined—to speak in behalf of his colleagues. In October alone, he spoke in nine different states, and among these was Missouri.[5] McCarthy entered the Missouri contest on October 23, when between 750 and 800 voters attended a meeting in the auditorium of Jefferson City's Junior College, at which he spoke on communism. Hennings, showing little fear of the Senator from Wisconsin, directed the Democratic State Committee to insert as an advertisement in the local newspaper, the day before the speech, excerpts from a recent anti-McCarthy editorial of the *Madison* (Wisconsin) *Capital Times*. The editorial accused McCarthy of income tax evasion and of granting "quickie" divorces to clients of political supporters and charged him also with the destruction of court records detrimental to important Wisconsin business interests.[6]

Apparently undisturbed by the advertisement, McCarthy launched into his well-worn speech attacking the State Department. Secretary of State Dean Acheson and Ambassador-at-large Philip C. Jessup were "at the very least Red sympathizers," and Hennings' party became "the Commiecrats" for supporting them. According to the Senator from Wisconsin, the Communists' infiltration of the federal government demanded a full-scale investigation such as only a Republican Congress could accomplish, since Democratic committee chairmen were presently blocking it. Turning to the Hennings-inspired advertisement, he observed that, elsewhere, such "propaganda" came from Young Communists,

[5] On Republican strategy: *New Republic,* 123 (October 9, 1950), 9; *Kansas City Star,* October 26, 1950; *Nation,* 171 (October 28, 1950), 385; *New Republic,* 123 (October 30, 1950), 7; *Nation,* 171 (November 4, 1950), 405; *New York Times,* November 10, 1950; *Time,* 56 (November 13, 1950), 19; *Newsweek,* 36 (November 13, 1950), 23; *U.S. News & World Report,* 29 (November 17, 1950), 14, 34; *New Republic,* 123 (November 20, 1950), 7; *Christian Century,* 67 (November 22, 1950), 1382. Benjamin Ginzburg, at one time a staff member of Hennings' Subcommittee on Constitutional Rights, essayed a completely political explanation of the rise of congressional investigations of subversion or disloyalty in *Rededication to Freedom.*

[6] Jefferson City *Daily Capital News,* October 24, 1950; *Jefferson City Post-Tribune,* October 24, 1950; *Jefferson City Sunday News and Tribune,* October 22, 1950.

but this was the first time it had appeared under the Democratic party's sponsorship. He then declared that his investigators had proved that Judge Thomas C. Hennings, Sr., father of the Democratic candidate, had paid for the advertisement. Howard Hannah, the treasurer of the Democratic State Committee, replied for Hennings by inviting McCarthy to inspect the check for $53, signed by himself and the Democratic State Chairman, with which the State Committee had paid for the advertisement. The next day, in St. Louis, Judge Hennings dismissed the accusation as ridiculous.[7]

Prior to McCarthy's invasion of Missouri the question of subversion had received only minor attention from Hennings and his Republican opponent, Forrest C. Donnell. Donnell refused to accuse the Administration of harboring subversives, on the grounds —odd indeed in 1950—that he had no evidence to support such an accusation. He merely urged increased vigilance, in view of the report from the Federal Bureau of Investigation that 54,174 Communists and ten times that number of fellow-travelers infested the nation.[8]

Hennings reached beyond his Missouri opponent to condemn the widespread charges that there were many Communists in sensitive positions in the government—the heart of McCarthyism. On September 15, the opening day of his campaign, he warned an audience in Moberly that an obligation to preserve fundamental liberties coexisted with the duty of maintaining internal security. He condemned as unjust the attacks made on citizens in the name of internal security and the tendency to punish individuals for their thoughts and associations. The real sources of these unfair practices, he asserted, were institutional as well as political; abuses of congressional immunity and of the investigative powers of Congress accounted for these injustices. Legislation like the In-

[7] See note 6 and: *Kansas City Star, St. Louis Globe-Democrat, St. Louis Star-Times, Kirksville Daily Express,* and *Joplin Globe,* all of October 24, 1950.

[8] Ernest Kirschten, "Donnell Luck and Missouri Scandal," *Nation,* 171 (October 14, 1950), 332; *New York Herald-Tribune,* October 15, 1950; *Los Angeles Examiner,* October 17, 1950; *Newsweek,* 36 (October 23, 1950), 36; *St. Louis Globe-Democrat,* October 24, 1950; *Mexico Evening Ledger,* October 25, 1950; *St. Louis Globe-Democrat,* October 31, 1950.

ternal Security Act of 1950 enabled the government to practice
thought control and to pass judgment on a citizen's associations.
The moving force behind this "McCarthyism," Hennings charged,
was merely political; it was, simply, the naked desire for partisan
political advantage and for newspaper headlines. And underneath
it all lay a national fear that was leading the people into "pander-
ing to the demands of those who have little regard for democracy
and its processes." As a solution, Hennings proposed a citizens
committee to investigate all charges of disloyalty, and a Presidential veto of the Internal Security Act.[9]

▶The hysteria welling up elsewhere in the nation seemed to
leave Missourians unmoved, for they approved Hennings' attack
on McCarthy and McCarthyism. The press discounted Donnell's
statistics from the FBI and reacted coolly to McCarthy's speech.
One of the state's four metropolitan newspapers, the *St. Louis
Post-Dispatch,* ignored the Senator's speech at Jefferson City entirely. The *St. Louis Star-Times* chided the Senator from Wisconsin for not answering the accusations of the *Madison Capital
Times.* The *Globe-Democrat,* also of St. Louis, observed that
McCarthy's speeches drew nationwide headlines before the Korean
War but had now become pointless. Of thirteen outstate regional
newspapers, only four paid any attention to the speech, and none
regarded it as significant. One of the four, the *Jefferson City Post-
Tribune,* characterized it as McCarthy's "traveling medicine
show." Press endorsements of the candidates indicated the same
tendency. The *Star-Times* condemned Donnell for not opposing
McCarthy in the Senate and for bringing him into Missouri. The
other Hennings paper, the *Post-Dispatch,* backed the Democratic

[9] Professor Eric F. Goldman attributes the origin of the term "Mc-
Carthyism" to the *Washington Post*'s cartoonist Herbert Block (*The
Crucial Decade—and After, America 1945-1960,* 145), while McCarthy's
backers attributed it to the *Daily Worker* (*Commonweal,* 56, September
12, 1952, 547). Hennings Papers, Box 30, Speech, Moberly, Missouri,
September 15, 1950; *St. Louis Post-Dispatch,* September 18, 1950. On the
implications for civil liberties in the Internal Security Act of 1950: John D.
Crawford, "Free Speech and the Internal Security Act of 1950," *Georgetown Law Journal,* 39 (March, 1951), 440. Truman vetoed the bill,
H.R. 9490, in the interest of civil liberties (*Congressional Record,* 81st
Cong., 2d Sess., 1950, 91, Part 11, 15629), but Congress passed the bill
over the veto the following day.

candidate for opposing the Internal Security Act. Even the Republican papers, the *Kansas City Star* and the *Globe-Democrat*, refrained from praising Donnell's position on domestic communism. In short, Missouri newspapers remained singularly unshaken by the threat of domestic communism, in or out of government.[10]

Judged by the election returns, Missouri voters shared the press's detachment from the antisubversive hysteria. Hennings defeated Donnell by 92,593 votes, making the Missouri Republican his party's only senatorial casualty of 1950. In the congressional contests, eight of Missouri's ten representatives who voted to uphold Truman's veto of the Internal Security Act won re-election. The other two lost by narrow margins, and a third lost for reasons unconnected with either civil liberties or internal security. This loss occurred in the Twelfth District, where St. Louis County, after a two-year interlude, returned to its traditional Republicanism.[11]

In its analysis of the Missouri election, the *Post-Dispatch* saw Hennings' victory as a mandate against the rising hysteria over internal security. The St. Louis newspaper submitted as evidence the voters' obvious disregard of McCarthy's speech at Jefferson City and of his "histrionic, last-minute radio appeal." In view of the voters' expressed attitudes, the liberal daily advised Hennings to "oppose smearing and hysteria in Congress." The *Globe-*

[10] *St. Louis Star-Times,* October 23–25, 1950; *St. Louis Globe-Democrat,* October 24, 1950. The following newspapers were consulted as indication of opinion in outstate Missouri: Cape Girardeau *Southeast Missourian, Columbia Tribune, Hannibal Courier-Post, Jefferson City Post-Tribune, Joplin Globe, Kirksville Daily Express, Macon Chronicle-Herald, Mexico Evening Ledger, Moberly Monitor-Index,* Poplar Bluff *Daily American Republic, St. Joseph News-Press, Sedalia Democrat, Sikeston Daily Standard, Springfield Leader-Press.* The four that reported McCarthy's speech were the newspapers in Hannibal, Jefferson City, Joplin, and Kirksville, on October 24, 1950. The quotation is from the *Jefferson City Post-Tribune* of October 24, 1950. On endorsements: *St. Louis Star-Times,* October 23, 1950; *St. Louis Post-Dispatch,* October 15, 1950; *Kansas City Star,* November 1, 1950; *St. Louis Globe-Democrat,* October 20, 1950.

[11] *Official Manual of the State of Missouri, 1951–1952,* 951 (the total vote in the senatorial election was 1,279,631). The ten congressmen, all Democrats, were: Bolling, Cannon, Carnahan, Christopher, Irving, Jones, Karst, Karsten, Sullivan, and Welch (*Congressional Record,* 81st Cong., 2d Sess., 1950, 96, Part 11, 15632–33, 15726). On the Republicanism of St. Louis County: Morron D. Harris, "Political Trends in Missouri," unpublished Master's thesis, University of Missouri.

Democrat, less susceptible to seeing the vote as a liberal mandate, nevertheless implied a similar interpretation of the election results. The pro-Donnell paper compared the results in Missouri with those in Maryland and pointed to their inconsistency. In Maryland, Senator Millard E. Tydings lost because the voters believed he had whitewashed the Communists-in-government issue; in Missouri, Hennings won because he opposed McCarthyism and the Internal Security Act of 1950.[12]

The strength of Missouri's mandate against McCarthyism was uncertain. The inconsistent national reaction to the Communists-in-government charge made the state's liberalism difficult to measure. In California, for example, Richard M. Nixon defeated Helen Gahagan Douglas with a campaign described by the *Nation* as, simply, "Helen Douglas is a Red." Yet, Connecticut returned Democratic Senator Brien McMahon, a close associate of Tydings in debunking McCarthy's accusations against the State Department, and New York re-elected Democratic Senator Herbert Lehman in spite of his having told Alger Hiss in August of 1948 that he had complete confidence in his loyalty.[13]

Additional uncertainty over the strength of Hennings' mandate against hysteria stemmed from the gentlemanly Donnell's refusal to play heavily on the antisubversive theme. The fair-minded Republican candidate's reluctance "to take off the gloves"—as it came to be called—kept the Communists-in-government issue from being brought into sharper focus in Missouri.

Nevertheless, Missouri's response to Hennings' initial effort at taking an aggressive stand in support of civil liberties held great importance for his future. The newly elected senator knew that the powerful *Post-Dispatch* would support him if he took a strong position in defense of civil liberties. More importantly, the *Post-Dispatch* could be counted on to rally enough popular support to make such a position politically feasible, if not advis-

---

12 *St. Louis Post-Dispatch,* November 8, 1950; *St. Louis Globe-Democrat,* November 9, 1950.
13 Carey McWilliams, "Bungling in California," *Nation,* 171 (November 4, 1950), 411. Sam Halper, "New York: Mud-Slinging Derby," *Newsweek,* 36 (October 30, 1950), 17. "Candidates Explain Outcome," *U. S. News & World Report,* 29 (November 17, 1950), 34. "The Elections," *Nation,* 171 (November 18, 1950), 451.

able. He discovered also that the more conservative *Star* and *Globe-Democrat* would be reluctant to oppose him in this position; in fact, two days after the election the *Star* leveled its own broadside at McCarthyism. This reaction of the press of the state held special importance for Hennings. He felt rather secure of his position with St. Louis voters, since, in four St. Louis elections, he had never failed to win; in the primary for the election to the Senate, the city's overwhelming support had swung the close contest his way; similiarly, it had provided a large share of the margin of victory in the general election. Now, at the beginning of his career in the Senate, the press of the state as well as of the city gave him an invitation, if not a mandate, to implement its belief in civil liberties. The Eighty-second Congress, Hennings' first, had scarcely opened when such an opportunity presented itself.[14]

The case of Ellen Knauff defies brief summary. Its essence, however, is clear enough. From August of 1948 to November of 1951, the U. S. Immigration Service, with the concurrence of the Attorney General, denied admittance into the country to Ellen Knauff, the alien wife of an American citizen, Kurt W. Knauff, on the grounds that she was a security risk. For most of these three years, Mrs. Knauff remained on Ellis Island, uninformed of the evidence against her. Early in 1950, the *Post-Dispatch,* joined shortly by the *New York Post* and the American Civil Liberties Union, began a crusade to secure a hearing for Mrs. Knauff. The crusade centered on the fact that she had been convicted as a security risk without knowing the evidence against her and without opportunity to refute it. The fact of her guilt or innocence was not the issue, asserted the *Post-Dispatch,* but the practice of arriving at exclusion decisions behind closed doors, without showing cause and without benefit of a hearing. Such a policy, maintained the St. Louis paper, violated the constitutional rights of the accused person and invited arbitrary judgments.[15]

[14] *Kansas City Star,* November 9, 1950. St. Louis furnished 70,501 votes of Hennings' 92,593 plurality. Professor James A. Burkhart presented an explanation of Missouri's liberalism in "Hennings of Missouri," *Frontier,* 8 (April, 1957), 13.

[15] Ellen R. Knauff, *The Ellen Knauff Story,* 101-6. For a briefer account, see Jean Begeman, "What Ellen Knauff Won," *New Republic,* 126 (January 7, 1951), 14–15.

The *Post-Dispatch*'s interest in the case developed when the Supreme Court, in January of 1950, denied Mrs. Knauff's appeal from the exclusion order. Speaking for the Court, Justice Sherman Minton held that the Attorney General had the right to exclude an alien without showing cause and without a hearing, if he judged that showing cause would harm the national interest. Since Attorney General J. Howard McGrath had stated that revealing the case against Mrs. Knauff would require uncovering secret sources of information essential to the government's intelligence, the Court dismissed the appeal. The three dissenting justices, however, strongly objected to Minton's ruling and, in the process, touched the crusading spirit of the *Post-Dispatch*.[16]

For a full year Hennings had read about the case of Ellen Knauff in the pages of the *Post-Dispatch*. When he arrived in Washington to be sworn into the Senate, the Knauff dossier of Ed Harris, the reporter assigned to the case, supplied the gaps in his information on the case. After Representative Francis Walter, determined to get the facts behind Mrs. Knauff's exclusion, introduced for the second successive year a bill for relief of Ellen Knauff, Hennings joined Walter's crusade by introducing a companion bill in the Senate. This measure, the first to be introduced in the Senate by the Missourian, directed the Attorney General to cancel all exclusion proceedings against Mrs. Knauff and to refrain from future use of the evidence that underlay the exclusion.[17]

Upon introducing the Knauff bill, Hennings questioned Attorney General McGrath's reasoning. The new senator argued that a secret hearing before a Senate committee would protect intelligence sources and, at the same time, safeguard Mrs. Knauff's rights. By introducing their private bills, Hennings and Walter hoped to force the Attorney General either to admit Mrs. Knauff into the country or to conform to the minimum demands of due

16 Knauff v. Shaughnessey, 338 U.S. 537 (1950). For a brief analysis of the opinions, see "Case Notes," *Alabama Law Review*, 2 (Spring, 1950), 357–61. For the *Post-Dispatch*'s entry into the case, see Knauff, *The Ellen Knauff Story*, 101–6.

17 Hennings Papers, Box 131, memorandum of Thomas Yarbrough (Hennings' first administrative assistant), January 17, 1951; Walter's first bill was House, 81st Cong., 2d Sess., 1950, H.R. 7614, and his second was 82d Cong., 1st Sess., 1951, H.R. 893 and S. 372.

process by granting her a secret hearing. Less than this, Hennings claimed, amounted to arbitrary action that violated fundamental human rights and basic democratic processes.[18]

While the Knauff bill lay pending in the Judiciary Committee, Hennings pressed McGrath further. By letter, he asked assurance from the Attorney General that everything possible was being done to hasten a final determination of the case. McGrath replied by special messenger, informing Hennings that, since part of the evidence against Knauff could now be revealed without harm to the public interest, he had arranged a hearing; a board of special inquiry would hear the case on March 26, 1951. The special board met as promised, and although it upheld the decision to exclude Mrs. Knauff, Hennings was satisfied. In a letter to Mrs. Knauff's attorney Alfred Feingold, Hennings declared it pointless to pursue further the Hennings-Walter bill. For Mrs. Knauff, however, the case eventually ended on a happier note. In the summer of 1951 the Attorney General sent the case to his own department's Board of Appeals. On August 29 its chairman, Thomas G. Finucane, announced that the five-man board had decided, with but one dissent, that the evidence did not justify excluding Mrs. Knauff as a security risk. On November 2 McGrath affirmed the recommendation, and the bizarre incident came to an end. For Hennings, the significance of the case continued, since it brought him closer to the *Post-Dispatch,* whose crusade he had espoused, and drew him further into a deepening concern over violations of civil liberties that stemmed from the nation's increasing emphasis on internal security.[19]

Hennings' concern for civil liberties that were being violated in the name of internal security now received a much stronger jolt from a conflict that had begun shortly after he entered the Knauff case, When applying for committee posts in the Eighty-second Congress, he indicated that he wished to continue the specializa-

[18] Hennings Papers, Box 131, press release, January 11, 1951.
[19] Hennings Papers, Box 131, Hennings to McGrath, March 10, 1951, McGrath to Hennings, undated, Hennings to Alfred Feingold, April 9, 1951; U. S. Department of Justice, Board of Immigration Appeals, August 29, 1951, and Office of Attorney General, November 2, 1951 (photostatic copies of each may be found in the Appendix of Knauff, *The Ellen Knauff Story*).

tion in foreign affairs that had marked his career in the House. The day after Congress opened, he informed Senator Carl Hayden, Democrat from Arizona and chairman of the Committee on Rules and Administration, of his committee preferences. The list read: Armed Services, Foreign Relations, Interstate and Foreign Commerce, Agriculture and Forestry, Interior and Insular Affairs. Since they came from a freshman senator, his suggestions received scant notice, and the Democratic Steering Committee rejected his entire list. Instead, Hennings received assignments to the Committee on Public Works and the Committee on Rules and Administration. The latter appointment was to become most important, since Hayden put the Missourian on the Subcommittee on Privileges and Elections, which promptly embarked on the investigation of the 1950 senatorial election in Maryland—an explosive project.[20]

On the first day of the new Congress, some probe of the Maryland election appeared likely. Democratic Majority Leader Ernest W. McFarland of Arizona successfully moved to have the oath of office administered to John Marshall Butler, Maryland's newly elected Republican senator, "without prejudice." This meant that the Senate, if it later chose, could refuse to seat Butler on a simple majority vote. Commenting on this move, Columnist Drew Pearson reported that the Democratic caucus had directed McFarland's motion in order to push investigation of the Maryland election. Early in February the Subcommittee on Privileges and Elections, an arm of the Rules Committee, confirmed Pearson's prediction. The subcommittee voted in executive session to press the investigation, and Chairman Guy M. Gillette, Democrat from Iowa, appointed a special hearings committee to begin work immediately. Freshman Democrat Mike Monroney of Oklahoma chaired the committee, which consisted of himself, Hennings, and two Republicans, Mrs. Margaret Chase Smith of Maine and Robert C. Hendrickson of New Jersey.[21]

The roots of the investigation of the Maryland election extended

---

[20] Hennings Papers, Box 159, Hennings to Hayden, January 4, 1951; *Congressional Record,* 82d Cong., 1st Sess., 1951, 97, Part 1, 218; *ibid.,* Part 17, D14 and D49.

[21] *Congressional Record,* 82d Cong., 1st Sess., 1951, 97, Part 1, 3; *ibid.,* Part 17, D49; *St. Louis Star-Times,* January 9, 1951.

back to McCarthy's initial outburst against the State Department. In Wheeling, West Virginia, on February 9, 1950, the Senator from Wisconsin accused the State Department of knowingly harboring Communists. On his return to Washington, McCarthy repeated this charge on the Senate floor, and the Upper Chamber responded by directing the Committee on Foreign Relations to investigate the merits of the accusation. With Millard Tydings, Democrat from Maryland, as chairman, the investigating committee concluded, in a majority report, that McCarthy's charges were unfounded. In violent reaction to this report, the Senator from Wisconsin accused the Senator from Maryland of whitewashing the issue to protect the Administration from embarrassment. In July of 1950 McCarthy pursued Tydings further by joining forces in the Maryland campaign with John Marshall Butler, Tydings' Republican opponent in the forthcoming November election. The combination of McCarthy and Butler proved successful, but on two counts it inspired a Senate investigation: the Upper Chamber questioned the propriety of outsiders interfering in a state campaign and the ethics of Butler's and McCarthy's electioneering techniques.[22]

The official participants in the Maryland election, Tydings and Butler, provided the Monroney special hearings committee with its first testimony in mid-February. In the following two months a stream of witnesses, with heavy emphasis on McCarthy's staff members, paraded before the committee. The grim narrative ended in April, but not until August did the special committee submit its report to the full subcommittee. Meanwhile, the Republican

[22] *Congressional Record,* 81st Cong., 2d Sess., 1950, 96, Part 2, 1952–81. Majority Leader Scott Lucas introduced S. Res. 231 on February 21, and it was agreed to, with amendments, on February 22 (*ibid.,* 2062, 2150). The subcommittee appointed to make the investigation included: Tydings (chairman), Theodore Green and Brien McMahon (Democrats), Bourke Hickenlooper and Henry Cabot Lodge (Republicans). The subcommittee was instructed to investigate all past and present personnel of the State Department against whom charges were made. McCarthy's reaction to the report of this committee can be read in his speech in Milwaukee on August 6, 1950, which was reprinted in the *Congressional Record,* 81st Cong., 2d Sess., 1950, 96, Part 18, A7246–49. The McCarthy-Butler collaboration came from Senate, Committee on Rules and Administration, 82nd Cong., 1st Sess., 1951, Report No. 647.

Committee on Committees, anticipating a harsh report, strategically replaced Senator Ralph Flanders, Republican from Vermont, on the parent Rules Committee, with McCarthy. This shift in the Rules Committee's personnel was a transparent maneuver to influence the subcommittee to tone down its criticism of McCarthy's involvement in the Maryland campaign.[23]

After the hearings closed in April, the Monroney Committee delayed submitting its report. In July, Chairman Gillette of the Subcommittee on Privileges and Elections angrily threatened to resign because the special hearings committee had not completed its report. Drew Pearson interpreted Gillette's action as response to pressure by "the *Chicago Tribune* group," whose involvement in the Maryland affair was becoming clear. The Senator from Iowa denied the accusation, claiming that the press of other committee work made him impatient with the hearings committee's failure to end the Maryland matter. Hennings, to whom the newspapers increasingly attributed the energy behind the investigation, made no effort to appease Gillette. Instead, he told Gillette that the special committee's report, as it now stood, was not clear enough to be understood by the public. Placing the blame on Gillette's failure to furnish the group with adequate counsel, he promised that the report would be forthcoming as soon as this was provided. His bluff called, Gillette simmered down, furnished the committee with acceptable legal assistance, and eventually joined the other four members in approving the final report.[24]

The Maryland Report, as it came to be called, aimed its biggest guns at McCarthy rather than at Butler. The latter escaped almost unscathed—he retained his seat in the Senate—because, as the subcommittee reasoned, the vagueness of the election laws made unseating him tantamount to ex post facto legislation. The subcommittee further argued that the unethical practices in the campaign were used, not in the front-street effort carried on by Butler,

[23] *Congressional Record,* 82d Cong., 1st Sess., 1951, 97, Part 17, D75–D190; *ibid.,* Part 5, 6935; *St. Louis Post-Dispatch,* June 24, 1951.
[24] On Hennings' part in the Maryland investigation: *St. Louis Post-Dispatch,* April 18, 1951; *Washington Post,* July 15, 1951; *St. Louis Post-Dispatch,* July 19, 1951. On Gillette's threat to resign: *Washington Times-Herald,* July 6, 1951; *Washington Post,* July 5, 1951; *St. Louis Post-Dispatch,* July 7, 1951.

but in the back-street campaign waged by McCarthy. As being guilty with McCarthy the subcommittee named Fulton Lewis, Jr., radio commentator for the Mutual Broadcasting System, and the two McCormick newspapers, the *Chicago Tribune* and the *Washington Times-Herald*. While the subcommittee did not free Butler from responsibility for this part of the campaign, it placed the greatest blame on the McCarthy forces. The group's most publicized technique, the four-page tabloid *From the Record,* received special condemnation. Along with considerable misleading copy, this tabloid presented a composite picture of Tydings listening attentively to the Communist party's leader Earl Browder. Beneath the picture, the caption, though admitting that the picture was a composite, represented Tydings as saying to Browder, "Oh, thank you, sir," in response to Browder's assurance that Owen Lattimore and others accused of disloyalty were not Communists. In the last days of the campaign, when shortness of time precluded adequate reply, 303,206 copies of the tabloid were distributed to Maryland's voters.[25]

Two facets of the Maryland Report later became the subject of comment: First, although the report strongly condemned those who waged the back-street campaign, it stopped short of recommending action against McCarthy; second, the report received unanimous approval by the five-man subcommittee. Initial reaction to the report did not connect these two facets. Centering on the first, the failure to recommend action, early press comment attributed mildness on the part of the subcommittee to the presence of McCarthy on the parent Rules Committee. As time went on, a more probable interpretation of the report focused attention on its second facet, the unanimity with which the subcommittee approved it. In this view, Hennings cleverly toned down the report in order to ensure unanimous support in the Subcommittee on Privileges and Elections. Against this interpretation opponents argued that the two Republicans on the subcommittee needed no inducement to vote against McCarthy. One, Mrs. Smith, had expressed her famous "Declaration of Conscience" against McCarthyism in the previous session of Congress, and the other, Hendrickson, had signed the declaration. Yet, the fact remained

[25] Report No. 647, *op. cit.*

that while Smith and Hendrickson felt personal antipathy for McCarthy and publicly condemned his methods, both had party responsibilities. For this reason, each would have hesitated to approve a report recommending expulsion of either Butler or Mc-Carthy. Moreover, unanimity in the subcommittee held great importance. Strictly partisan voting in the subcommittee would have inspired similar action in the Rules Committee, enfeebling the report when it reached the Senate floor. Hennings' responsibility for this strategy became clear a few weeks later when McCarthy favored him with one of his by-now patented attacks.[26]

On August 2, 1951, the Subcommittee on Privileges and Elections unanimously accepted the Maryland Report. Four days later the Rules Committee formally accepted the report but delayed final action. That same day Democratic Senator William Benton of Connecticut, unwilling to await official action by the committee, took the report to the Senate floor and called for immediate expulsion of McCarthy. The Senator from Connecticut based his proposal primarily on McCarthy's activities in the Maryland campaign but pointed in addition to "other acts since his election to the Senate." The carefully drawn Maryland Report had become the basis for a move toward censure of the Senator from Wisconsin.[27]

Republican response in the Senate to Benton's proposal came first from Minority Leader Kenneth Wherry of Nebraska and then from McCarthy himself. The Nebraskan objected to Benton's using the Maryland Report prior to its approval by the Rules Committee. Wherry attributed Benton's action to the Democratic National Committee's desire to take the heat off its chairman, William M. Boyle, then under fire for a loan made by the Reconstruction Finance Corporation to a company he formerly represented as counsel. McCarthy's response went far beyond that of the Minority Leader. On the floor of the Senate he first confused the

[26] *St. Louis Post-Dispatch,* September 19, 1951; Louisville *Courier-Journal,* September 30, 1951; *Kansas City Star,* August 3, 1951. On the "Declaration of Conscience," see: *Congressional Record,* 81st Cong., 2d Sess., 1950, 96, Part 6, 7894–95.
[27] For action by the Rules Committee, see *Congressional Record,* 82d Cong., 1st Sess., 1951, 97, Part 17, D499 and D505. For the Benton resolution, see *ibid.,* Part 7, 9498–500.

issue by dropping more names of State Department "Communists." Then, admitting his interference in the Maryland election, he defended it as a patriotic service to Maryland and the nation. If Tydings had not whitewashed the investigation of the State Department, asserted McCarthy, then he had indeed treated the Senator from Maryland unfairly. But the central question remained: Was the State Department a nest of communism? Turning to the Elections Subcommittee, he cast doubt on the objectivity of Smith and Hendrickson, both of whom, he recalled, had signed the "Declaration of Conscience." As for Benton, McCarthy suggested that, in view of the Democrat's earlier career in the State Department, he was trying to prevent the exposure of former subordinates, such as William T. Stone. Finally, in defense of Fulton Lewis, Jr., and the McCormick newspapers, he asked why Drew Pearson and the *Washington Post* incurred no criticism for their activities in Maryland in support of Tydings.[28]

Initial reaction indicated that Benton's resolution would quickly die in committee. On August 8, when the Rules Committee voted to accept the Maryland Report, the members implied that the matter had ended. On learning that Senator Carl Hayden, Democrat from Arizona and chairman of the Rules Committee, had sent the Benton proposal to the Subcommittee on Privileges and Elections, Gillette said he planned no action. Other members of the subcommittee agreed with the Chairman. As late as August 31, Hennings, and perhaps Benton, also appeared inclined to drop the matter. In an intriguing letter to Tom F. Baker, president of the Missouri Cotton Producers Association and an ardent supporter of the Benton resolution, Hennings wrote:

We had quite a time on this [the Maryland investigation]—over three months and beginning the second week I was here—taking testimony and conducting hearings. . . . It practically immobilized me at the very outset of my term and I am still trying to catch up and do many things which I had to postpone doing earlier. . . . I am taking an active interest in this [the Benton resolution] and there is no question but that, in a

[28] *Ibid.,* 9500–501; *New York Times,* August 9, 1951; *Congressional Record,* 82d Cong., 1st Sess., 1951, 97, Part 7, 9703–13; Report No. 647, *op. cit.,* for view of McCarthy.

matter of principle, the views which you so clearly and eloquently express are accurate. There are some complications, however, in terms of party policy and even Bill Benton has suggested that he would be happy to see his resolution somewhat modified.[29]

In *The Reporter,* Douglass Cater pinpointed the complications in terms of party policy mentioned by Hennings. Cater professed that many Democratic senators were wishing Benton had left McCarthy alone. Their reasons centered both on the timing of the move and on its probable repercussions. According to Cater, these Democrats felt that McCarthy should have been expelled from the Senate the previous year, if at all, since August of 1951 was too near the elections. Moreover, they were reluctant to create a modern precedent for the Senate's expelling its own members. Cater concluded that these feelings, plus Gillette's vexation at receiving another sticky assignment, made action on the Benton resolution unlikely.[30]

Despite these predictions of early death for the Benton resolution, another series of events pointed in the opposite direction. In mid-August the White House chose to take a strong position against McCarthy. Anticipating the strategy for the 1952 election, President Truman lashed out at McCarthyism at the dedication of the new national headquarters of the American Legion. In his speech on this occasion the President denounced "this terrible business" of smear and accusation. Though Truman refrained from mentioning any names, McCarthy understood the President's implications and demanded equal time to reply to them. Then, in early September, the unpredictable Benton confirmed Hennings' analysis of the Maryland Report. The Senator from Connecticut shifted his objective from expulsion of McCarthy to censure. "A resolution of censure," he stated, "would provide the moral grounds to encourage the voters of Wisconsin to expel him in 1952." Having shifted to a more realistic goal, Benton ex-

[29] *New York Times,* August 9, 1951; "Democrats Fume at McCarthy, But He Has Them Terrorized," *Newsweek,* 38 (August 20, 1951), 19; Douglass Cater, "Is McCarthy Slipping?" *Reporter,* 5 (September 18, 1951), 25. Hennings Papers, Box 73, Hennings to Tom F. Baker, August 31, 1951.
[30] Cater, "Is McCarthy Slipping?" *op. cit.*

pressed utter disbelief that "this committee" with "this Chairman" would, as the press predicted, pigeonhole his resolution.[31]

The final event leading to the subcommittee's decision to consider the Benton resolution began with McCarthy himself. On September 19 the Subcommittee on Privileges and Elections planned to meet in executive session to decide the fate of Benton's motion. The previous day Hennings, having entrusted his proxy to Monroney, prepared to leave Washington for a three-day meeting of a law association in New York City. As he was boarding the plane for New York, he received from McCarthy a letter, already in the hands of the press, suggesting that Hennings should disqualify himself from considering the Benton resolution. The judgment of the Senator from Missouri, McCarthy bluntly asserted, was biased. His alleged prejudice, according to McCarthy, stemmed, first, from the fact that Hennings' law firm in St. Louis was counsel for the *Post-Dispatch,* a fervent anti-McCarthy organ. In addition, Hennings' senior law partner John Raeburn Green had recently concluded an appeal before the Supreme Court on behalf of John Gates, one of the Communist leaders convicted under the Smith Act. In closing the letter, McCarthy added a patronizing piece of advice: "I understand, Tom, that your father has a record as a fine lawyer and jurist. May I urge that you phone him and follow his advice on whether you should insist upon taking part in this administration-conceived version of a loyalty board for Senators."[32]

Hennings' reaction was instantaneous. Before boarding the plane, he wired McCarthy the bristling and ominous threat: "I propose to discuss you in the Senate on Friday. I hope that you will have time to be there even if it requires your temporary absence from inventing smears and lies about others."[33]

---

[31] "This Terrible Business," *Nation,* 173 (August 25, 1951), 142; "The McCarthy Issue," *U. S. News & World Report,* 31 (September 7, 1951), 24; "Benton v. McCarthy," *New Republic,* 125 (September 17, 1951), 8.

[32] Hennings Papers, Box 159, Hennings to Monroney, September 19, 1951; *Congressional Record,* 82d Cong., 1st Sess., 1951, 97, Part 17, D598. McCarthy's letter is reprinted *ibid.,* Part 9, 11857.

[33] Reprinted in *Congressional Record,* 82d Cong., 1st Sess., 1951, 97, Part 9, 11858.

The content and timing of the McCarthy letter invite specula-
tion. For Hennings it was a firsthand taste of pure McCarthyism,
but the network of imputation was already familiar to him. From
the *Daily Worker* McCarthy had learned that Green acted as
counsel for John Gates. This professional relationship proved,
he concluded, that Green was pro-Communist. Pursuing his own
kind of logic, McCarthy reasoned that Green's partner Hennings
was also pro-Communist, because he shared in the "Communist
fee" supposedly earned by Green. As to the *Post-Dispatch,* the
newspaper's major sin consisted of objecting to McCarthy; it had
objected also to the Supreme Court's upholding Gates's initial
conviction. The newspaper's retainer paid to Hennings' law firm
increased the Senator's vested interest in communism. The firm's
pattern of "softness" on communism, McCarthy charged, proved
that Hennings was biased against the Senator from Wisconsin
because of his fight against communism.

The letter's closing allusion to Judge Hennings contained its
own curious element. Less than a year earlier, McCarthy had
attacked the Senator through his father. On that occasion he accused Judge Hennings of picking up the tab for the anti-McCarthy
advertisement published on the eve of the latter's Jefferson City
speech. The rationale behind this strategy is difficult to fathom.
Perhaps McCarthy, with his "instinct for the jugular," felt he was
touching an exposed nerve developed at times by children of illus-
trious parents. The mention of Judge Hennings might have been
intended as a warning of personal attacks to come. It may be
that McCarthy believed that Judge Hennings, out of his long
experience in politics, might persuade "Tom" to back away from
the Benton resolution. Judging from what followed, the personal
allusion did little more than hone the edge of Hennings' reply.

McCarthy's attack on Green in the letter had the same effect.
Toward John Raeburn Green, Hennings felt a filial affection that
was reciprocated by his fatherly senior partner. The only thing
"red" about Green was the reddish tinge, intermingled with gray,
in his hair and mustache. Although he scrupulously avoided anything that might injure his junior partner's political career, Green
still felt compelled to undertake the Gates appeal. For him the
issue was not communism but the constitutional right of free

speech, which Gates's conviction under the Smith Act seemed to deny. An able and scholarly attorney, Raeburn Green threw down the gauntlet to the nation's witch-hunters by publicly asserting that "the liberty of each of us can be no greater than the rights of the Communists. . . . Our freedom stands or falls with theirs." Green accepted the Gates case after numerous leaders of the American bar had refused the task as too explosive and made good his boast.[34]

On Friday Hennings took the Senate floor as promised. After recounting the essence of McCarthy's accusations, he turned first to a defense of Raeburn Green. In anticipation of just such an attack, Green had provided Hennings with ample explanation of his motives in accepting the Gates case. Both in a letter to Hennings and in the preface to his Gates brief, he expressed his personal disdain for Gates and his Communist colleagues. It would be better, Green wrote, if there were no Communists in our midst, but, since there were, the future of the American constitutional system demanded that they be afforded the same rights as are guaranteed to all citizens by the Constitution. Then Green stated the conditions under which he took the case: He would accept no fee, and he would have complete independence from earlier counsel. To cap his defense of Green, Hennings was able to draw on the current issue of the *American Bar Association Journal,* in which an editorial eloquently praised Green for his effort in the Gates case as an example of "what is pure and noble in our profession."[35]

Green's defense accomplished, Hennings turned on the absent McCarthy with a denunciation that was described by the *New York Times* as "skirting the edges of Senatorial conduct":

It is perfectly obvious . . . that the suggestions contained in his [McCarthy's] letter are a thinly veiled attempt—and not the first one—to discredit the work of the subcommittee and invalidate its findings by devious means and irrelevant attacks on its members. It is a perfectly

---

[34] *Missouri Law Review,* 15:1, 111–14; interview, John Raeburn Green, June, 1962; Green Papers, Green to Hennings, June 15, 1951.

[35] *Congressional Record,* 82d Cong., 1st Sess., 1951, 97, Part 9, 11855–57; Green Papers, Brief for Gates, July 9, 1951; *American Bar Association Journal,* 37 (September, 1951), 673.

transparent effort to divert the attention of the Senate and the American people from the real issue at stake in the resolution of the Senator from Connecticut. The Benton proposal is directed to the activities of the junior Senator from Wisconsin in the 1950 Maryland senatorial election and to his fitness to be a member of this body. . . . Repeated shabby attempts to discredit the honest efforts of a subcommittee of the United States Senate and to undermine the trust the American public should have in this body can and must be met by frank and forthright answers.[36]

Hennings' dramatic speech breathed new life into the Benton resolution. The press noted that, as the Senator from Missouri finished his speech, Senators Brien McMahon, Democrat from Connecticut, and Paul Douglas, Democrat from Illinois, stepped forward to shake his hand. More significantly, veteran newsmen reported that non-Administration Democrats, some of them Southerners, were poised to aid Hennings if McCarthy's supporters retaliated. Taking their cue from William S. White, the *New York Times's* analyst of senatorial behavior, editorialists interpreted the attack on Hennings as McCarthy's biggest blunder to date. With near unanimity, newsmen concluded that by attacking Hennings the Senator from Wisconsin had alienated the one group in the Senate which, though opposed to McCarthy's style, would be the last to allow the dirty business of expulsion. For them, senatorial legend was at stake. This group, so the story went, consisted of conservative Democrats, heavily weighted with Southern members of the "Senate Club." A number of reasons were advanced to explain their strong reaction to the attack on Hennings: The Missourian was himself a conservative and a member of the club; he had bested Truman in the 1950 primary, making him a hero to anti-Administration Democrats; he had done nothing to antagonize McCarthy; and, finally, the harsh attack on a senator, unlike attacks on the State Department, indicated that McCarthy had now become intolerable.[37]

[36] *Congressional Record,* 82d Cong., 1st Sess., 1951, 97, Part 9, 11855–57.
[37] *New York Times,* September 22 and 23, 1951; *Christian Science Monitor,* September 22, 1951; *St. Louis Post-Dispatch,* September 23, 1951; *Miami Daily News,* September 25, 1951; *St. Louis Globe-Democrat,* September 26, 1951; *Manchester Guardian,* September 27, 1951; *Kansas City Star,* September 27, 1951; Louisville *Courier-Journal,* September 30, 1951; "Joe Stubs His Toe," *Nation,* 173 (October 6, 1951), 271.

Giving the myth chapter and verse, White reconstructed the following conversation with a "distinguished but unnamed" Southern senator:

McCarthy will never be got by the Bentons. He will never be got, here, by the State Department. But a while back, in June, he made a big mistake by attacking Marshall. He made a mistake down in Georgia the other day by asserting that some Senators have Communists on their payrolls. But he has made the biggest mistake of all now in taking on Tom Hennings. Tom is one of us. He didn't come to Washington fighting anybody and he hasn't done anything to McCarthy.[38]

This pronouncement, while making a fine story, contained numerous errors of judgment. Senator Herman Welker, Republican from Idaho and a McCarthy backer, did retort to Hennings, and no Southern Democrat stood up to defend the Missourian. Welker cited Hennings' telegram to McCarthy, insisting that its venom would lead many Americans, himself included, to agree with McCarthy's adverse opinion of the Senator from Missouri. Only New Englander Benton spoke in Hennings' defense. The "distinguished but unnamed" senator's statement that Hennings had done nothing to antagonize McCarthy needed qualification. A major plank in the Missouri Democrat's 1950 platform was a scathing denunciation of McCarthyism; during the campaign, the two had crossed swords in Jefferson City; finally, strong rumor painted Hennings as the influence behind the Maryland Report. Similarly, the insistence on Hennings' conservatism missed the mark. The Missourian was a conservative in matters pertaining to fundamental law, but not in economics. Throughout the 1950 primary and general elections Hennings never failed to support Truman's Fair Deal and strong civil rights proposals. Yet the myth did contain a germ of truth. Insofar as the Senate had a club,

---

[38] *New York Times,* September 23, 1951. See also William S. White, *Citadel, passim.* White's thesis on the ultimate censure of McCarthy centers on the revolt of the "Senate Club" against him when he wore out the club's patience. An interesting analysis of the White Senate Club thesis, as given me by a former administrative assistant to Hennings, suggested that White creates senatorial myths that become at least partially true when some senators try to conform to the myth. Like White's Southern senator, this informant is distinguished, and he will remain unnamed (interview, May, 1962).

Hennings received membership early, but not because of his conservatism. Courtly manners, charm, brilliance, and reluctance to allow differences in policy to become personal conflicts paved Hennings' acceptance into the club. In short, the Missourian was widely liked and respected by his colleagues. Hence, an attack on him brought greater revulsion than, for example, an attack on those senators who made a practice of preaching liberalism to their colleagues.[39]

Not all commentators favored Hennings. The *Chicago Tribune* and Columnist Constantine Brown strongly sided with McCarthy. The *Tribune* felt that the Senator from Missouri, along with Smith and Hendrickson, should leave the subcommittee. Brown agreed, citing Hennings' telegram as both injudicious and indicative of true bias.[40]

Hennings was correct in anticipating support from his Missouri constituency. While defending the *Post-Dispatch* on the Senate floor, the Missouri Democrat asserted that many Missourians agreed with the St. Louis newspaper. Thoughtful and responsible citizens, he said, in Missouri and elsewhere, deplored McCarthy's techniques of distortion and misrepresentation. Letters from constituents immediately confirmed his statement, for three out of four of those who wrote applauded his attack on the Senator from Wisconsin. Similarly, the St. Louis newspapers had nothing but praise for the action of their freshman senator.[41]

After the dust settled, the disastrous consequences of his attack on Hennings struck McCarthy. Backing down somewhat,

[39] *Congressional Record,* 82d Cong., 1st Sess., 1951, 97, Part 9, 11857– 58; interviews with former staff members, May, 1962. Robert L. Riggs stated that an attack on, for example, Herbert Lehman or Hubert Humphrey would have created little stir in the Senate. He remarked that some conservative Democrats would have welcomed such an attack (Louisville *Courier-Journal,* September 30, 1951). Later, observers of senatorial behavior placed Humphrey in the club, prior to his election as Vice-President.

[40] *Chicago Tribune,* September 29, 1951; *Washington Evening Star,* September 24, 1951; *St. Louis Globe-Democrat,* September 26, 1951.

[41] Hennings Papers, Box 51, letters pro-McCarthy; Boxes 115, 152, letters anti-McCarthy; *Congressional Record,* 82d Cong., 1st Sess., 1951, 97, Part 9, 11855–58; *St. Louis Globe-Democrat,* September 26, 1951; *St. Louis Post-Dispatch,* September 25, 1951. By this date the *St. Louis Star-Times* had ceased publication.

he announced to the press that if "Tom" and "Margaret" felt they could remain unbiased in their judgments, he would not press the matter further. Unfortunately for him, Tom, Margaret, and the rest of the subcommittee refused to back down. Hennings curtly announced that he had no intention whatsoever of disqualifying himself from the subcommittee. In response to Mrs. Smith's courteous appeal for a vote of confidence, the subcommittee assured her that she should also remain. On September 24 the subcommittee voted to take action on the Benton resolution. The following Friday Benton appeared as requested and read to the members a 30,000-word indictment of the Senator from Wisconsin.[42]

The investigation by the Subcommittee on Privileges and Elections, begun on September 28, 1951, proved fateful for McCarthy. At first, his major concern was neither expulsion nor censure, but the Republican primary in Wisconsin, which presented the only real obstacle to his return to the Senate. Of potential opponents, only Governor Walter J. Kohler, Jr., seemed capable of displacing him. Though Kohler had not indicated he would run, McCarthy feared that the Benton investigation would be just the encouragement he needed. This fear proved unfounded, but the Benton resolution held other grief for the Wisconsin Republican, since it initiated a probe that led to his censure by the Senate in 1954.[43]

In justice to McCarthy's political acumen, it seems likely that his attack on Hennings was not unconsidered. He realized that of those on the Gillette Subcommittee, Hennings had played the key role. A public attack on Hennings during his absence from the crucial meeting on September 19, he reasoned, would stampede Gillette and Monroney into dropping the resolution. Gillette, who was already committed to ignoring Benton's move, and Monroney, who held Hennings' proxy, could easily have disposed of the sticky business for good. Assuming this reasoning was cor-

[42] *New York Times,* September 22–30, 1951; *Congressional Record,* 82d Cong., 1st Sess., 1951, 97, Part 17, D612, D620, D629.
[43] *Kansas City Star,* September 27, 1951; Graham Hovey, "McCarthy Faces the Voters," *New Republic,* 125 (December 3, 1951), 15. On Kohler's refusal to oppose McCarthy, see Carey McWilliams, "Wisconsin Previewed," *Nation,* 174 (March 22, 1952), 269.

rect, it becomes evident that Hennings' telegram to McCarthy was crucially effective; it gave the subcommittee pause and halted the voting. After Hennings' speech on Friday on the Senate floor, the momentum against the Senator from Wisconsin made turning back impossible.

The opening of the hearings on the Benton proposal marked the end of a full year since Hennings had instituted his campaign against Donnell. He had begun the campaign with a clear diagnosis of the nation's illiberal state of mind, and from the beginning he had recognized the main sources of this mentality. Abuse of congressional investigating power, abuse of congressional immunity, and the demagogic practice of exploiting the nation's fear of subversion all played a part. Significantly, he leveled no criticism at the executive branch of government, later to be the subject of great concern on his part. The legislative branch was his target this first year, except for the Knauff case. Late in the first session of Congress, Hennings made a beginning at controlling investigating committees. With Senator Estes Kefauver, Democrat from Tennessee, he jointly sponsored a resolution to establish a fair code for congressional committees. But more importantly in this first year, he moved into the center of the conflict with the legislator most closely connected with "playing on the nation's fear of subversion in order to gain headlines or political advantage."[44]

The liberal mind eventually arrived at three solutions to abuses of civil liberties during the Cold War. One centered on establishing a stricter code to govern congressional investigating committees; the second concentrated on ridding the Senate of McCarthy; the third solution came later in the fifties, when executive departments led the hunt for subversives. In these later years of the decade, liberals attempted to create countervailing institutions in the federal government to hunt, in their turn, violations of civil liberties. In his first year Hennings participated in an effort to govern committees by fair rules. In a larger way, he came near to assuming effective leadership in removing McCarthy from the Senate. His part in creating a countervailing institution had to await three more years of involvement in the first two solutions.

44 For the Kefauver resolution, see *Congressional Record,* 82d Cong., 1st Sess., 1951, 97, Part 8, 10602–5.

III

The Hennings Report on McCarthy

THREE DOCUMENTS of the Senate underlay the body's ultimate censure of Senator McCarthy. Two of these, the Maryland Report and the Hennings Report, bear the signature of Senator Hennings. The third, the Watkins Report, is little more than a restatement, at a more propitious time, of Hennings' views. Hence, the crucial elements in the quasi-legal case against McCarthy came from the pen of the Missouri Democrat.[1]

The same subcommittee that produced the Maryland Report had nominal responsibility for the Hennings document. In actual fact, it was a one-man project, tenaciously pursued by Hennings in the closing minutes of the Eighty-second Congress. Since it appeared at a time when McCarthy seemed least vulnerable, the report had no immediate effect. Later, when the behavior of the Senator from Wisconsin became unbearable even to Republicans, the Hennings Report provided the strongest base for a move against him. The

---

[1] U. S., Congress, Senate, Committee on Rules and Administration, 82d Cong., 1st Sess., 1951, Report No. 647 (henceforth cited as *Maryland Report*). Senate, Committee on Rules and Administration, Subcommittee on Privileges and Elections, 82d Cong., 2d Sess., 1952, Report on S. Res. 187 and S. Res. 304, Committee Print (henceforth cited as *Hennings Report*). The complete report was reprinted in U. S., Congress, Senate, Select Committee to Study Censure Charges, *Hearings*, 83d Cong., 2d Sess., 1954, Part 2. The committee's Report No. 2508 is hereafter cited as *Watkins Report*.

eventual success of the document rested on the author's lawyer-like caution in stating the evidence against McCarthy and his thorough recital of facts.

In theory, none of the three arms of the federal government exercises functions reserved to another; the judiciary does not legislate, nor does Congress judge. In practice, the courts make law and Congress passes sentence, and among these quasi-judicial actions of Congress are the judgments it makes on its own members. Article I, Section 5 of the Constitution gives to each house of Congress the right to "punish its own members for disorderly behavior, and, with the concurrence of two-thirds, expel a member." In line with its committee system, such action ordinarily begins with an investigation in committee of the questioned behavior. When faced with the recommendation of its respective investigating committees, each house of Congress determines whether to punish. From 1871 to the Reorganization Act of 1946, the Senate assigned the task of investigating its members either to the Committee on Privileges and Elections or to a special committee created for the purpose. Since 1946, in the absence of any *ad hoc* special committee, the investigation has rested with the Subcommittee on Privileges and Elections, an arm of the Rules Committee. In the Eighty-second Congress, this was the Gillette Subcommittee, to which the Senate successively referred the tasks of investigating the Maryland election of 1950 and the Benton resolution of August 6, 1951.[2]

The fifteen-month struggle over the Benton resolution began on September 28, 1951, with Benton's long indictment of McCarthy before the Gillette Subcommittee. It ended with the Hennings Report of January 2, 1953, as the Democratic Eighty-second Congress gave way to its Republican successor. The conflict divided into two unequal periods: Gillette held the reins of the subcommittee from Benton's indictment to McCarthy's smashing victory in the Wisconsin primary one year later; during the final three months of its existence Hennings guided the battered remnants of the five-man subcommittee. Significantly, the effective report came from this second period, at a time when the anti-McCarthy forces had

---

[2] U. S., *Congressional Record,* 82d Cong., 2d Sess., 1952, 98, Part 3, 3701–5.

despaired of stopping the career of the Senator from Wisconsin. When Hennings became chairman, the subcommittee had dwindled to two members, Hennings and Robert Hendrickson, Republican from New Jersey. Since Hendrickson was reluctant to draw on himself any more abuse from McCarthy, Hennings supplied what energy the subcommittee possessed.[3]

During Gillette's tenure as chairman of the subcommittee McCarthy consistently eluded or cleverly countered its every effort to examine Benton's charges. Since McCarthy knew that the completion of the investigation prior to the September primary would endanger the success of his campaign for re-election, his basic strategy was delay. His controversial methods had involved him in a number of suits in addition to Benton's charges, but so long as these were not resolved before September 8, the date of the Wisconsin primary, he would escape unscathed. In July, when confusion still crippled the Gillette Subcommittee's investigation, McCarthy's position in Wisconsin remained secure. His popularity continued unabated while he recuperated in the surgery ward of Bethesda Naval Hospital after an operation that conveniently obviated the need to face Wisconsin voters. Under these circumstances, Governor Walter J. Kohler, potentially his strongest rival in the primary, chose to seek another term as governor rather than to challenge him. While McCarthy's popularity soared, the Gillette Subcommittee could show little for its year of effort save its own distraught condition and a damaged reputation.[4]

The tactics with which the Senator from Wisconsin fended the

[3] For a summary of Benton's indictment: *New York Times,* September 29, 1951. For a chronological account of subcommittee action: *Watkins Report,* 7-19.
[4] On the political situation in Wisconsin: Carey McWilliams, "Wisconsin Previewed," *Nation,* 174 (March 22, 1952), 269; "Benton Invades Wisconsin," *Christian Century,* 69 (July 16, 1952), 821; Robert H. Fleming, "Can McCarthy Win Again?" *Nation,* 175 (August 16, 1952), 147; Bernard Hennessy, "The Chance of McCarthy's Defeat," *New Republic,* 127 (August 18, 1952), 14; "McCarthyism: Is it a Trend?" *U. S. News & World Report,* 33 (September 19, 1952), 21; "Wisconsin: Wave of the Future," *Nation,* 175 (September 20, 1952), 223; "Why They Voted for McCarthy," *Nation,* 175 (September 20, 1952), 225; "The Wisconsin Primary," *Time,* 60 (September 22, 1952), 23; John B. Oakes, "Report on McCarthy and McCarthyism," *New York Times Magazine* (November 2, 1952), 12.

Gillette Subcommittee were familiar to people who had watched his career. Only once did he accept the subcommittee's invitation to appear before it to shed some much-needed light on the investigation. On that lone occasion he appeared merely to offer a bill of particulars in support of his own resolution calling for the expulsion of Senator Benton. Barging into the hearing room followed by a hand-truck loaded with papers and files, he regaled the members with five hours of innuendo directed against Benton. In effect, he questioned both the integrity and the loyalty of the Democrat from Connecticut, but said nothing about the evidence that called his own integrity into question. One such item concerned McCarthy's relationship with the Lustron Corporation, a manufacturer of prefabricated houses. Ostensibly as a means to sell more houses, Lustron agreed to buy a pamphlet on housing compiled by McCarthy. For his journalistic effort the Senator from Wisconsin received seventy cents per word, or $10,000. Skeptical of this high value placed on McCarthy's literary talents, the subcommittee found that Lustron had been under investigation by the Senate to evaluate the huge loans it had received from the Reconstruction Finance Corporation. Since McCarthy was a member of both congressional committees making the investigation, the subcommittee had obvious reasons to suspect McCarthy's relationship with Lustron. Was the fee a payment for the pamphlet or for "other services rendered"? As did many of the questions raised by the subcommittee over McCarthy's personal finances, this one went unanswered.[5]

Distraction of attention from the real issue was another tactic of the Senator from Wisconsin. To keep the subcommittee in turmoil and diverted from the Benton resolution, McCarthy instituted a debate over the group's right to investigate his personal

[5] On McCarthy's indictment of Benton: *New York Times,* July 4, 1952; "McCarthy on Benton," *Newsweek,* 40 (July 14, 1952), 32. On McCarthy's relations with Lustron: *New York Times,* September 29, 1951; Senate, Committee on Rules and Administration, Subcommittee on Privileges and Elections, *Hearings,* 82d Cong., 1st and 2d Sess., 1951, 1952, Part 1, 23 ff., 65 ff.; *Hennings Report,* 15–19; *Congressional Record,* 83d Cong., 2d Sess., 1954, 100, Part 10, 12959, 12963; Jack Anderson and Ronald W. May, *McCarthy, the Man, the Senator, the "Ism,"* 336 ff.; Richard H. Rovere, *Senator Joe McCarthy, passim.*

finances. Irritated by the diversionary scheme, Mike Monroney, Democrat from Oklahoma, suggested that McCarthy ask the Senate to discharge the subcommittee from further consideration of the Benton resolution. Monroney reasoned that a Senate vote against this motion would amount to a vote of confidence in the subcommittee as well as an affirmation of its jurisdiction. In addition, such a motion would force other senators to take a position on their controversial colleague. The strategy backfired, however. When McCarthy refused to make the motion, the subcommittee itself presented it, and the Senate voted unanimously not to discharge the Gillette group. McCarthy upset the maneuver, however, by joining the majority that approved the investigation of his personal finances and then calling for a similar investigation of Senator Benton. The net result was the addition of another distracting probe to the subcommittee's agenda.[6]

Further delay arose from the subcommittee members' preoccupation with defending themselves from McCarthy's attacks. Never one to leave the initiative to his opponents, McCarthy charged the members of the subcommittee with parroting the Communist line and with furthering what he modestly asserted was the Kremlin's primary aim, "getting McCarthy." In their study of the Senator from Wisconsin, Jack Anderson and Ronald W. May claimed that McCarthy desperately but futilely attempted to discover a taint of communism in Hennings' staff in order to disrupt the subcommittee's investigation. But besides accusations of disloyalty, the Wisconsin Republican charged the Democratic members of the subcommittee with wasting Senate funds in an attempt to dig up anti-McCarthy material for the party's national committee. Chairman Gillette became especially vulnerable to this charge after anti-McCarthy material from a secret subcommittee report mysteriously began appearing in the press. Although it remained unclear whether those releasing the information wished to embarrass

---

[6] The Monroney resolution was Senate, 82d Cong., 2d Sess., 1952, S. Res. 300, which Senator Carl Hayden, chairman of the Rules Committee, introduced. For the Senate vote on S. Res. 300: *Congressional Record*, 82d Cong., 2d Sess., 1952, 98, Part 3, 3954. The McCarthy resolution was Senate, 82d Cong., 2d Sess., 1952, S. Res. 304. On the Monroney scheme: Anderson and May, *McCarthy, the Man, the Senator, the "Ism,"* 323 ff.

McCarthy or the subcommittee—by making the latter liable to charges of smearing—further delay and confusion resulted.[7]

Prior to the Wisconsin primary, several incidents within the subcommittee gave added comfort to McCarthy. Late in 1951 Daniel Buckley, an investigator for the subcommittee, complained to the press that the Gillette group had dismissed him because he had opposed its anti-McCarthy bias. The day before the primary another investigator, Jack Poorbaugh, resigned in protest against the same alleged bias. Finally, with remarkably effective timing, on the day of the primary Senator Herman Welker, a Republican from Idaho who had replaced Mrs. Smith on the subcommittee, submitted his resignation with the statement that he wanted no part of the smear being prepared for the Wisconsin Republican. The effect of these protests on Wisconsin voters was telling, for on September 8 they gave McCarthy more votes than his seven opponents combined.[8]

In the wake of Welker's resignation and McCarthy's easy victory, the harried Gillette submitted his resignation, with the suggestion that, since his departure balanced Welker's, the subcommittee should return to its pre-1951 membership of three senators. Hayden agreed and named Hennings to replace Gillette as the new chairman. No sooner had the Senator from Missouri started to overcome the effects of these distractions, however, than Monroney left on a European vacation. Furious, Hennings urged Hayden to tell the Oklahoman either to return to his duties or to resign from the subcommittee. When Monroney chose the latter

---

[7] On McCarthy's accusations against the subcommittee: *Hennings Report,* 1–15; *Watkins Report,* 5–19, 28–31. On the press leak, see *Hennings Report,* 13; *New York Times,* April 22, 1952; Anderson and May, *McCarthy, the Man, the Senator, the "Ism,"* 323. On the alleged effort to find Communist infiltration of Hennings' staff: Anderson and May, 321.

[8] For the resignation of Welker: *Watkins Report,* 18; Senate, Select Committee to Study Censure Charges, *Hearings,* 83d Cong., 2d Sess., 1954, Part 1, 291; *New York Times,* September 27, 1952. On Welker's replacing Mrs. Smith: *New York Times,* January 24, 1952. For Poorbaugh's resignation: *Hennings Report,* 8, 14–15. For Buckley's statement: *Hennings Report,* 14. For the results of the Wisconsin primary: *U. S. News & World Report,* 33 (September 19, 1952), 21; H. H. Wilson, "Why They Voted for McCarthy," *Nation,* 175 (September 20, 1952), 225; "The Wisconsin Primary," *Time,* 60 (September 22, 1952), 23.

alternative, Hayden placed himself on the subcommittee in order to make it the legal threesome.[9]

The new chairman chose Paul J. Cotter from the staff of the parent committee as counsel for the subcommittee, with orders to conclude the investigation as soon as possible. Without the knowledge of Hennings, and using a rubber stamp of Hennings' signature, Cotter placed a mail cover on the Senator from Wisconsin and his key staff members. The mail cover consisted of directing the postmaster at Washington to give Hennings a daily listing of the names and return addresses of everyone from whom McCarthy and his staff received mail. With the fruits of this information and the evidence gathered from the hearings and staff investigations, Hennings prepared a final attack on McCarthy. He wrote McCarthy in November, requesting that he appear before the subcommittee to refute the evidence it had gathered, but McCarthy, relaxed and encouraged by his re-election, was hunting deer in northern Wisconsin. With only a month remaining before the Benton resolution was to expire officially at the close of the Eighty-second Congress, Hennings decided to make his report without McCarthy's testimony.[10]

The day before the Eighty-third Congress convened on January 3, 1953, Hennings sent a copy of the completed report to each

[9] For Gillette's resignation and Hennings' assignment as chairman: Hennings Papers, Box 159, Gillette to Hennings, September 10, 1952; copy of Gillette's letter to Hayden, September 10, 1952; telegram from Hayden to Hennings, September 23, 1952; copy of letter, Hayden to Gillette, September 23, 1952. On Monroney's resignation and Hayden's appointment of himself: *Hennings Report,* 8; *Washington Post,* November 20, 1952; *Watkins Report,* 25–26.

[10] On Cotter's appointment: *Hennings Report,* 11. On Cotter's use of the mail cover: Senate, Special Committee on Investigation of Cover on Mail of Senators, 83d Cong., 2d Sess., 1954, Report No. 2510. The respective responsibilities of Cotter and two of the subcommittee investigators, Francis X. Plant and Robert Shortly, remain obscure. In fact, only Hennings, of the subcommittee members, was definitively absolved from having approved the device. Cotter privately claimed that one of the other senators on the subcommittee gave him express approval. Hence, it was either Hendrickson, Monroney, or Hayden (Hennings Papers, Box 159, desk memo to Hennings from "Mac," November 16, 1954). For Hennings' final correspondence with McCarthy: *Hennings Report,* 8–9, 15; *Watkins Report,* 13–16, 19, 28–29.

senator. Later the same day he released it to the press. The next day, despite the incriminating exposé, McCarthy was sworn into the Senate without protest. Striding down the Senate aisle on the arm of his Wisconsin colleague Alexander Wiley, he gave Hayden, in passing, a friendly slap on the back. Hayden, who had signed the subcommittee's report with Hennings and Hendrickson, grimaced, but said nothing. When the new Senate organized its committees, William Jenner, Republican from Indiana and a McCarthy ally, replaced Hayden as chairman of the Rules Committee. The report was now referred to Jenner's committee, which quickly stopped further distribution of the document, so damaging to the Republican Senator from Wisconsin. To frustrate Jenner's action, a number of liberal organizations reproduced all or part of the report and made it available to the public.[11]

For a document that had stimulated such frantic efforts at quashing, the Hennings Report was unexpectedly restrained. Its four hundred pages contained mostly factual exhibits; only fifty pages were devoted to Benton and McCarthy. The smaller section on Benton seemed insignificant, since the subcommittee charged only that he had badly managed a campaign contribution of $600, a fact the Connecticut Democrat had earlier admitted. The subcommittee refrained from making any recommendations in the larger portion of the text that concerned McCarthy; it was simply a concise and well-documented narrative that suggested two conclusions: First, that McCarthy had obstructed the whole investigation and had repeatedly abused the members of the subcommittee; second, that the subcommittee had gathered a considerable body of unrefuted evidence indicating highly irregular financial transactions on McCarthy's part.

In addition to the questions raised by McCarthy's acceptance of a $10,000 fee from the Lustron Corporation, the subcommittee's investigation led to other queries. It asked, for example, whether "funds supplied to Senator McCarthy to fight Communism or for other specific purposes were diverted to his own use," and if "Senator McCarthy's activities on behalf of certain

[11] *New York Times,* January 3–4, 1953; Willard Shelton, "The Shame of the Senate," *Progressive,* 17 (February, 1953), 7; *St. Louis Globe-Democrat,* January 22, 1953.

special interest groups, such as housing, sugar, and China, were motivated by self-interest." One sequence of questions extended as far back as 1944 and implied that McCarthy had violated federal and state corrupt practice acts during his senatorial campaigns of 1944–1946. "What," asked the subcommittee, "was the source of funds totalling $17,600 allegedly contributed by Senator McCarthy's relatives to his 1944 primary campaign?" In conjunction with this same campaign, the subcommittee asked:

What disposition was made by Senator McCarthy of stock market profits in excess of $40,000 realized in 1943 and withdrawn from time to time in 1944? Why did Senator McCarthy, who had $40,000 at his disposal in 1944 call upon his relatives for financial assistance in connection with the 1944 primary campaign?

To explain the absence of recommendations, the subcommittee asserted that the issues transcended partisan politics and should be decided by the whole Senate. In conclusion, the group announced that the report would be turned over to the Department of Justice and the Bureau of Internal Revenue for any action they deemed appropriate.

Initial reaction to the Hennings Report was unanimous: Nobody liked it. McCarthy's supporters condemned it as an obvious smear attack on their hero. Columnist David Lawrence accused the subcommittee of further entrenching the congressional right to smear. The report, he said, was full of implications of wrongdoing, yet furnished no actual proof or evidence of such actions. The report only proved, he concluded, that there was no real difference, in fundamental principle, between those who shouted the loudest about McCarthyism and those at whom they shouted. Hendrickson, though he had signed the report, expressed similar misgivings over the report's raising questions without answering them. Welker termed the report "outlandish," implying that the Rules Committee would certainly reject it when Republicans assumed control.[12]

McCarthy was irate. The subcommittee, he charged, struck "a new low in dishonesty and smear." He called Hayden and Hennings "Truman lackeys," who were trying to frighten those sena-

[12] *St. Louis Globe-Democrat,* January 5 and 10, 1953.

tors who were about to "break the hold which the pinkoes, Communists and crooks have had upon this government." In an unfortunate statement that was to haunt him later, he characterized Hendrickson as "a living miracle in that he is without question the only man in the world who has lived so long with neither brains nor guts."[13]

Liberals expressed equal annoyance over the weakness of the Hennings Report and the failure of the Senate to act on it. Admitting that the dilemma of the subcommittee made controversy inevitable, the liberal journal *Commonweal* criticized it for raising the very issues it was supposed to solve and for refusing to subpoena McCarthy. The Senate's failure to take action on the report came under equally vehement fire. The *Nation* called the body's inaction "a Senate sellout," while Willard Shelton, in the *Progressive,* termed it "the shame of the Senate." The *New Republic,* which deplored the seating of McCarthy also, dramatically described the scene: "When his name was called to take the oath there was a hush. The cowed Senate sat mute."[14]

Hennings ignored the complaints of McCarthy's backers, but the criticism from liberals infuriated him. Especially annoying to him were the attempts in the press to explain the mildness of the report. Hennings specifically rejected the explanation given in the *Nation* by a political scientist at Princeton University, H. H. Wilson, who attributed the report's mildness to "a concession by Senator Hennings to overcome the resistance of Senator Hendrickson." Professor Wilson, Hennings asserted privately, had little understanding of the situation in the Senate. The simple truth was that the votes needed to sustain a move against McCarthy did not exist, and any attempted showdown would have resulted

13 *St. Louis Post-Dispatch,* January 3, 1953; *New York Times,* January 3, 1953; *Watkins Report,* 17.
14 "Report on McCarthy," *Commonweal,* 57 (January 23, 1953), 393; H. H. Wilson, "The Senate Sellout," *Nation,* 176 (January 24, 1953), 64; Willard Shelton, "The Shame of the Senate," *op. cit.; New Republic,* 128 (January 12, 1953), 3. Not all of the liberal press failed to analyze the situation as Hennings saw it. For example, Marquis Childs, in the *St. Louis Post-Dispatch* of January 6, 1953, shared Hennings' analysis. (Note also: Hennings Papers, Box 73, letter from Walston Chubb to Hennings on February 24, 1953, indicates that Marquis Childs spread the story on Hennings' motive in making the report the way he did.)

in a vote of confidence in the Wisconsin Republican and a repudi-
ation of the subcommittee. Such a result, Hennings concluded,
would have been disastrous for the Senate and for the country.
To intimates he expressed the opinion that henceforth the problem
of McCarthy rested squarely in the hands of the Republican party,
since a partisan move against him was doomed to failure.[15]

In the Congress that opened with this controversial seating of
McCarthy, Hennings' private analysis was confirmed. Impatience
with the controversial Senator grew steadily among Republicans
until finally, near the end of the second session, McCarthy's own
party, as Hennings had hoped, successfully moved against him.
Republican satisfaction with McCarthy because of his vote-getting
ability in 1950 and 1952 gradually diminished during the Eighty-
third Congress, when the Senator from Wisconsin repeatedly
embarrassed his own party. President Eisenhower, except on a
single occasion, refused to tangle with him, although he congratulated Republicans in the Senate after their move against McCarthy
succeeded. But despite the absence of overt pressure from the
Administration, the majority party in the Senate developed a
distaste for McCarthy when, as Hennings correctly noted, he ran
out of Democratic targets and turned on Republicans.[16]

During the fifteen months that disenchantment with McCarthy
grew within his party, the Hennings Report remained effectively
buried. Acceptance of the document by the Rules Committee became unthinkable after Jenner replaced Hayden as chairman, and
under the new Administration neither the Justice Department nor
the Bureau of Internal Revenue found anything in the report to
merit prosecution. Even the educational value of the document

[15] H. H. Wilson, "The Senate Sellout," *Nation, op. cit.;* Hennings
Papers, Box 85, Hennings to George C. Vournas, February 12, 1953. Also,
see Drew Pearson, *St. Louis Post-Dispatch,* January 7, 1953; Hennings
Papers, Box 85, Hennings to Ralph Torreyson, February 7, 1953.

[16] On the position of McCarthy in the Republican party and his relationship with the Eisenhower Administration: Robert J. Donovan, *Eisenhower: The Inside Story,* 246 ff.; Richard H. Rovere, *The Eisenhower
Years, passim;* Eric F. Goldman, *The Crucial Decade: America, 1945-
1955, passim;* Herbert Agar, *The Price of Power: America since 1945,* 147
ff.; Richard H. Rovere, *Senator Joe McCarthy, passim;* Walter Johnson,
1600 Pennsylvania Avenue; Presidents and the People, 1929-1959, 287 ff.;
Progressive, 18 (November, 1954), 3; Hennings Papers, Box 18, Speech
at Jefferson-Jackson Day Dinner, Danville, Virginia, June 3, 1954.

labored under severe handicaps. In accord with Senate practice, the report received an initial printing of 2,500 copies. From this supply, Hennings had immediately distributed a copy to each senator. For several weeks thereafter he filled numerous requests for copies, many of which came in response to publicity given the report by Eleanor Roosevelt in her syndicated column. But by March of 1953, Hennings' supply was exhausted, and the requests that continued to pour in went unfilled. When questioned about the supply of copies, the Senator asserted that the number he distributed had barely dented the original printing; in April he began referring requests to the *New Republic,* which reprinted major portions of the text. Republicans showed little zeal for widening the report's distribution. Senator Wallace Bennett of Utah, for example, sent a significant reply to a constituent who requested a copy. In the main body of his letter, Bennett explained that the report was a biased effort, but he promised to send a copy anyway. In a footnote, dated a day after the text of the letter, he regretfully informed the constituent that the supply of reports had just run out. Since the date of the footnote was January 27, 1953, when ample copies should have been available, Bennett's statement seemed an obvious ruse to limit circulation of the report. Another request, this one to Hennings, complained that the subcommittee's office, soon after publication of the report, had advised the applicant that no copies were available. In desperation, Hennings threw open his office to those who wished to read the only remaining copy of the report. It is easy to understand how the rumor that Jenner had pigeonholed the report gained substance.[17]

[17] For executive action on the Hennings Report: *Christian Century,* 70 (September 23, 1953), 1068; *U. S. News & World Report,* 35 (October 30, 1953), 99. For Mrs. Roosevelt's column and Hennings' reaction: *Washington Daily News,* January 30, 1953; Hennings Papers, Box 84, Hennings to Roosevelt, February 10, 1953. On the distribution of the report: Hennings Papers, Box 159, Hennings to Mrs. Clifford Ellsworth Conry, March 6, 1953; Hennings to Hon. Allen McReynolds, March 19, 1953; Box 82, Hennings to Robert E. McWilliams, January 28, 1953; Hennings to James F. McNamara, February 13, 1953; William C. Noonan to Hennings, March 14, 1953; Phillip Gelb to Mrs. Rose Zimmerman (Hennings' staff), March 11, 1953; Box 30, Robert G. Moore, Salt Lake City, to Hennings (with enclosure of Senator Wallace Bennett's letter), February 2, 1953; Doris Fleeson, *St. Louis Post-Dispatch,* March 18, 1953. The reprint in the *New Republic:* 128 (March 30, 1953), 12 ff.; *Labor's Daily,* July 21, 1953.

Further action on Hennings' exposé of McCarthy and his methods had to await the motion of Senator Ralph Flanders, Republican from Vermont, to censure McCarthy. In the subsequent proceedings, which met, eventually, with success, two significant facts stood out: First, the initiative for Flanders' move against his fellow Republican came primarily from McCarthy's own party; second, each motion against the Senator from Wisconsin took substance from evidence contained in the Hennings Report.

Flanders began his assault amid the clamor surrounding McCarthy's controversy with the Army. In March of 1954, the Vermont Republican read a lecture to McCarthy on the floor of the Senate, questioning his value to the Republican party. It seemed, he said, that McCarthy had become a satellite of the Democratic party, since he gave the opposition so much cause for glee. Flanders returned to his theme in June, observing that the Senator from Wisconsin was dividing his party by urging colleagues to seek evidence of subversion in the Republican Administration. A few days later, Flanders remarked that he had recently received a copy of the Hennings Report and found it interesting. "A bootlegged edition," he explained, "was sent me months ago . . . but I paid little attention to it." The Senator from Vermont then startled his colleagues by moving that, until McCarthy answered the questions raised by Hennings in the report, he be stripped of the chairmanship of the Committee on Government Operations. Although he was elaborately ignored by McCarthy, Flanders pressed on. He explained his delay in openly opposing the Senator from Wisconsin by confessing to only "a gradual accumulation of uneasiness" over McCarthy's antics. He now, however, made the motion to censure McCarthy. The first item in his supporting bill of particulars was McCarthy's treatment of the Gillette-Hennings Subcommittee, as documented in the "newly discovered" report.[18]

Democrats swiftly joined the hunt, none more gleefully than Senator J. William Fulbright of Arkansas. The man whom Mc-

[18] *Congressional Record,* 83d Cong., 2d Sess., 1954, 100, Part 3, 2886; Part 6, 7389–90, 8032–33; Part 8, 10992–93; Part 10, 12729–34. Flanders' first resolution was Senate, 83d Cong., 2d Sess., 1954, S. Res. 301, and the second was S. Res. 261.

Carthy called "halfbright" presented his own bill of particulars in support of the Flanders resolution. Of his six items, Numbers One and Two came directly from the Hennings Report. Senator Wayne Morse, an Independent by now, quickly followed suit. Of his seven reasons for censure, the first two closely resembled the charges Fulbright had culled from the Hennings Report.[19]

Although the Flanders resolution anticipated an immediate Senate vote on its merits, a majority of senators felt that a special committee should investigate the charges before any voting took place. Hennings, as might be expected, disagreed with the majority decision. He recounted his long and arduous experience on such a committee, terming it a distasteful and frustrating task, and he argued that another investigation would be a mistake. After his first three years in the Senate, the Missourian explained, he came to feel that his only purpose in being sent there was to observe the activities of the Senator from Wisconsin. From the experiences of those three years, he predicted that a special committee would receive no more cooperation and no less abuse from McCarthy than had the Gillette-Hennings Subcommittee.[20]

Despite appeals by Hennings, Fulbright, and others, the majority prevailed. With twelve members dissenting, the Senate voted on August 2 to appoint a bipartisan committee to investigate the Flanders resolution and the Morse-Fulbright amendments. Democrats selected for the committee included Edwin C. Johnson of Colorado, John C. Stennis of Mississippi, and South Carolinian Sam J. Ervin, the latter two high-ranking members of the so-called "Senate Club." The Republican members were Frank Carlson of Kansas, Francis Case of South Dakota, and Arthur V. Watkins of Utah. With Watkins as chairman, the committee began hearings in late August and completed its report in time for the special session on November 8.[21]

In its report the Watkins Committee recommended that the Senator from Wisconsin be censured on two counts. The first

[19] *Congressional Record,* 83d Cong., 2d Sess., 1954, 100, Part 10, 12903–19, 12927, 13732.

[20] *Ibid.,* 12946–51, 12985.

[21] *Ibid.,* 12989, 13394; *Watkins Report,* 2; *Congressional Record,* 83d Cong., 2d Sess., 1954, 100, Part 10, 15486. On the work of the Watkins Committee: Rovere, *Senator Joe McCarthy,* 223 ff.

count charged him with refusing to appear before the Gillette-Hennings Subcommittee and with abusing the members of that body. The second condemned McCarthy's abusive treatment of Brigadier General Ralph Zwicker during his controversy with the Army. On both counts the recommendation was unanimous, although Senator Case, a week later, withdrew his vote on the charge related to Zwicker, attributing his change of heart to new evidence unearthed after he signed the report.[22]

Three weeks after the Watkins Committee submitted its recommendations, the Senate voted 67 to 20 to accept the first charge, but demurred on the indictment related to Zwicker. In its place the senators substituted a final count and voted 64 to 23 to censure McCarthy for the abuse he heaped upon the Watkins Committee in the course of its investigation. Thus, of the forty-six original charges leveled against the Senator from Wisconsin, the only one ultimately to stand was the charge documented in the Hennings Report.[23]

The censure indictment based on the Hennings Report did not go unchallenged. The Watkins Committee gave McCarthy and his attorney Edward Bennett Williams ample opportunity to refute it. Their defense appeared in McCarthy's testimony before the committee as well as in the brief Williams filed with the Watkins group and, some years later, in Williams' reflections on the proceedings. The elaborate defense shed additional light on the work of the Gillette-Hennings Subcommittee and on its fruit, the Hennings Report.[24]

Williams' legal defense of McCarthy's treatment of the subcommittee rested, first, on the assertion that the subcommittee lacked official status and jurisdiction to investigate the financial affairs of the Senator from Wisconsin. Since the competence of the

[22] *Watkins Report,* 31, 61, 67–68, filed with Senate on November 8, 1954 (*Congressional Record,* 83d Cong., 2d Sess., 1954, 100, Part 11, 15851); *Congressional Quarterly Almanac,* 10 (1954), 456–69.

[23] *Congressional Record,* 83d Cong., 2d Sess., 1954, 100, Part 12, 16392.

[24] Senate, Select Committee to Study Censure Charges, *Hearings,* 83d Cong., 2d Sess., 1954, Part 1, Part 2, 554–74; Edward Bennett Williams, "The Final Irony of Joe McCarthy," *Saturday Evening Post,* 235 (June 9, 1962), 21, and *One Man's Freedom,* 59 ff. (The magazine article and the relevant part of the book are identical.) For a brief description of this defense: Rovere, *Senator Joe McCarthy,* 227 ff.

subcommittee extended only to elections, Williams charged that it exceeded its jurisdiction when it investigated McCarthy's personal finances. Further, the subcommittee lost its status as an arm of the Senate when three of its five members resigned. Moreover, even if the group had jurisdiction and official status, McCarthy had no obligation to testify before it, since he was never subpoenaed. Turning to the Watkins Committee, Williams questioned its jurisdiction also. By what right, he asked, could a committee of the Eighty-third Congress pass judgment on matters pertaining to a previous Congress? The people of Wisconsin, Williams asserted, approved McCarthy's actions in the Eighty-second Congress by re-electing him in November of 1952, and the Senate, by seating McCarthy on January 3, 1953, ratified that verdict.[25]

Williams' second argument concerned the fairness of the methods employed by the Gillette-Hennings Subcommittee. Even in a legislative trial, he declared, the accused has the right to cross-examine adverse witnesses. Although McCarthy requested this right, Gillette refused him. The subcommittee's methods of investigation constituted a further violation of individual rights. The device known as a mail cover, Williams charged, invaded the Senator's right to privacy and disregarded the constitutional prohibition against unreasonable search and seizure. Moreover, since the mail cover demanded at least a momentary delay of the mail, the practice had violated federal law. But apart from the mail cover, Williams claimed that the subcommittee had been biased against McCarthy, and he pointed to the protests registered by Welker, Poorbaugh, and Buckley as proof. In summarizing this part of the defense, he contended that, in light of the subcommittee's bias and unfairness, McCarthy's refusal to cooperate and his attacks on the members were understandable.[26]

Several questions of fact were raised in Williams' defense of McCarthy. McCarthy's failure to appear before the subcommittee, Williams argued, was the latter's fault. Only once, he asserted, did the subcommittee request the Senator from Wisconsin to testify, and on that occasion its members knew that McCarthy

[25] Senate, Select Committee to Study Censure Charges, *Hearings,* 83d Cong., 2d Sess., 1954, Part 2, 554 ff.
[26] *Ibid.,* Part 2, 554–63; Williams, *One Man's Freedom,* 64–71.

would be out of town on the day specified for his appearance. McCarthy did not even learn of the request, said Williams, until after the deadline had passed. Moreover, the Senator from Wisconsin had made it clear in 1952 that he would testify only if served with a subpoena, and yet at no time did he receive a subpoena from the subcommittee. With regard to the mail cover, Williams expressed the opinion in later years that if McCarthy and the Senate had known about the notorious device before the censure proceedings, the vote on censure would have failed.[27]

The extensive legal and factual defense engineered by McCarthy and Williams demanded a reply. In making its reply, the Watkins Committee stated that the Gillette-Hennings Subcommittee had jurisdiction to investigate McCarthy's financial affairs and that the Senate affirmed this jurisdiction when it voted unanimously not to discharge the subcommittee from further consideration of the Benton resolution. In addition, McCarthy himself had sent a request to the same subcommittee to investigate the financial affairs of Benton, and the group had dutifully fulfilled his request.[28]

The Watkins Committee also concluded that the loss of three members from the five-man subcommittee did not destroy the group's official status as an arm of the Senate. Quoting the Senate parliamentarian, Watkins reasoned that Hayden, as chairman of the full Rules Committee, had the power during the Senate's adjournment to appoint himself as the third member of the subcommittee and Hennings as chairman without consulting the full committee.[29]

To justify its own jurisdiction to pass judgment on the events of the previous Congress, the Watkins Committee ruled that Congress is a continuing body, and it denied the legal implications that Williams asserted as following from McCarthy's reelection and the Senate's seating him. In the first place, some of McCarthy's questionable behavior occurred after one or both of these decisions. Moreover, the Senate had only a few hours to examine the Hennings Report before the question of seating McCarthy arose. Finally, the committee concluded that the power to

27 Williams, *One Man's Freedom*, 64–71.
28 *Watkins Report*, 24.
29 *Watkins Report*, 25–26.

censure, unlike the contempt power, belongs to the Senate without regard to the time and place of a Senator's misconduct.[30] The most trenchant objection raised by Williams and McCarthy concerned the latter's obligation to testify before the Gillette-Hennings Subcommittee. The subcommittee never subpoenaed him and only once requested that he appear before it. The single request came in a telegram from Hennings on November 21, 1952, when McCarthy was hunting deer in northern Wisconsin. Through a clerical error the Hennings Report contained an exhibit that erroneously indicated that another request was sent to McCarthy at a different time.[31]

Nevertheless, McCarthy's failure to testify before the subcommittee to refute the evidence it had gathered constituted a serious breach of senatorial conduct. While the subcommittee withheld a subpoena because, according to Hennings, it lacked the power to enforce it, and only once requested McCarthy to appear, it had, on six occasions between September 25, 1951, and November 7, 1952, invited him to explain the incriminating evidence it had gathered. Moreover, the members of the subcommittee denied that McCarthy ever told them he would respond only to a subpoena. But even without a subpoena, the Watkins Committee concluded, McCarthy owed it to himself and the Senate to answer charges that cast serious doubt on his honor and to cooperate with a Senate subcommittee.[32]

[30] *Watkins Report,* 20–23, 30.
[31] *Watkins Report,* 15, 26–28.
[32] *Watkins Report,* 26–28; *Hennings Report,* 9–10; Hennings Papers, Box 51, John Howe to Hennings, August 31, 1954; Mary K. Garner to Hennings, September 13, 1954; copy of telegram from Benton to Arthur V. Watkins, September 13, 1954; letter from Mary K. Garner to Langdon West, September 13, 1954; Mary K. Garner to Hennings, September 14, 1954; Mary K. Garner to Langdon West, September 14, 1954; copy of letter from Benton to Watkins, September 15, 1954; Benton to Hennings, September 15, 1954; copy of telegram from Gillette to Mary K. Garner, September 15, 1954. (The above correspondence was between the offices of former Senator Benton and Hennings. In effect, Benton told Hennings that the information he had gathered from Gillette, Hayden, Hendrickson, and Monroney proved that none of them could recall McCarthy's having said he would not testify unless subpoenaed to do so.) *Watkins Report,* 26–27; *Hennings Report,* 15.

The attack Williams made on the fairness of the subcommittee was at least misleading. The behavior of Welker, Poorbaugh, and Buckley surely admitted another explanation. Welker, ardently pro-McCarthy, had regularly demonstrated a bias that made his protest against the subcommittee's methods highly questionable. Three days before the Wisconsin primary, Poorbaugh had requested a brief leave of absence from the subcommittee, pleading the necessity of attending to some personal matters. When he suddenly resigned the day before the primary and denounced the subcommittee, the suspicion that he had committed himself to assisting in McCarthy's campaign became plausible. Buckley's protest contained its own peculiarities. He publicly denounced the subcommittee at 5:00 P.M. on December 27, 1951, but the telephone company's records indicated that he had been in contact by long-distance telephone with McCarthy's office at 3:00 P.M. that day and that other calls occurred throughout the following month. In short, the three protests against the alleged unfairness of the subcommittee came from persons whose objectivity was, at best, questionable.[33]

The Watkins Committee conceded too much when it allowed McCarthy to condemn the subcommittee for refusing to permit him to cross-examine adverse witnesses, though it denied that this refusal justified the abuse that McCarthy heaped on the members of the subcommittee. The subcommittee had invited McCarthy to be present during all relevant hearings and repeatedly offered him the opportunity to refute adverse evidence. Moreover, the subcommittee acted wisely in not allowing McCarthy to cross-examine its witnesses. In a court of law this right belonged to the Senator from Wisconsin, but the Subcommittee on Privileges and Elections was not a court of law, nor was the accused an ordinary citizen. He was a senator, and, therefore, he possessed extraordinary privileges, such as congressional immunity and the power to compel testimony from others. The major restraint that could prevent the abuse of these privileges was the control exercised by

[33] On Poorbaugh and Buckley: *Hennings Report,* 14–15. On Buckley and Welker: Anderson and May, *McCarthy, the Man, the Senator, the "Ism,"* 319, 322, 339.

his senatorial peers, who operated through a legislative trial without need of observing all the procedures so necessary in a court of law. Their judgment, not the rules of a law court, governed the proceedings and created an extraordinary power to balance the extraordinary privileges enjoyed by all senators. The subcommittee, on the basis of past experience, judged it unwise to allow McCarthy the right of cross-examination; the full Senate unanimously approved this decision by its vote of confidence in the subcommittee. In a trial before a court of law, this judgment would have been unfair; in a legislative trial, when the case revolved around conduct censurable within the Senate and when the accused had a past history of twisting committee hearings into a one-man pursuit of irrelevancies, this judgment was understandable and not, at least patently, unfair.[34]

The final objection registered by Williams concerned the mail cover instituted by the subcommittee's counsel Paul J. Cotter. The imposition of this device by Cotter or by an investigator subject to him was done subsequent to the institution of several charges against McCarthy. One charge accused him of speculating on the stock market with funds given him to fight communism. Another charge, later proven false, intimated that McCarthy was engaging in some kind of racket that involved a printer. In the absence of clarification of these charges by the Senator from Wisconsin, Cotter imposed this investigative device on first-class mail directed to McCarthy's Washington residence between October 24 and November 16, 1952. Mail directed to McCarthy's secretary Miss Jean Kerr and staff men Donald A. Surine and Ray Kiermas came under the same surveillance.[35]

Although he freed the subcommittee members of knowledge of Cotter's action, Williams objected to the mail cover on two grounds. The use of mail cover, he argued, violated McCarthy's right to privacy, an objection that most senators believed was

34 *Watkins Report,* 28.
35 Senate, Special Committee on Investigation of Cover on Mail of Senators, 83d Cong., 2d Sess., 1954, Report No. 2510; *Congressional Quarterly Almanac,* 10 (1954), 469; *Congressional Record,* 83d Cong., 2d Sess., 1954, 100, Part 12, 16276–77; also, see note 10.

justified. In addition, Williams reasoned that the vote of censure would have failed of a majority if McCarthy and the members of the Senate had known about the mail cover beforehand. Williams' reasoning on this point was not accurate, for both McCarthy and the Senate knew of the mail cover before the vote on censure; McCarthy knew about it at least a month before December 2, the date of the vote, for on October 30, 1954, he released to the press in Iowa a letter he was sending to Gillette, querying him on the matter. Gillette received the letter on November 1, 1954, and the next day lost his Senate seat in the Iowa election.[36]

The Senate learned of the mail cover on December 1, the day before the vote on censure, when McCarthy precipitated discussion of it on the floor of the Senate. Hayden explained then that Cotter considered the device a normal investigative technique and had imposed it without either the approval or the knowledge of the subcommittee's members. Senator Jenner objected to Hayden's points, emphasizing the unfairness of a mail cover, but Hayden defended Cotter on the ground that any able investigator would have used it. Jenner countered that use of the device to apprehend criminals differed from its use to investigate a United States senator's activities, but Hayden curtly dismissed the distinction as being inapplicable in McCarthy's case.[37]

The debate concerning the mail cover, which took place on December 1, ended with the creation of a two-man committee that was empowered to make an immediate investigation. Senators Homer Ferguson, Republican from Michigan, and Walter George, Democrat from Georgia, completed the probe in one day, and, while exonerating Hennings of blame for using the mail cover in the subcommittee's investigation of McCarthy, they condemned past and future use of the device in the investigation of senators. Perhaps the Ferguson-George report, if it had appeared earlier, would have altered the recommendations of the Watkins Committee. Beyond this slender possibility, there is little reason to believe that the controversy over the mail cover could have done

36 Williams, *One Man's Freedom,* 59–71; *Congressional Record,* 83d Cong., 2d Sess., 1954, 100, Part 12, 16274.
37 *Ibid.,* 16331–32, 16276–77.

more than delay the Senate's gradual closing in on Joseph Mc-
Carthy.[38]

While Williams maintained later that censure did little to limit
McCarthy's subsequent activities and that his client wore the
Senate's punishment as a badge of courage, McCarthy's influence
declined steadily thereafter. And, of comfort to the liberals, was
evidence that down with him went much of the hysteria responsible for shrinking the scope of civil liberties.

The responsibility for McCarthy's decline rested with no single
senator, since the proper conditions for curbing McCarthy's power,
by no means inevitable, were essential. Nevertheless, it must be
noted that Hennings made singular contributions to McCarthy's
ultimate fall. The Maryland Report, the contents of which stimulated the Benton resolution, gained much of its force from the
Missourian's guidance; the decision to pursue the Benton resolution rested heavily on Hennings' stiffening in the face of Mc-
Carthy's personal attack; it was the Missouri Democrat who took
charge of the investigation of McCarthy in September of 1952,
after Gillette had given up in despair; and he worked night and
day in the closing hours of the Eighty-second Congress in order
to produce his report on McCarthy before the Republican Eighty-
third Congress began.[39]

The impact of the Hennings Report indicated the value of these
efforts. Repeatedly, in subsequent investigations of McCarthy, its
sound accumulation of evidence was to provide a springboard for
motions to discipline the Senator from Wisconsin. Hennings himself claimed that the evidence in the report provided a sufficiently
strong prima-facie case against the Senator from Wisconsin to take
before a jury. Though the Watkins Committee refused to pass
judgment on McCarthy's alleged financial irregularities, the accumulation of evidence forced him into continual evasion and
abuse of the subcommittee. The bipartisan character of the report
on that evidence, a character that Hennings had insisted upon,

[38] *Ibid.,* 16342–44. The resolution was Senate, 83d Cong., 2d Sess., 1954,
S. Res. 332; Special Committee on Investigation of Cover on Mail of
Senators, 83d Cong., 2d Sess., 1954, Report No. 2510.
[39] Williams, *One Man's Freedom,* 68. For another view of McCarthy's
postcensure behavior: Rovere, *Senator Joe McCarthy,* 232 ff.

ultimately made McCarthy's evasions and abuse grounds for bipartisan censure. Undoubtedly, the Hennings Report had educational value also. The public ultimately took notice of its contents, despite its months of burial, for liberal groups reproduced it and liberal journals based articles on it. Efforts to suppress the document quite possibly added to its effectiveness by undermining confidence in McCarthy and by lessening the fears of those who might oppose him. It is significant that when Senator Flanders rose in the Senate to make his motion of censure, he held in his hand a copy, published by Americans for Democratic Action, of the Hennings Report.[40]

[40] *Congressional Record,* 83d Cong., 2d Sess., 1954, 100, Part 10, 12946–51. For an example of the way the journals drew on the Hennings Report: *Progressive,* 18 (April, 1954), entire issue. On the various publications of the Hennings Report: *Labor's Daily,* July 21, 1953. On the document used by Flanders: Clifton Brock, *Americans for Democratic Action,* 146.

IV

The Problem: Preventive Law

THE CONTROVERSIES over civil liberties in the early 1950's involved much more than Senator McCarthy and his machinations. Zeal for security, with its accompanying disregard of freedom and justice, burned in Congress, in the White House, and in the public consciousness. Filtering down from the federal level, loyalty-security programs touched state and local governing bodies and private corporations. By 1955 statutes and executive orders, private agreements and loyalty oaths had created a new body of law; John Lord O'Brian has called it "preventive law." With it, law in the United States acquired a new dimension. Heretofore, criminal law had aimed at punishing a person only when his *mens rea*—criminal intent—led to some overt act or to conspiracy to act. The loyalty-security program, however, attempted to anticipate subversive action by probing a citizen's mind in search of subversive ideas. In the beginning, this search affected only the six million employees of federal, state, and local governments. Gradually, it spread to the professions and to employees of private industry. Brought into being by the fears engendered by the Cold War, preventive law soon enveloped one-fifth of the nation's working force.[1]

[1] John Lord O'Brian, *National Security and Individual Freedom,* 24-26; Ralph S. Brown, "6,000,000 Second-Class Citizens," *Nation,* 174 (June 28, 1952), 644, and "Loyalty-Security Measures and Employment Opportuni-

The new system of law needed new procedures, developed by trial and error. New norms of evidence concentrated on a man's conversation, his reading habits, and his associations. Logically extended, this kind of evidence could emerge even from the conversation, reading materials, and associations of his family, friends, and acquaintances. A citizen's personal associations became particularly significant under this new system. Judgment of "guilt by association" presently achieved a mechanical efficiency when the Attorney General prepared a list of organizations, membership in which served as a touchstone for identifying subversive thinking. With this cue from the federal government, state and local officials, private industries, and self-appointed vigilantes prepared lists of their own. In time, list-making became, as one commentator described it, a "roll your own" procedure.[2]

The new system of law also required new punishments. The usual penalty, imprisonment, could not be used. Jailing a citizen who was "guilty by association" of subversive ideas was not feasible in peacetime. Of the new punishments developed for the new system, exposure was the most common, and, through the use of modern media of communication, it was also the most effective. Besides exposure, for the citizen in government service dismissal became the usual penalty. Employees in private industries that held government contracts suffered the same punishment. Such dismissals became widespread after war broke out in Korea, for defense mobilization expanded government contracts and their accompanying security regulations. Faculties and staffs of universities became subject to the same examination and penalties when they undertook research programs for the government. Even in private industries that held no government contracts, an unofficial black-

ties," *Bulletin of the Atomic Scientists,* 11 (April, 1955), 113. For a complete catalogue of coverage prior to 1958, see Brown's *Loyalty and Security Employment Tests in the United States,* 164 ff.

[2] For an excellent insight into laws of evidence followed in security procedure, see Adam Yarmolinsky, *Case Studies in Personnel Security.* For the history of the Attorney General's list, see Eleanor Bontecou, *The Federal Loyalty-Security Program,* 157 ff. Chronological File of the Subcommittee on Constitutional Rights (henceforth: CRS File), 1955, memorandum of Benjamin Ginzburg, October 20, 1955. For examples of private listing: Merle Miller, *The Judges and the Judged.*

list developed as a weapon of punishment. In the last group, fear of public reaction, rather than federal regulation, inspired the practice.[3]

Other thorny problems appeared when the new system of law went into operation. Accuracy in convicting a citizen of subversive intent was difficult to attain. Even in the most rigid system of criminal law errors take place. The Constitution of the United States guarantees a fair trial, not an accurate one, and the new practice of judging ideas rather than actions greatly increased the possibilities for error. Moreover, finality in judging thoughts is in all circumstances elusive and, perhaps, impossible to achieve. Passing judgment on a man's thought patterns can seldom be definitive, for the person who is adjudged innocent at one moment may imperceptibly become guilty the next. Should he, then, be haled back into court? Also, in the trials that took place under the new system of law a new hurdle was set in the path of justice, for a judge who found too many accused persons innocent became suspect himself. Perhaps he harbored the subversive idea of protecting his fellow subversives. Who, then, was to judge the judge's thoughts?[4]

A moment's reflection reveals that the nation's courts were not adequate to enforce preventive law. Each department of government and each corporation needed its own security system. Personnel, often untrained in judging criminal action, undertook to judge criminal ideas as the task, risky enough for a practitioner of law, fell to laymen. At times, laymen of one political party passed judgment on members of the opposing party, and such judgment became a weapon in personal vendetta in all areas of the nation's life. Possibly, the accused stood in the path of the accuser's

[3] On the extension of the loyalty-security system into private industry and universities: Brown, *Loyalty and Security,* 61 ff., 119 ff. On the security measures of private industries without government contracts: John Cogley, *Report on Blacklisting: Movies* and *Report on Blacklisting: Radio.*

[4] Bontecou, *The Federal Loyalty-Security Program,* 245. Commenting on the lack of finality in a security decision, Max Ascoli stated: ". . . no man who has been the object of prolonged widely publicized security investigation has ever succeeded in gaining a decisive, unalterable clearance. This is the first principle of the Jurisprudence of Security." ("The Jurisprudence of Security," *Reporter,* 11, July 6, 1954, 8.)

advancement within a department or opposed the opinions of an adverse witness. In the climate provided by the new system of law, judging a man's ideas or testifying about them provided opportunity for strategic, vengeful action in the personal and political battles within departments of government and private industry.[5]

Besides being founded on a questionable basis, preventive law suffered from the lack of exact definitions of the subversive ideas it proscribed. Traditionally, the statutes that forbid criminal acts have developed through a slow process of legislative action. In this process, the crime has received exact definition, citizens have learned what behavior is punishable, and judges have learned what evidence indicates commission of the crime. Preventive law contained little or none of this definition. What, for example, is a disloyal thought? What evidence indicates that a person has harbored disloyal thoughts? What constitutes the nation's security? The new system of law never answered these questions because it never received the benefit of normal legislative action. It simply appeared, the frantic offspring of the Cold War.[6]

Enforcing preventive law proved to be as difficult as understanding it. On the federal level, both Congress and the President contributed their energies to enforcement. This joint effort in itself was novel, for in theory the legislative branch of the government makes laws and the executive branch enforces them. By 1954 congressional committees, operating on the principle of exposure for its own sake, vied with the President for the title of major

[5] In the case of Bailey v. Richardson, 341 U. S. 918 (1951), the Supreme Court affirmed, without an opinion, the decision of the United States Court of Appeals for the District of Columbia (182 F. 2d 46, 1950) which said, in effect, that in loyalty cases involving a government employee the courts have no function to perform (Milton R. Konvitz, *Bill of Rights Reader,* 329–30). On the personnel operating the security program: Bontecou, *The Federal Loyalty-Security Program,* 40–48, 250–52. On use of the security program for partisan political objectives: Hennings Papers, Box 20, Speech at Jefferson-Jackson Day Dinner, April 13, 1953, Pittsburgh, Pennsylvania.

[6] Interview with Sadi Masé, May, 1962. (Mr. Masé is a professor of jurisprudence and was a close friend of Senator Hennings.) On the absence of strict definitions of loyalty and security violations: Bontecou, *The Federal Loyalty-Security Program,* 241 ff.; Brown, *Loyalty and Security,* 4 ff., 383 ff.

executor of security law. While investigating subversive ideas, the committees exposed to public censure the citizens accused of harboring the ideas and demanded their dismissal. Cowed into submission, heads of government agencies and of private industries dutifully carried out the sentences.

The general public shared the responsibility for the growth and success of the loyalty-security network. Some citizens, of course, were critical of the network and its operation. Others acquiesced to its existence with reluctance, disliking its methods but thinking its ends were necessary. A few eagerly demanded more extreme measures in pursuing subversives, but the vast majority of the public simply did not understand the complex creation, at least in meaningful terms. Brooding over this fact, John Lord O'Brian, former prosecutor for the Justice Department, complained of the absence of leaders willing to speak out and capable of touching the native fairness of Americans. The nation needed statesmen, he said, with the ability to explain the loyalty-security program in the moral terms the people could understand.[7]

The historical emergence of preventive law in the executive branch began with President Truman, but it reached its peak during the Eisenhower Administration. In March of 1947 President Truman issued Executive Order 9835, creating a loyalty program for federal employees. Under its provisions any employee could be dismissed if "reasonable grounds" existed for questioning his loyalty. Truman directed the Attorney General to compile a list of subversive organizations whose members would automatically come under suspicion and appointed the Loyalty Review Board to oversee the entire program. In 1951 the review board pressed Truman for a more stringent norm for federal employment. The President responded with a new executive order, which demanded dismissal if "reasonable doubt" existed about the employee's loyalty. Before its expiration under Eisenhower, nearly two million civil servants had gone through the loyalty mill set up by Truman.[8]

[7] On the attitude of the public and the extent of the so-called hysteria: O'Brian, *National Security and Individual Freedom,* 82–84. Compare, however, with Samuel A. Stouffer, *Communism, Conformity and Civil Liberties.*

[8] The best book-length analysis of the Truman loyalty program is Bontecou, *The Federal Loyalty-Security Program.* For a brief, accurate

Alongside this loyalty program a separate security system, instituted during World War II, continued to function. This security program gave to heads of certain executive departments and agencies the power to suspend or, if necessary, dismiss at a moment's notice any employee they felt was a security risk. While restricted primarily to military departments during the war, this "summary dismissal" power was extended by Congress in 1950 to the heads of eleven sensitive departments and to any other department head the President designated. The most glaring weakness of this program—perhaps a necessity in wartime—was that it gave to the department head the power of suspending at will any employee he suspected might be a security risk. In many cases the suspended employee, deprived of his income, had no choice but to seek other employment without waiting for the final decision on his security status.[9]

In his first "State of the Union" message, President Eisenhower, in an effort to forestall any accusations of "softness" on communism, intimated that he would revise the loyalty-security program. He promised that no disloyal citizen would any longer draw his salary from the federal government, and that his Administration would dissipate, once and for all, the public's fears over Communists-in-government. To accomplish these goals, he asserted, no additional legislation was needed. Unnoticed at the time, this last statement indicated that the President had decided to base his entire program on the "summary dismissal" power left over from World War II.[10]

In April of 1953 the Eisenhower security program appeared as promised. From the President came Executive Order 10450 and from Attorney General Herbert Brownell, Jr., sample instructions for enforcing it. At first blush, the Eisenhower–Brownell program satisfied a major complaint long registered by liberal critics of

description: Leonard D. White, "The Loyalty Program of the United States Government," *Bulletin of the Atomic Scientists,* 7 (December, 1951), 363 ff. The second norm of dismissal came in Executive Order 10241. My interpretation of Executive Order 10241 came from: Brown, *Nation,* 644 ff.

[9] Reprints of these summary dismissal statutes may be found in Bontecou, *The Federal Loyalty-Security Program,* Appendix 2 (B).

[10] *Congressional Record,* 83d Cong., 1st Sess., 1953, 99, Part 1, 748 ff.

Truman's program. Defenders of civil liberties had repeatedly protested the Truman Administration's failure to distinguish the problem of security from that of loyalty. Loyalty is a personal quality, they pointed out, while security involves a person and an objective situation. Not every disloyal person constitutes a threat to national security, nor, conversely, is every security risk a disloyal citizen. The most discussed example of this distinction was the homosexual. In a sensitive position, a homosexual threatens national security because of his susceptibility to blackmail; by threatening to expose his condition, foreign agents could possibly force him into disloyal acts. Therefore, the homosexual is indeed a security risk but not essentially disloyal.[11]

The Administration solved the dilemma of loyalty versus security by abolishing the Truman loyalty program. To take its place, the President, on the basis of the 1950 "summary dismissal" statute, expanded the security program to cover every department and agency of the federal government. The Loyalty Review Board, with its regional and agency miniatures, received a curt notice of dismissal, and nothing took its place. Eisenhower thereby decentralized the security system and put the ultimate power of decision in the hands of federal department and agency heads. Assisting the department heads were hearings boards that drew their personnel from within the departments. The Civil Service Commission partially filled the role exercised earlier by the Loyalty Review Board, since the commission supervised the administration of the program and reported every six months to the National Security Council. The Attorney General served as adviser to the various department heads in matters pertaining to security. In sum, the Eisenhower security program gave the summary dismissal power, which in World War II only military departments possessed, to the more than sixty heads of executive departments and agencies.

Underlying the new security program was the assumption that every federal employee, down to the last game warden, worked in a sensitive position. In consequence, every department or agency head received the power to suspend any employee on a moment's

11 Eleanor Bontecou, "President Eisenhower's 'Security' Program," *Bulletin of the Atomic Scientists,* 9 (July, 1953), 215 ff. For a comparison of the programs under Truman and Eisenhower, see: Brown, *Loyalty and Security,* 21 ff.

notice and to dismiss him without the right of appeal to a higher authority. At the same time, the norm of dismissal as a security risk became so amorphous that it could exclude from federal service *as a security risk* anyone who, for example, talked or drank excessively. Thus, in disentangling security from loyalty, Eisenhower merged it with the vast suitability program. As a consequence, the norm and process of dismissal became easier, but the effect on the reputation of the dismissed remained the same. While security chiefs found it easier psychologically to brand a man a security risk than a disloyal citizen, the public saw little difference between the two. To the public, the Eisenhower Administration, with its increased volume of alleged security separations, seemed to be striking sound blows to end the "twenty years of treason." This deceptive caricature of the Eisenhower security program led easily to the "numbers game," a Republican political device aimed at convincing the public that the Eisenhower Administration was busy ridding the federal government of Communists and fellow-travelers left over from the Truman era.

The political advantage implicit in the "numbers game" began to emerge in October of 1953, when the Administration announced the initial results of the new security program. The White House stated that, under the program, 1,456 persons had thus far left the government payroll. Two weeks later, this vague announcement received "clarification" when Bernard M. Shanley, special counsel to the President, claimed in a speech at Newark that "1,456 subversives had been kicked out of government jobs since the President assumed office." After considerable questioning of the figures by Democrats and numerous requests for an official breakdown on the reasons for individual employees' being "kicked out of government," Shanley confessed that he was mistaken only in using the term "subversives."[12]

As the 1954 elections approached, Shanley's figure rose to 2,200, and Democrats continued to press for a breakdown of cases and

[12] For the chronology of the "numbers game" see: *Congressional Quarterly Almanac*, 10, 378-83. For Hennings' reaction: Hennings Papers, Box 18, Speech, October 14, 1954, Nevada, Missouri; Speech, October 16, 1954, Kansas City, Missouri; Box 19, Speech, October 23, 1954, Moberly, Missouri. On the facts underlying the "numbers game," see: Brown, *Loyalty and Security*, 57-59; Hennings Papers, Box 160, memo from William D. Patton to Charles H. Slayman, Jr., August 8, 1956; p. 123 ff.

reasons. Representative Robert Sikes protested that the Administration's failure to provide a breakdown of this useful statistic
indicated that some Republicans believed "a security risk is any
Democrat who has a government job and the only security that is
involved is that of the Republican Party." Finally, Philip Young,
chairman of the Civil Service Commission, appeared before the
Senate Post Office and Civil Service Committee to give the requested breakdown. While Young's figures helped somewhat to dissipate the fog surrounding the dismissals, Eisenhower, the next day,
March 3, 1954, drew even thicker, more confusing clouds about
the issue when he repeated that the 2,427 separations from government service—the number had jumped again—were all security
risks. As the November election drew closer, the Vice-President
drained the final drop of partisan politics from the "numbers
game." In September of 1954, Mr. Nixon proclaimed that the
Administration was kicking Communists, fellow-travelers, and
security risks out of the government by the thousands, and in
October he added that all but one of the 165 security separations
from the State Department had been hired under Truman.[13]

The Truman and Eisenhower administrations were not the
only users of preventive law. In Congress, the roving committees
that were investigating subversion both made the new system of
law and enforced it. From 1945 to 1950 the House Un-American
Activities Committee had this field of endeavor to itself, but in
1950 Senator McCarthy began his one-man crusade of exposure
from the floor of the Senate. The next year Senator Patrick A. Mc-
Carran's Subcommittee on Internal Security took its place in the
lists next to HUAC and the Senator from Wisconsin. This trium-
virate prevailed over the legislative branch of the United States
government throughout the Eighty-second Congress.[14]

When the new administration tightened its security early in
1953, the congressional investigators of subversion also stepped up

[13] *Congressional Quarterly Almanac,* 10, 712; 11, 16, 27, 40.
[14] On congressional investigations after World War II: Robert K. Carr,
*The House Committee on Un-American Activities, 1945–1950; Federal Bar
Journal,* 14, issues 1 and 2; Alan Barth, *Government by Investigation;*
Telford Taylor, *Grand Inquest, the Story of Congressional Investigations;*
William F. Buckley *et al., The Committee and its Critics;* Association of
the Bar of the City of New York, *Report of Special Committee to Study
Committee Procedures.*

their pace. In the new Congress, Representative Harold H. Velde, Republican from Illinois, led the House Un-American Activities Committee, and Senator Jenner, Republican from Indiana, replaced McCarran as chairman of the Subcommittee on Internal Security. McCarthy, the new chairman of the Committee on Government Operations, named himself chairman of its Subcommittee on Investigations. This awesome group searched for communism in schools, entertainment, labor unions, religion, government, the State Department's information service, the Voice of America, and the armed forces. It was the last-named investigation, as conducted by McCarthy's Permanent Investigations Subcommittee, that led to McCarthy's estrangement from the part of the public that supported him, the Administration, and the Republican party and provided the context for his censure by the Senate.[15]

Appalled by this proliferation of the uses of preventive law, Hennings answered John Lord O'Brian's plea for a statesman capable of explaining the situation in moral terms the people could understand. Even during his first term, when his investigations of Senator McCarthy occupied much of his time and energy, the Missouri Democrat showed concern for the broader movement the Senator from Wisconsin symbolized. But after completing his report on McCarthy in January of 1953, Hennings turned his attention more closely to the implications of preventive law. He severely criticized the new law because it tended to limit freedom of thought by punishing free expression. The loyalty-security program, said Hennings, suppressed freedom of thought in the only way possible—by placing limitations on the free communication of ideas amongst citizens. In such an atmosphere, thoughts remained within the individual, unshared by others and powerless to continue the progress America had achieved in the past.[16]

[15] For scope of these three committees: *Congressional Quarterly Almanac,* 9, 70, 316–24, 334–50, 354–60; *ibid.,* 10, 362–74. For Hennings' reaction: Hennings Papers, Box 18, press release, May 7, 1954; Speech, May 4, 1954, Haverford, Pennsylvania. For the Army-McCarthy hearings: Michael Straight, *Trial by Television.*

[16] For example, Hennings Papers, Box 3, Speech at Jackson Day Banquet, January 12, 1952, Springfield, Missouri; Speech to Women's National Democratic Club, March 17, 1952, Washington, D. C.

Under similar siege, according to Hennings, was the justice Americans were accustomed to expect. The process of enforcing preventive law violated the traditional American sense of fair play, which students of law call due process. Guaranteed by the Fifth and Fourteenth amendments, due process constitutes the essence of criminal justice by extending to an accused person a network of safeguards developed over the centuries by Anglo-Saxon law. These safeguards prevent arbitrary verdicts and provide an environment from which an accurate judgment is most likely to emerge. The existing administration of loyalty-security programs unnecessarily violated due process, since a citizen accused of disloyalty often failed to receive the minimum opportunity to defend himself. In some cases, the accused learned neither the identity of his accuser nor the nature of the evidence against him. Arbitrary and inaccurate judgments, Hennings concluded, were the inevitable result.[17]

Turning specifically to the Truman loyalty program, Hennings questioned both its value and its operation. Even though the Democratic President and fellow Missourian took great pains to safeguard civil liberties threatened by his loyalty program, he failed to escape Hennings' denunciation. The fact that traitors and hard-core Communists seldom turned up in the sweep of a loyalty net, said Hennings, cast considerable doubt on its effectiveness. In addition, the program's arbitrary procedures violated due process and had already made men in public office cautious in their thoughts and hesitant in expressing them. Hennings recommended that the loyalty program be dropped or, if it had to remain, that its procedures be modified in accord with due process of law.[18]

[17] For example: Hennings Papers, Box 18, Speech at Haverford College, May 4, 1954, Haverford, Pennsylvania; Speech to alumni of Washington University of St. Louis, May 20, 1954, Washington, D. C.

[18] Hennings Papers, Box 3, Speech to members of B'nai B'rith, November 5, 1951, Mount Vernon, New York; Speech at Jackson Day Banquet, January 12, 1952, Springfield, Missouri; Speech to the Women's National Democratic Club, March 17, 1952, Washington, D. C. On the fairness of the Truman Loyalty Program, see: Bontecou, *The Federal Loyalty-Security Program*, 239–40; Richard P. Longaker, *The Presidency and Individual Liberties, passim.*

Hennings reserved his strongest criticism for congressional investigators of subversion who, he said, constituted the main source of infringements on civil liberties. Unsubstantiated accusations of disloyalty streamed from investigating committees and from lone congressmen, uninhibited because of their immunity from libel suits. Witnesses, haled before a committee and thoroughly browbeaten, were accorded little opportunity to defend themselves and were forced to answer "Yes" or "No" to questions that could not be answered so simply. Such committees allowed witnesses to make derogatory statements about third persons who, accused *in absentia,* had little opportunity to defend themselves; their damaged reputations were seldom fully rehabilitated by later retractions. These probes, Hennings warned, would appear like inquisitions, in the pages of history. As a remedy to abuses by committees, he offered a Senate resolution creating a fair code of procedure, and he suggested that the press and radio might provide the opportunity for the committees' victims to tell their side of the story.

Turning to the People, Hennings asserted that much of the blame for violations of civil liberties rested on the public conscience. In a national crisis the majority tends to limit free expression, not through political suppression, but by refusing employment to the unorthodox. In the existing crisis, he continued, fear made many citizens think that ideas are somehow dangerous and led people to believe that the nation could not meet the Communist threat without violating freedom of expression. This fear was gradually undermining the traditional viewpoint in the law that a man is innocent until proven guilty. In its place had arisen the attitude that a citizen is disloyal until he proves his loyalty. An essential element of communism, Hennings observed, is thought control. With the federal loyalty program filtering down to the state and local levels; with universities demanding loyalty oaths of faculty and students; and with character-assassination and name-calling dominating the news, who could doubt, asked Hennings, that thought control had already arrived? In its hysteria, he concluded, the nation had fostered the very thing it was fighting.

But something more concrete than speeches was needed to

reverse the infringements on individual rights. Hennings saw little opportunity for making any immediate changes in the Truman-Eisenhower security system, but congressional committees seemed more amenable to remedial action. In fact, a movement within Congress for a code of fair procedure in committees had antedated Hennings' arrival in the Senate. Democratic Majority Leader Scott Lucas of Illinois and Representative John McCormack, Democrat from Massachusetts, introduced fair-code measures in 1949. Since neither resolution became law, Senator Estes Kefauver, Democrat from Tennessee, introduced a similar bill in 1951, and Hennings cosponsored it, but to no avail. In 1953, liberals in the Senate introduced a wide variety of resolutions aimed at solving the worsening problem of unfair procedures in committees, but the members of the two parties failed to agree on a unified means of enforcing the code, so little progress was made.[19]

The drive for a code of fair procedure reached a climax in 1954, when the Senate was swamped from all sides by demands for action. Bar associations, religious and civic groups, and private citizens pleaded for such a code after witnessing the televised spectacle of the Army-McCarthy hearings. Responding to these pressures from every direction, nineteen Democrats in the Senate agreed to sponsor a single resolution for a fair procedure code. Pooling their talents, they formulated Senate Resolution 256 and held hearings on it in June of 1954.[20]

In the hearings on Senate Resolution 256, as well as in an

[19] On the background of the 1954 fight for a code: *Congressional Quarterly Almanac,* 10, 375 ff. The Kefauver bill was Senate, 82d Cong., 1st Sess., 1951, S. Con. Res. 44. The second Kefauver bill, which Hennings' again cosponsored, was Senate, 83d Cong., 1st Sess., 1953, S. Con. Res. 10. For the Republican strategy: *New York Times,* February 27–28, March 3–4 and 10–12, and July 2, 1954.
[20] On public pressure for fair committee code: *New York Times,* March 18 and 25, April 24, May 29, June 26, and August 18 and 26, 1954. For the pressure exerted on Hennings: Hennings Papers, Box 29, Congressional Investigations correspondence in 1954; Box 30, McCarthy censure correspondence in 1954; Box 36, Congressional Investigations correspondence in 1954; Box 50, Correspondence on S. Res. 256, 83d Cong., 2d Sess.; Box 52, Congressional Investigating Committees in 1954.

extensive series of speeches, Hennings made his contribution to the fair code movement. The questions concerning the procedures used in congressional investigations, he stated, arose from a failure to distinguish two types of committee investigations. In the first, which he termed *legislative* investigations, no code of procedure was needed, since Congress merely sought information needed to frame statutes. In this type of probe, an individual's personal beliefs and associations came under inspection only if they affected the policy or the conduct of public office. In short, since the individual was not on trial, he had little need to quarrel with committee procedures.[21]

The second type Hennings labeled an *inquisitional* investigation, and in this type the individual was actually on trial. His thoughts and actions came under scrutiny, and he became in fact an accused person. The question of fair procedure arose when the committee employed procedures in an inquisitional investigation that were fair only in a legislative probe. Hennings suggested that rights similar to those granted the accused in a court of criminal law were apropos in an inquisitional hearing. The accused should have the right to counsel, the right to cross-examine adverse witnesses, the right to present evidence and witnesses in his own behalf, and the right to be protected from premature release of damaging evidence. In short, he urged Congress to grant due process to the accused, insofar as this could reasonably be followed outside of a court of law.[22]

The move for a code of fair procedure never succeeded in the Senate. After the censure of McCarthy the steam went out of the movement. Many senators began to doubt the wisdom of establishing a strict code of conduct, since it would unreasonably hamper the wide-ranging work of congressional investigations. Hennings, too, admitted that Congress needed broad powers to investigate

[21] Hennings Papers, Box 18, Speech, March 30, 1954, Miami, Florida; Speech, May 4, 1954, Haverford, Pennsylvania; Speech, May 20, 1954, Washington, D. C.; testimony of Hennings before Subcommittee on Rules on S. Res. 256, June 28, 1954; Box 19, Speech, December 3, 1954, St. Louis, Missouri.

[22] See note 21.

effectively and that his distinction between inquisitional and legislative investigations contained insurmountable difficulties in practice. Yet, the movement did not fail entirely. Most senators agreed that, in the last analysis, fair procedures came primarily from fair men. They agreed also that the long debate over codes served to bring to light the ways in which congressional committees, deliberately or inadvertently, treated witnesses unfairly. In these educational terms, Hennings' distinction between different types of committee investigations had the desired effect.[23]

The result of Hennings' vigorous criticism of preventive law was his gradual emergence as the Senate's leading defender of civil liberties. By the close of the Eighty-third Congress in 1954, his influence in other areas had increased also. To his membership on the Rules Committee was added, in the spring of 1953, assignment to the Judiciary Committee, the parent body of the Subcommittee on Internal Security, and unanimous election by fellow Democrats as secretary of the Party Conference. With the latter post went membership on the thirteen-man Steering Committee and the ten-member Policy Committee as well as floor leadership behind Majority Leader Lyndon B. Johnson of Texas and Party Whip Earle C. Clements of Kentucky. In short, Hennings had become a member of what William S. White termed the Democrats' "Board of Directors."[24]

Hennings' influence within the Senate continued to increase in the Eighty-third Congress, during which he made two of the most significant contributions of his career in the Senate. The first of these concerned the long-simmering debate over the so-called Bricker Amendment, which would have limited the treaty-making powers of the President. With Senator John W. Bricker, Republican from Ohio, and Senator Walter George, Democrat from Georgia, leading the bipartisan majority, the proposed amendment seemed assured of passage. Greatly disturbed by this attempt at invading the President's power over foreign affairs, Hennings led a strenuous campaign against the measure and gradually won

23 Hennings Papers, Box 19, Speech on Senate floor, January 5, 1955.
24 Hennings Papers, Box 3, press release, January 6, 1953; William S. White, "Democrats' Board of Directors," *New York Times Magazine* (July 10, 1955), 10.

support for his position. When the issue came to a vote late in February of 1954, the Missourian's learned constitutional argument tipped the scales against the amendment by the slender margin of one vote. The drama of a first-term senator besting Senator George, who ranked highest among the Democrats in respect to seniority, in an appeal for votes constituted what many considered Hennings' most brilliant triumph and the major source of his reputation as the intellectual leader of Democratic liberals in the Senate.[25]

A second accomplishment, which Hennings himself considered his greatest achievement, resulted from the conflict over seating Senator Dennis Chavez, Democrat from New Mexico. In the election of 1952, Chavez had defeated Patrick J. Hurley in an extremely close contest. Since peculiar circumstances surrounded the balloting, Hurley promptly contested the outcome. However, on January 3, 1953, the day after the release of the Hennings Report on McCarthy, no one questioned Chavez when he appeared to take his oath. According to reporters, Chavez was seated without contest because Democrats in the Senate decided to heed the threat of Senator Robert Taft, Republican from Ohio, to move against Chavez if Democrats refused to seat McCarthy because of the Hennings Report. Hurley's appeal ultimately proved effective, however, for in March of 1954 the Subcommittee on Privileges and Elections produced a majority report recommending that Chavez be unseated. But Hennings, the lone minority member of the subcommittee, had anticipated the move by insisting on having his own minority counsel to conduct a separate investigation of the New Mexico election. With information supplied by the newly hired attorney Myron G. Ehrlich, Hennings countered with a scathing attack on the majority report of the Republican Senators, Frank A. Barrett of Wyoming and Charles E. Potter of Michigan. Moved by the well-researched minority view, the Senate rejected the subcommittee's recommendation to unseat Chavez. Among his colleagues, who fully appreciated the importance of the contested

[25] William S. White, *New York Times,* February 28, 1954; Edward V. Long, "Tom Hennings—The Man from Missouri," *Missouri Law Review,* 26 (November, 1961), 408 ff.; interview with Bernard Fensterwald, Jr., May, 1962; White, *New York Times Magazine* (July 10, 1955), 10.

seat in the closely divided Upper Chamber, Hennings added several cubits to his increasing stature.[26] In view of his growing prominence within the Senate, Hennings' defense of civil liberties during the Eighty-third Congress took on added significance. His criticism of attacks on due process and freedom of expression received wider acceptance and deeper respect. The fight over the Bricker Amendment assured his reputation as a brilliant student of the Constitution, and the conflict over the Chavez election stamped him as a shrewd and resourceful party man, capable of probing the weak points of Republican strategy. Months earlier, in conflict with McCarthy, the Missourian had proved his courage. For these reasons, Hennings' views on civil liberties carried more weight within the Senate than outsiders suspected.[27]

The aristocratic Hennings wore his increasing prestige easily but unobtrusively and used it to advantage in defense of civil liberties. Few opportunities to pinpoint the nation's illiberal preoccupation with security escaped him. His almost comical brush with President Eisenhower over "bookburning" illustrates the point. Underlying the conflict was Hennings' immediate concern with the power the Velde-Jenner-McCarthy tandem seemed to wield over the Administration and his deeper fear that Eisenhower was destroying the fundamental balance of power within the federal government by allowing Congress to run roughshod over him. To reverse this trend Hennings tried to force Eisenhower to stiffen his resistance toward what the Missourian called the "know-nothing wing" of the Republican party.

Eisenhower's surprising reference to "bookburning," in a speech at Dartmouth College during the summer of 1953, provided the

26 On Hurley's petition for an investigation: *Congressional Record,* 83d Cong., 1st Sess., 1953, 99, Part 1, 147. On the rumored threat of Taft: Marquis Childs, *St. Louis Post-Dispatch,* January 6, 1953. Senate, Committee on Rules and Administration, 83d Cong., 2d Sess., 1954, Report No. 1081, Parts 1 and 2; *Congressional Record,* 83d Cong., 2d Sess., 1954, 100, Part 3, 3630 ff., 3732; Hennings Papers, Box 4, press release, June 8, 1953. Apart from the vacillating Senator Wayne Morse, the division of the Senate in 1953–1954 was 49 Republicans to 46 Democrats; in 1955–1956, the division was 48 Democrats to 47 Republicans.

27 White, *New York Times Magazine* (July 10, 1955), 10–11. Interview with Charles H. Slayman, May, 1962.

opening Hennings required. In condemning the censorship of books placed in the United States overseas libraries, Eisenhower found himself in the paradoxical position of castigating a policy of his own State Department. In June of 1953 the State Department, in an obvious reaction to McCarthy's investigation of the department's Overseas Information Service, directed that all books having even the most tenuous connection with political unorthodoxy be removed from overseas libraries. When Eisenhower made his disparaging allusion to "bookburning," Hennings pounced on the inconsistencies between the President's actions and statements and suggested that he could stop the "bookburning" any time he wished. In a series of publicized letters to Secretary of State John Foster Dulles, Hennings invited the nation to view the spectacle of the President and the Department of State cowed into submission by Senator McCarthy and his roving Subcommittee on Investigations. Eventually, the original and more sensible policy on books was restored, but not before Eisenhower felt the consequences of not taking a firmer stand against McCarthy and congressional investigating committees.[28]

Hennings' burgeoning power in the Senate and his acknowledged leadership in the defense of civil liberties placed him in an advantageous position for the showdown over preventive law that began in 1955. The censure of McCarthy on December 2, 1954, and the movement for a fair code of procedure for congressional committees during the same year blunted the edge of the worst abuses of individual rights. The real stronghold of preventive law was not Congress, however, but the loyalty-security program of the executive branch. Unobtrusively dispersed throughout the many executive departments and agencies, it remained firmly entrenched and totally intact despite the more public curtailments of its practice. As long as Republicans controlled Congress and its committees, liberals

---

[28] For McCarthy and the O.I.S.: *New York Times,* March 25–28, April 2–3, June 15–18, 21–23, and 28, and July 3, 5, 9–10, and 16, 1953. For Hennings' part in the controversy: Hennings Papers, Box 4, press release, June 16, 1953; Box 20, press releases, June 25 and July 2 and 10, 1953. For Eisenhower's reaction: Robert J. Donovan, *Eisenhower: The Inside Story,* 89 ff. For an account of the two McCarthy staff men involved in the library investigation: Richard H. Rovere, *The Eisenhower Years,* 125 ff., and *Senator Joe McCarthy,* 199 ff.

could do little more than make speeches that voiced their criticisms of the Administration's program, but when the Democrats regained control of Congress in 1955, the way was clear for a full-scale assault on the Eisenhower security system. The goals were obvious: to make Republicans pay in full for playing the "numbers game" in the previous Congress and to erect a countervailing force that would overwhelm the numerous forces that sought to maintain the nation's security by curtailing its most treasured freedoms. While Hennings had no aversion to partisan politics, the latter goal provided the major stimulus that led him to create the Subcommittee on Constitutional Rights.

V

The Changing Tide

WHEN THE Eighty-third Congress opened in 1955, its Democratic members were poised to attack the Eisenhower security program. The "numbers game" had been only the latest in a series of charges by Republicans that Democrats were hopelessly "soft on communism." Since the 1950 congressional campaign, Democrats had suffered from the image created by the Republicans that depicted them as naïve about problems of internal security. Now, after two years of a Republican Congress in the Capitol and a Republican General in the White House, the tables had turned.

The surprising feature of this attack on the Administration's security program was its unexpected scope. A mere listing of the critics indicates that the wide range of nonpartisan concern for individual rights played as large a role as party politics. The Ford Foundation's Fund for the Republic subsidized the New York Bar Association to undertake a complete analysis of the legal implications of the security program. Adam Yarmolinsky, a Washington lawyer and a guardian of civil liberties, busied himself with publishing fifty case histories of victims of the security system. Rowland Watts, secretary of the Workers Defense League, was publishing similar case histories that had been given him by attorneys who defended soldiers enmeshed in the Army's security program. The federal courts began hearing more and more cases emerging from the security practices of executive departments.

On Capitol Hill, Senator Hubert Humphrey, Democrat from Minnesota, and Senator Olin Johnston, Democrat from South Carolina, were holding extensive security hearings prior to appointing the bipartisan Wright Commission to make a complete study of the security network. From within the inner sanctum of the Justice Department came a strident critique by Harry P. Cain, a former Republican senator and McCarthyite, but now a member of the Subversive Activities Control Board. Some, but not all, of these voices, to which Hennings added his own, were impelled by a desire for partisan political advantage.[1]

As the critics prepared their case, the Administration made their task easier by exposing several skeletons that had been tucked away in its security closet. In late December of 1954, the Federal Employee Security Program disclosed one of its worst blunders. The victim was Wolf I. Ladejinsky, a Russian-born American working as an agriculture attaché for the State Department in Tokyo and an expert in land reform. When Ladejinsky applied for an administrative transfer from the State Department to the Department of Agriculture, Secretary of Agriculture Ezra Taft Benson refused to accept him. After explaining that the transferee was no longer suitable to discharge the responsibilities of an agriculture expert, Benson added that Ladejinsky was, moreover, a security risk.

Had the Secretary omitted the latter charge, the incident would have merited little publicity. No sooner had Benson made the charge that Ladejinsky was a security risk, however, than Clark

[1] On the Fund for the Republic: *New York Times,* December 22 and 23, 1954, and August 22, 1955; *Commonweal,* 63 (December 2, 1955), 211; *American Mercury,* 78 (June, 1954), 109; *ibid.,* 80 (June, 1955), 71 ff. On Harry Cain: L. Edgar Prina, "The Harry Cain 'Mutiny,' " *Collier's,* 136 (September 2, 1955), 32 ff.; "The Road to Damascus," *Reporter,* 12 (February 12, 1955), 4; *Newsweek,* 45 (March 28, 1955), 24; *Nation,* 180 (April 9, 1955), 298; Willard Edwards, "The Reformation of Harry Cain," *American Mercury,* 81 (October, 1955), 39 ff.; Harry P. Cain, "I Could Not Remain Silent," *Coronet,* 39 (November, 1955), 29 ff.; Ernest K. Lindley, "Of Harry Cain," *Newsweek,* 47 (May 28, 1956), 41; "Cain's Conscience," *New Republic,* 135 (November 5, 1956), 2. On the Court: Walter F. Murphy, *Congress and the Court;* James Reston, *New York Times,* December 25, 1955; Chapters VII and VIII below. For an analysis of the Yarmolinsky and Watts studies: Anthony Lewis, "Security: Interim Reports," *Reporter,* 13 (September 8, 1955), 27 ff.

Mollenhoff, Washington correspondent for Cowles Publications, revealed that the State Department had cleared Ladejinsky a few months earlier, using the same information upon which Benson now based his refusal to clear him. The Administration's uneasiness increased when Republican Congressman Walter Judd of Minnesota asserted that Benson, should he examine Ladejinsky's writings carefully, would find proof that their author had for twenty years been staunchly opposing communism. While serving as a missionary in Asia, Judd had seen the land reformer's work firsthand and had concluded that Ladejinsky had caused for communism some of its most serious setbacks in that part of the world. Benson's security chief J. Glenn Cassity agreed with Judd that Ladejinsky's writings were anti-Communist, but asked, how could the Agriculture Attaché write so strongly against communism while his father and three sisters remained as hostages in Russia? Answering his own question, Cassity concluded that Ladejinsky knew his relatives were safe because he was acting on orders from Moscow.[2]

The obvious contradictions in the Administration's security system and the more obvious nonsense that Cassity employed to justify his action presented to the eager Democrats a perfect object of attack. The nebulous task of divining a man's thoughts had led to an imputation of disloyalty from conduct that was vigorously anti-Communist. The incident illustrated, in addition, that the Administration's overzealous caution could be self-defeating as well as contradictory. Democratic land reform, an effective antidote to the constant pressures of Communists preparing to take an underdeveloped nation into the Marxist camp, was to suffer because an astigmatic security officer labeled a land reformer of proven ability a security risk. A system that could produce such a decision suddenly appeared to weaken rather than strengthen the nation's defense against communism. Harold E. Stassen, the director of the Foreign Operations Administration, brought this facet of the incident into sharp focus when he gave security clearance

[2] *New York Times,* December 19, 21–27, 29, and 31, 1954, January 4, 6, 10, 19, and 31, June 28, and July 3, 1955. On the Ladejinsky case: Clark R. Mollenhoff, *Des Moines Register,* December, 1954, and January, 1955; Mollenhoff, *Washington Cover-Up,* 79 ff.

to Ladejinsky and assigned him to the important work of land reform in Communist-threatened South Vietnam.[3]

Soon after the Ladejinsky fiasco, the Administration's security network received another stiff blow. From a federal district court in El Paso, Texas, came news that one of the government's star witnesses in loyalty-security cases, Harvey M. Matusow, confessed that he had lied in the government's successful prosecution of Communist labor leader Clinton E. Jencks. The confession accompanied Jencks' appeal from his 1954 conviction for falsely making a non-Communist oath before the National Labor Relations Board. Several days later, Matusow submitted a similar confession in conjunction with an appeal by thirteen second-line Communist leaders who had been convicted in 1952 for violating the Smith Act. In early February, the embarrassing development reached a climax. At the Biltmore Hotel in New York City, ex-Communist Matusow held a press conference to announce, amid tinkling glasses of Scotch-and-soda, that his forthcoming book *False Witness* would expose the flow of lies he had produced during his five-year career as a government informer.[4]

Shocked by Matusow's confession, the Senate's Subcommittee on Internal Security subpoenaed the professed ex-Communist to explain his actions. The subcommittee, headed by Senator James Eastland, Democrat from Mississippi, had obtained considerable testimony from Matusow in 1952, and its members were no less chagrined at his present turn-about than were the courts and the Justice Department. To save face, the subcommittee sought to show that Matusow told the truth from 1951 to 1954; that he began lying only when he started recanting in 1955; and, finally,

3 Unfortunately, Ladejinsky became involved in a conflict-of-interest charge not long after the security episode (*New York Times,* February 11, 1956).

4 *New York Times,* January 29 and February 1, 1955. On Matusow's press conference: Richard H. Rovere, "The Kept Witnesses," *Harper's,* 210 (May, 1955), 25 ff. For an interesting explanation of the mentality of ex-Communists: Hannah Arendt, "The Ex-Communists," *Commonweal,* 57, 595 ff. Matusow's affidavit in *United States v. Jencks,* in Senate, Committee on Judiciary, Subcommittee on Internal Security, *Hearings,* 84th Cong., 1st Sess., 1955 (hereafter, *Eastland Subcommittee Hearings*), Part 2, 160 ff. Matusow's affidavit in *United States v. Flynn, ibid.,* 156 ff.

that his recantation was part of a Communist scheme to discredit the government's stable of ex-Communist witnesses.[5]

To achieve these ambiguous goals, the Eastland Subcommittee questioned Matusow in public hearings from February to May of 1955. Though little evidence emerged, the hearings kept the Administration on edge and the nation entertained. Matusow's fund of stories seemed limitless. He bluntly accused other former Communists, whose names were household words by now, of lying. Under questioning by Hennings, a new addition to the subcommittee, he confessed that McCarthy was responsible for his attempts in Montana and Washington to smear Senators Mike Mansfield and Henry M. Jackson during their 1952 campaigns. The bizarre hearings reached their ridiculous climax when Senator Welker queried Matusow about his finances. Hoping to prove that the witness's financial condition was now leading him to cooperate with the Communist party, Welker asked Matusow about his present financial status. The witness replied that it was adequate because of large royalties he was to receive from a toy he had recently invented. Pressing the point as a source of information essential to the nation's security, Welker asked Matusow about the nature of this toy. After first pleading the Fifth Amendment, the witness finally gave Welker his answer. The toy, said Matusow, was "a stringless yo-yo."[6]

To the satisfaction of all its members except Hennings, the Eastland Subcommittee established that Matusow's earlier testimony was reliable. In its report, with Hennings the lone dissenter, the group concluded that Matusow's recanting was a Communist plot to discredit the government's turncoat witnesses. In a brief statement, Hennings asserted that he could not accept the subcommittee's conclusions and that he would issue his separate view in the near future. Though fully prepared for delivery, this separate view never appeared. In this unpublished dissent, the

[5] *Eastland Subcommittee Hearings,* Part 1, 1–86.
[6] *Eastland Subcommittee Hearings,* Parts 1–12. On Matusow's accusations against ex-Communist witnesses: *ibid.,* Part 2, 112. For Hennings' questioning Matusow about the 1952 campaign: *ibid.,* Part 2, 187 ff. For Welker's questioning Matusow: *ibid.,* Part 4, 377 ff.

Missourian took the position that Matusow was a liar from start to finish and that his testimony in 1951–1954 was just as unreliable as his recanting in 1955. The closely reasoned reply devastated the logic and selective use of evidence in the majority report. Its failure to appear was probably the result of the strategy employed by Eastland and his chief counsel Jay Sourwine. Well aware of Hennings' viewpoint, they held up the majority report until December 31, 1955. By that time Hennings had lost interest in the incident, and, his campaign for re-election being at hand, he withheld his minority report.[7]

While the Administration reeled from the Ladejinsky and Matusow episodes, Harry P. Cain began delivering another series of jarring blows from his position on the Subversive Activities Control Board. The "Cain Mutiny," as the press called it, began unexpectedly in January of 1955 in a speech given by the ex-Senator to the Fifth District Republican Club of Spokane. The Ladejinsky case, said Cain, illustrated the "shortsightedness, ruthlessness, smugness and brutality of bureaucracy" at its worst. To reform the system, he suggested that a new standard of security clearance replace the impossible criterion that federal employment must be "clearly consistent with national security." In addition, he demanded that the same standard should apply to all federal agencies and departments and that the Administration should clearly indicate that a security risk was not necessarily a disloyal citizen.[8]

The antagonism Cain created against the existing security program was tremendous. His party affiliation, his reputation as a staunch guardian of the nation's internal security, and his official position within the antisubversive system gave weighty authority

[7] *New York Times,* December 31, 1955. There is no record of this report in published government documents, but a committee print of the report, dated April 6, 1955, may be found in the Hennings Papers, Box 163. Hennings Papers, Box 163, draft of minority report on Matusow, undated; Box 7, letter from Hennings to Senator Eastland, July 27, 1955; Box 10, press release from Hennings' office, December 29, 1955. Interview with Sadi Masé, May, 1962. For another critical evaluation of the majority report: Murrey Marder, *Washington Post* and *Times-Herald,* December 31, 1955.

[8] *Washington Post* and *Washington Star,* January 16, 1955; *New York Times,* January 20, 1955.

to his criticism. Realizing this, the Administration's security chiefs bristled with anger at Cain when newspapers in the nation's capital gave the unexpected blast front-page coverage. The Administration's men let it be known that they felt Cain had betrayed his trust; they insisted that he should have brought his complaints to responsible officials in the Justice Department or else should have resigned his position before speaking out publicly. Cain retorted that he had complained to the proper officials, but without their taking action. Now, he would be silent and await reforms in the program.

The reforms appeared on March 4 in a memorandum of Attorney General Herbert Brownell, Jr., but they failed to satisfy Cain. Viewing them as little more than an urgent request to department heads to be more cautious in their application of security measures, the ex-Senator returned to his public attack on the security program. In a speech at the National Civil Liberties Clearing House, he called for more radical reforms. He recommended that both Republicans and Democrats divorce the security program from politics; that security officers disregard pre-1947 membership in subversive organizations; that department heads stop suspending, without pay and prior to a hearing, employees in nonsensitive positions who were under security investigation; that the Attorney General's list be abolished; that schools be organized for security officers; and that the Administration cease basing security judgments on "casual informers" who were unwilling to face the accused and submit to cross-examination. With this speech, Cain's break with the Administration became irreparable.[9]

The chain of events that began with Ladejinsky's case placed the Eisenhower Administration in a defensive position on security matters. The tide had definitely turned, and by March of 1955 congressional demands for a large-scale inquiry on the security

[9] For the memorandum of Brownell: Senate, Committee on Post Office and Civil Service, Subcommittee to Investigate the Government Employee Security Program, *Hearings,* 84th Cong., 1st Sess., 1955 (hereafter, *Johnston Subcommittee Hearings*), Part 1, 56 ff. For Cain's speech: Senate, Committee on Government Operations, Subcommittee on Reorganization, *Hearings,* 84th Cong., 1st Sess., 1955 (hereafter, *Humphrey Subcommittee Hearings*), 667 ff.

system had become irresistible. Senator Humphrey had already opened hearings in the Subcommittee on Reorganization to air his proposal for a bipartisan commission to examine the security system. Senator Olin Johnston had received $125,000 in Senate funds for his Post Office and Civil Service Committee to examine complaints registered by victims of the Federal Employee Security Program. At this point, Hennings decided to approach the security problem from a more radical perspective by focusing attention on the individual rights it endangered and the legal revolution it was effecting.

Hennings intimated his intentions in a speech to the Law Club of Chicago in March. He placed the current security controversy in the framework of the larger problem of a steady erosion of the freedom and justice guaranteed by the First and Fifth amendments to the Bill of Rights. Responsibility for this unfortunate development involved both the legislative and the executive branches, both Democrats and Republicans. The First and Fifth amendments, said Hennings, were the cornerstones of the Bill of Rights, since they protected freedom and justice, respectively. Freedom of speech and thought, guaranteed by the First Amendment, suffered serious limitations from such legislation as the Internal Security Act of 1950; justice, the due process of law guaranteed by the Fifth Amendment, was being increasingly disregarded because of the novel development of administrative criminal law implicit in the security program of the executive branch. The result was a steady erosion of the Bill of Rights.[10]

To reverse this process of erosion Hennings envisioned the Subcommittee on Constitutional Rights, a permanent group to act continuingly as a force in support of the Bill of Rights. An increased sense of urgency attached to the plan from a speech by Chief Justice Earl Warren, shortly before Hennings' speech in Chicago. In an address during February at Washington University in St. Louis, Warren had suggested that if the nation were asked in 1955 to ratify the Bill of Rights, a majority of the people would quite possibly reject it. The apprehension shown by the

[10] Hennings Papers, Box 19, Address to the Law Club of the City of Chicago, March 25, 1955.

Chief Justice brought to a climax Hennings' own concern and led to his speech on the need for a subcommittee on constitutional rights.[11]

Fortunately, Hennings had at hand a convenient foundation for the new subcommittee. Since the beginning of the Eighty-third Congress, the Missourian had been a member of the Subcommittee on Civil Rights, an arm of the Judiciary Committee. During 1953 and 1954 this body served primarily as the burial ground for stalemated civil rights legislation. Early in 1955, however, Senator Harley Kilgore, Democrat from West Virginia and chairman of the parent committee, named Hennings as chairman of the nearly forgotten group. Since the subcommittee's name seemed to limit its jurisdiction to civil rights legislation, Hennings coined the title, Subcommittee on Constitutional Rights. Henceforth, the Chairman could reasonably claim jurisdiction over all Senate matters touching either civil rights or civil liberties.[12]

Once freed from the limitations implied in the discarded title, Hennings could chart his new course. The other two members of the subcommittee, Senator William Langer, Republican from North Dakota, and Senator Joseph O'Mahoney, Democrat from Wyoming, left the direction of the group in the Chairman's hands.

[11] *Case and Comment,* 60 (September–October, 1955), 3 ff. Interviews with former staff members, May, 1962.

[12] On the relation of the Subcommittee on Constitutional Rights to an earlier subcommittee of the Senate Committee on Education and Labor under the direction of Senator Robert M. LaFollette: Lawrence Speiser, "The Constitutional Rights Subcommittee: The Lengthened Shadow of One Man," *Missouri Law Review,* 26 (November, 1961), 499 ff. The relationship to the LaFollette Subcommittee, which Speiser mentions, seems merely accidental. Apparently, it exerted little or no causal connection with the Hennings Subcommittee. Speiser also stated that the Hennings Subcommittee was "suggested in the fall of 1954." Speiser based this statement on conversations with Langdon C. West after 1955 (interview with Lawrence Speiser, May, 1962). On the authority of a subcommittee of the Senate Judiciary Committee to investigate the Bill of Rights: *Rules and Manual of the United States Senate,* 84th Cong., Standing Committees, Rule XXV (K), (12); Hennings Papers, Box 161, press release, May 20, 1955. On the change of name from "Civil Rights" to "Constitutional Rights" in the Judiciary Committee's meeting of January 20, 1955: Subcommittee on Constitutional Rights, Chronological Files (hereafter: CRS Files), 1956, memorandum of Jane Williams to Charles Slayman, November 29, 1956.

In April, the Senate granted Hennings' request for a $50,000 appropriation to be spent on:

A general examination of the Bill of Rights and proposed legislation affecting it, to determine the appropriateness of its present-day application; with particular attention to matters concerned with due process, the right of privacy, freedom of speech, freedom of the press, freedom from unreasonable search and seizure, and the functions of administrative departments whose responsibilities particularly affect such rights.[13]

The first months of the new subcommittee's existence proved to be anything but smooth. Major problems arose from Hennings' efforts to assemble an adequate staff and from the difficulties involved in translating general goals into specific programs. The subcommittee's first chief counsel, a New York lawyer and sometime author, Marshall MacDuffie, failed to fulfill Hennings' expectations for a hard-hitting program. Research Director Benjamin Ginzburg, a social scientist, proposed the desired investigation of the security system, but was unable to organize it into an orderly and self-justifying program. Finally, Hennings called on a St. Louis lawyer, Lon Hocker, who was to be the Republican candidate for Governor of Missouri two years later. Hocker formulated an amendment-by-amendment, clause-by-clause examination of the Bill of Rights that satisfied Hennings.[14]

Hocker's proposal had many advantages. The clause-by-clause examination of the Bill of Rights forecast an almost unlimited agenda and a long life for the subcommittee. Moreover, since guilt

[13] Senate, Committee on Rules and Administration, 84th Cong., 1st Sess., 1955, Report No. 236.

[14] Hennings Papers, Box 160, memorandum from Marshall MacDuffie to Hennings, Langer, and O'Mahoney, June 8, 1955; CRS Files, 1955, memorandum of Marshall MacDuffie, June 30, 1955. On MacDuffie's writings, see: Marshall MacDuffie, *The Red Carpet,* and "The Khrushchev I Know," *Collier's,* 135 (April 15, 1955), 96 ff. Hennings Papers, Box 160, memoranda from Benjamin Ginzburg to Hennings, May 17, 1955; Ginzburg to Langdon C. West, June 9, 27, 1955; Ginzburg to Hennings, June 15, 1955; Box 19, press release, May 15, 1955; Box 160, copy of letter from Benjamin Ginzburg to Senator Brien McMahon, February 6, 1952. Benjamin Ginzburg, "Loyalty, Suspicion and the Tightening Chain," *Reporter,* 11 (July 6, 1954), 10 ff., and *Rededication to Freedom.* Hennings Papers, Box 160, memorandum from Hocker to Hennings, July 18, 1955; letters from Hennings to Langer and O'Mahoney, July 18, 1955.

by association was implicit in most security cases, the clauses related to freedom of speech and assembly in the First Amendment could reasonably serve as springboards for an immediate investigation of the security program, the prime target of the subcommittee. Such subterfuge was needed, Hennings felt, to obviate conflict with the Humphrey and Johnston subcommittees, which seemed to pre-empt the security field, and to forestall the adverse publicity that was to be expected from the defenders of a strong security system. Under Hocker's strategy, if anyone criticized Hennings for attacking the nation's defenses against subversion the Chairman could pass the blame to the Founding Fathers, who placed freedom of speech and assembly in the First Amendment.

The clever plan had one limitation, however, for the first clause of the First Amendment refers neither to freedom of speech nor to freedom of assembly, but to freedom of religion. To adjust to this inconvenient fact, the author of the plan, Chief Hearings Counsel Hocker, successfully urged Hennings to make at least a token examination rather than bypass the clause relating to religion. The Chief Hearings Counsel reasoned that, if handled properly, the public would respond calmly to an impartial examination of religious freedom in the nation.[15]

Hocker was dead wrong, and his study of religious freedom, coupled with MacDuffie's untimely and ungraceful resignation, nearly wrecked the subcommittee before it got off the ground. The Chief Hearings Counsel planned to conduct a survey by mail of the current status of religious freedom and then hold brief public hearings that would, he hoped, lead to the conclusion that the clause relating to religion needed no attention from the subcommittee. With his conclusion all but formulated, Hocker began searching for supporting evidence, but found, instead, that the clause contained constitutional issues that did, indeed, need examination. Of special interest was the conflict over the meaning of the so-called "establishment clause." What did the First Amendment mean when it said that Congress could make no law respecting the establishment of religion? Did it mean that Congress could

15 Interviews with former staff members, May and June, 1962; Hennings Papers, Box 160, letters from Hennings to Senators O'Mahoney and Langer, July 18, 1955.

give *no aid* of any type to any religion, or only that Congress could give *no preference* to any religion? The *no aid* interpretation, Hocker found, was common among Protestants and Jews, while the *no preference* position was common among Catholics.[16]

The Chief Hearings Counsel scheduled the hearings on the clause relating to religion for October and prepared a questionnaire soliciting opinions on the meaning of the "establishment clause" and factual instances of violations of the "freedom of religion" clause. The crucial question on the establishment clause invited the respondent to take either the *no aid* or the *no preference* position. On consulting with Washington representatives of Protestant and Catholic groups, Hocker was advised that though his questionnaire was impartial, the total plan held considerable danger of stimulating religious strife. Despite this advice, the St. Louisan chose to continue the project, believing he had constructed adequate safeguards against sectarian bickering. To forestall any sect from distorting the responses, he directed that the questionnaire be given out only on written request and that a control inquiry be conducted by sending the questionnaire to the 3,500 members of the American Political Science Association. All responses were to be sent to the Bureau of Social Science Research of the American University in Washington for tabulation and interpretation. To prevent sectarian diatribes in the public hearings, Hocker determined that no one should testify without advance approval of his statement.

To set the stage for the debate, he solicited testimony on the *no aid* interpretation from Leo Pfeffer, counsel to the American Jewish Congress and a spokesman acceptable to both Jews and Protestants, and on the *no preference* position from Edward S. Corwin, a Protestant whose reasoning on this point was generally accepted by Catholics. As a final safeguard, Hocker explicitly

16 Hennings Papers, Box 160, memoranda from Hocker to Hennings, O'Mahoney, and Langer, July 18 and August 11, 1955; letter from Hennings to O'Mahoney, July 18, 1955; letter from Hennings to Langer, July 18, 1955. CRS Files, 1955, letter from Hocker to the Right Rev. James A. Pike, August 18, 1955; letter from Hocker to Ray A. Billington, September 14, 1955; letter from Hocker to Leo Pfeffer, September 6, 1955; letter from Hocker to Rev. James W. Clarke, July 26, 1955. Interviews with former staff members, May and June, 1962.

warned witnesses that the subcommittee was interested only in evidence of current problems and would reject any testimony aimed at describing violations of the clause on religion at some future time.[17]

Public response to the proposed study of the clause on religion was heatedly divided. The liberal *Washington Post* opposed the plan because it would divert attention from more immediate problems and because the subcommittee apparently had no intention of trying to solve the problems it uncovered. Reaction among Jewish groups was mixed, though it later became clear that a majority favored the study. The *Christian Century,* a respected Protestant journal, opposed the investigation out of fear that it would arouse bitter controversy and because it felt that the *no aid* interpretation had already been established by the Supreme Court. Catholic publications favored the study because they felt it could clarify, and perhaps overturn, the trend the Supreme Court seemed to be following in its decisions on the establishment clause. With a view toward extending the *no aid* interpretation, an organization known as Protestants and Others United for the Separation of Church and State—popularly referred to as POAU—was enthusiastic over the planned study. As the hearings drew near, the *Christian Century,* despairing that the public hearings would be canceled, urged all non-Catholic groups and "individual Roman Catholics" to rally behind POAU, since that group was the perfect leader for the forthcoming battle.[18]

[17] Hennings Papers, Box 160, Report on Questionnaire Survey Conducted by the Senate Subcommittee on Constitutional Rights by the Bureau of Social Science Research of the American University (mimeo), November, 1955; memoranda from Hocker to Hennings, O'Mahoney, and Langer, August 11, 1955, from Hocker to Hennings, August 30, 1955; CRS Files, 1955, letter from Hocker to Rev. Joseph M. Snee, August 12, 1955; letter from Hocker to Edward S. Corwin, August 28, 1955; letter from Hocker to Dr. Robert T. Bower, August 29, 1955; letter from Hocker to Charles P. Taft, September 12, 1955; letter from Hocker to Richard Brown, September 13, 1955; letter from Hocker to Paul Blanshard, September 14, 1955. Interviews with former staff members, May, 1962.

[18] *Washington Post,* August 20, 1955. For the Jewish reaction: Hennings Papers, Box 160, letter from William H. Gremley to Richard Brown, October 3, 1955, and enclosed news release, American Jewish Congress, September 30, 1955, New York (favoring hearings); memo from Glenn

(Continued on next page)

Alarmed at this rapid build-up of sectarian battle lines, the subcommittee's members became increasingly apprehensive, as did some religious leaders. Senator O'Mahoney was especially disturbed, for he felt that a bitter sectarian fight would provide Communists with propaganda material. Apparently, too, Catholic religious leaders unofficially confirmed the misgivings conveyed to Hocker earlier by their Washington representatives. Faced with this opposition, Hennings began withdrawing support from his Chief Hearings Counsel. At first he postponed the October 3 hearings, explaining that more time was needed to digest responses to the questionnaire; finally, he announced that, since the written replies to the questionnaire indicated no major problems over the religion clause, he was canceling the public hearings.[19]

D. Everett to Langdon West, undated, and enclosed news release, Religious News Service, October 24, 1955 (American Jewish Committee and Anti-Defamation League of B'nai B'rith opposing hearings). In the November 12, 1955, issue of the *New York Times,* a news item stated that the Joint Advisory Committee of the Synagogue Council of America and of the National Community Relations Advisory Council had sent a letter to Hocker stating that the hearings on religion would have been helpful. This Joint Advisory Committee represented forty-three Conservative, Orthodox, and Reform Jewish bodies. The letter was sent on November 11, 1955. Herman Edelsberg, director of the Anti-Defamation League of B'nai B'rith, sent this clipping in a letter to Langdon West on November 17, 1955. Edelsberg concluded: "The record now indicates that the leading Jewish organizations representing all but a tiny fraction of American Jewry favored or did not oppose the hearings." (Hennings Papers, Box 160, letter from Edelsberg to West, November 17, 1955.) *Christian Century,* 72 (August 17, 1955), 940; (September 7, 1955), 1014 ff.; (October 12, 1955), 1163. The same reaction appeared in a press release from Baptist Joint Committee on Public Affairs, September, 1955, Washington, D. C. For the Catholic reaction: *America,* 93 (August 27, 1955), 503; *Our Sunday Visitor,* October 2, 1955. For the POAU reaction: press release, Protestants and Other Americans United for Separation of Church and State, October 4, 1955, Washington, D. C.; *Washington Post,* October 6, 1955; *St. Louis Post-Dispatch,* October 7, 1955; *St. Louis Globe-Democrat,* October 19, 1955.

[19] On sectarian controversy: CRS Files, 1955, letter from Hocker to the Right Rev. James A. Pike, August 18, 1955; letter from Hocker to Richard Brown, September 13, 1955; *Christian Advocate,* October 20, 1955. On the increased apprehension: Hennings Papers, Box 160, letter from Hennings to Editor of *Christian Advocate,* October 21, 1955; *Washington Post,* October 1, 1955; *St. Louis Post-Dispatch,* October 2 and 6, 1955;

The aftermath of the controversy left the subcommittee tottering on the edge of collapse. Seeing his weeks of exhaustive work going for naught, Hocker quietly prepared his resignation and his departure for St. Louis. The reputation of the subcommittee declined further when some sects spread stories of elaborate plots engineered by Catholics to reverse Supreme Court rulings on the religion clause. At this point, matters worsened when Chief Counsel MacDuffie announced that the division of authority between himself and Hocker had become intolerable. In tendering his resignation, MacDuffie stated that disagreement with Hocker over the religion survey and over a questionnaire prepared for the study of freedom of speech convinced him that he could no longer tolerate the division of authority. The resignation itself was relatively harmless, but the timing and the stories that followed it were nearly disastrous to the Hennings Subcommittee.[20]

After MacDuffie's resignation, a series of articles appeared in the *Chicago Tribune,* questioning the integrity and good sense of the subcommittee's members. The most serious charge accused the Hennings group of intending to destroy the Federal Bureau of Investigation. At times under the by-line of Willard Edwards, the *Tribune*'s series purported to reconstruct the efforts of MacDuffie to defeat a secret plot, engineered by Research Director Ginzburg, to ruin the FBI, discredit ex-Communist Elizabeth Bentley, a key government informer, and destroy the nation's internal security system. According to Edwards, both Hocker and Langdon C. West, Hennings' able administrative assistant and an architect of the subcommittee, were in collusion with Ginzburg, so MacDuffie, unable to prevent the plot, finally resigned in protest. Adding to

Washington Post, October 12, 1955; *New York Post,* October 12, 1955. On postponing and canceling hearings: Hennings Papers, Box 10, press release, September 30, and October 5, 1955. Interviews with former staff members, May and June, 1962.

20 Interviews with former staff members, May and June, 1962; *Christian Advocate,* October 20, 1955; Paul Blanshard, *God and Man in Washington,* 104; Hennings Papers, Box 160, press release, Marshall MacDuffie, October 11, 1955 (copy); *St. Louis Post-Dispatch, New York Times, Washington Post, New York Post, Washington Daily News, Chicago Tribune,* October 12, 1955.

the adverse publicity, the articles questioned Hocker's prudence by revealing that he had intended to make an investigation of Shintoism, a Japanese religious sect then on the Attorney General's list, and to dramatize the subcommittee's opening session by hiring a Hollywood actor to impersonate Thomas Jefferson.[21]

The subcommittee's staff felt certain that MacDuffie had inspired the *Tribune's* articles. The series was sufficiently accurate to indicate that the author knew even the smallest details of the subcommittee's plans. Ginzburg, for example, heartily opposed the government's use of informers and wanted to investigate discrepancies he felt existed in Miss Bentley's testimony. Hocker, as the *Tribune* stated, had considered investigating the Attorney General's listing of Shintoism in connection with the study of the religion and assembly clauses. Also, the Chief Hearings Counsel had attempted to induce actor Joshua Logan to impersonate Jefferson in the subcommittee's opening session. Moreover, the *Tribune's* series bore a striking resemblance to the viewpoint that MacDuffie expressed in his letter of resignation to Hennings. Although MacDuffie announced his resignation on October 11, his letter of resignation was dated October 6, and the *Tribune's* series began on October 7. Finally, the beneficiary of the articles, at the expense of the subcommittee, was its former Chief Counsel. The *Tribune* depicted him as a benevolent liberal who suddenly found himself surrounded by a new type of left-wing radicals. The pro-Communist connotations that Fulton Lewis, Jr., had seen five months earlier in Author MacDuffie's personal interviews with Chairman Nikita Khrushchev suddenly became charming sidelights on his career. In the fiasco over the religion clause, the former Chief Counsel was cleared of any responsibility. He had opposed the plan from the beginning, and subsequent events completely vindicated his prudence.[22]

[21] *Chicago Tribune,* October 4, 7, 12, and 23–24, 1955.

[22] This account of the reaction of the subcommittee has come from: Interviews with former staff members, May and June, 1962; Hennings Papers, Box 160, copy of a telegram from Langdon West to Hennings, October 29, 1955; CRS Files, 1955, letter from Hocker to Senator Harry P. Case, November 3, 1955. On Hocker's intention to investigate Shintoism: CRS Files, 1955, letter from Hocker to Frank S. Sterck, August 1, 1955; letter from Hocker to Howard F. Van Zandt, August 3, 1955; letter from

Contrary to the *Tribune*'s expectations, the blow aimed at the subcommittee not only failed to complete its destruction but started a reaction that stabilized the group and set it on the path of its greatest achievement. Convinced that MacDuffie was trying to destroy the subcommittee, Hocker tore up his resignation and plunged into the next project. While the press wrote the subcommittee's obituary, the staff closed ranks behind the Chief Hearings Counsel and began intensive preparation for the November hearings on freedom of speech, of the press, and of assembly. Hardened by criticism, the Hennings Subcommittee was in the mood for a stinging assault on its prime target, the security program.[23]

Sharing his staff's reaction to what it considered an unfair attack, Hennings approved plans for a mid-November public session and announced its objective. For that announcement he chose a meeting of the St. Louis Lawyers Association on November 3. To ensure accurate reporting of the closely reasoned and somewhat technical address, Langdon West sent a synopsis of the speech to newspapers several days in advance. In one of the most important speeches of his career, Hennings stated that the goal of the November hearings was an examination of a revolutionary phenomenon called administrative criminal law.[24]

While proudly terming himself a conservative in matters of traditional legal institutions, Hennings told the St. Louis lawyers that the real test of a society's worth was its treatment of citizens accused of crime. "The highest dignity of law," he stated, "finds its manifestation in the administration of criminal justice, because here the State pits its authority against the honor of human person-

---

Hocker to Edward S. Corwin, August 28, 1955 (in this letter Hocker indicated that he was dropping the Shintoism matter, on Corwin's advice). On Hocker's intention to induce Joshua Logan to impersonate Jefferson: CRS Files, 1955, letter from Hocker to Joshua Logan, August 15, 1955. MacDuffie's letter to Hennings is in: Hennings Papers, Box 160, letter from MacDuffie to Hennings, October 6, 1955. On the earlier comments of Fulton Lewis, Jr.: Hennings Papers, Box 160, typewritten transcript of broadcast of Fulton Lewis, Jr., Washington, D. C., May 22, 1955.

[23] This account of the reaction of the subcommittee staff has come from: Interviews with former staff members, May and June, 1962; CRS Files, 1955, letter from Hocker to Senator Harry P. Case, November 3, 1955.

[24] Hennings Papers, Box 160, memorandum of West to all editors, columnists, and reporters, November 1, 1955.

ality." In a democratic society, Hennings continued, "a criminal
trial is also the crucial test of dedication to the principles of democratic society."[25]

Applying this measuring rod to the nation, the Senator asserted
that criminal justice in America was falling prey to a revolutionary development that promised to destroy it. Since the 1930's, he
said, administrative law had been growing rapidly as a result of
the needed regulations in the economic and social spheres. This
development introduced into American law "a principle repugnant
to our notions of justice—the principle that an administrative
agency, which, as distinguished from a court, may be a party in
interest, has the power to decide controversies and to dispose of
property rights involving individuals and corporations." Recogniz-
ing this radical departure, the courts and the Congress set down
rules to protect property rights in the course of administrative
proceedings. Though far from perfect, these rules demanded some
measure of due process akin to the fair procedures of the courts.
With the rise of the security programs, administrative law began
branching out from civil proceedings over property rights to criminal procedures involving human personality. This second revolution, he concluded, was not only dangerous, but it was unrecog-
nized by Americans.

Hennings then pinpointed the legal deficiencies present in this
revolution. In general, the security system lacked the safeguards of
orthodox criminal law. The use of secret informers, for example,
destroyed the customary rights of the accused to confront the
sources of incriminating evidence and to cross-examine adverse
witnesses. Granting that informers are essential to law enforcement, Hennings objected to the fact that their identity, the basis
of their credibility, remained hidden. In security cases not only the
accused but even the security officer and the security board were
often ignorant of the informer's identity. Moreover, the norm for

---

25 Hennings Papers, Box 160, Address to St. Louis Lawyers Association,
November 3, 1955, St. Louis, Missouri. On administrative criminal law:
J. Malcolm Smith and Cornelius P. Cotter, "Freedom and Authority in
the Amphibial State," *Midwest Journal of Political Science,* 1 (May,
1957), 40 ff.

determining security dismissals—that retention of the accused be "clearly consistent with national security"—destroyed the principle of traditional criminal law that declared the accused was presumed innocent until proven guilty. In security law, the accused carried the burden of proving that his retention was "clearly consistent" with the nation's security. The logic of making security determinations violated another tenet of orthodox criminal law. The practice of using the Attorney General's list as a touchstone for security determinations led not only to assessing guilt by association, but even guilt by friendship and kinship. An accused person could be judged a security risk not only on the basis of his own membership in a listed organization, but merely on the basis of friends' or relatives' membership.

In another respect Hennings saw the security program's departure from orthodox criminal law. In modern criminal law, statutes defining criminal activity must either be based on traditional formulations of the common law or be the result of "considered legislative actions." As a corollary to this principle, criminal statutes are subject to strict interpretation, and there can be no prosecution "for analogically constructed offenses." Yet, in the security program, the definition of a security risk could be altered by arbitrary administrative action. An example of this was Truman's 1950 amendment of his own 1947 loyalty standard. With a stroke of the pen the President changed the norm from "reasonable grounds for belief that the person involved is disloyal" to "reasonable doubt" about his loyalty. Then, in 1953, with another stroke of the pen, Eisenhower changed the norm to retaining an employee only if "clearly consistent with national security." Such arbitrary changes in the definition of a crime are unknown in orthodox criminal law.

Anticipating the objection that the security program was not criminal law of any kind, since it levied no punishment, Hennings saw a precedent in primitive Anglo-Saxon law and early common law. He observed that after a conviction in proceedings that were "substantially trials for treason," the security program administered the ancient punishment of outlawry. By placing the accused "in jeopardy of infamy and punishment," and by stigmatizing him as a security risk, the program did, in effect, expel him from the community. This, Hennings concluded, was little more than the ancient punishment of outlawry.[26]

To emphasize the urgency of the situation, Hennings reminded his fellow lawyers that the security program was not just a limited phenomenon. Quoting a recent article in *Fortune* by Chief Justice Warren, Hennings estimated that twenty million Americans, if a worker's family were included, were affected by this new branch of administrative law. "This program," he warned, "is no longer remote; it has become a truly national problem. Now it touches you and me, our friends and our neighbors."[27]

Hennings offered no panacea for the problem he described. He asserted, however, that the Subcommittee on Constitutional Rights, by exposing the problem in its full dimensions, was taking the first step toward a solution, and for one part of the problem he suggested a specific remedy. Noting that even in administrative civil law the parties at interest could scrutinize the sources of incriminating evidence, Hennings called attention to a recent decision of the Court of Appeals condemning the use of secret informers in the Port Security Program. In order to make administrative criminal law as fair as its civil counterpart and to abide by this recent court decision, the Senator repeated a plan he had suggested as early as 1950. He proposed the appointment of attorneys to be public examiners of secret informers. These "public defenders," as he termed them, would be paid by the government and would be available to citizens undergoing security investigation. By cross-examining, in closed session, the government secret informers, the public defender could evaluate the credibility of the testimony and, at the same time, safeguard the government's informing system. Though this suggestion never won acceptance, it called attention to the security program's most severe breach of

[26] Perhaps Hennings found this allusion to outlawry in Telford Taylor, *Grand Inquest,* Chapters 14 and 15 and Appendix 3.

[27] Chief Justice Earl Warren, "The Law and the Future," *Fortune,* 52 (November, 1955), 106; compare with: Ralph S. Brown, "Loyalty-Security Measures and Employment Opportunities," *Bulletin of the Atomic Scientists,* 11 (April, 1955), 113 ff.

traditional criminal law and silenced critics who claimed that the Hennings Subcommittee wanted to destroy the FBI.[28]

Nearly eight months had passed since Hennings' opening speech to the Chicago Law Club, and the Subcommittee on Constitutional Rights had accomplished little. But the long period of gestation had its bright side. The determination and enthusiasm of the staff were at fever pitch. The Chairman and his brain trust, Langdon C. West and Russian-born legal scholar Sadi Masé, had sufficient time to mull over the implications of administrative criminal law. The case histories published by Adam Yarmolinsky and Rowland Watts were now available, and the federal courts were moving against the security practices of some federal departments and agencies.

Chief Justice Warren, speaking for the Supreme Court in *Peters v. Hobby,* caught Ginzburg's attention with his methodical approach to the vagaries of the security system. Warren invalidated the security-inspired removal of Peters from his position with the Department of Health, Education, and Welfare on the ground that the department's procedure violated the Eisenhower executive order establishing the program. Although most liberals criticized the Court for not examining the validity of the executive order itself, Ginzburg accepted Warren's approach as a blueprint for the subcommittee. Let the subcommittee, he asserted, examine the procedures of executive agencies to see if they conformed to Executive Order 10450; then, examine Executive Order 10450 to see if it conformed to the congressional statute on which it was based; finally, examine that statute to see if it conformed to the Bill of Rights. The advantage of this approach, Ginzburg con-

---

28 The recent decision Hennings alluded to was Parker v. Lester, 227 F. 2d 708 (9th Cir. 1955). A few weeks later, Hennings applauded a similar decision by Judge Luther V. Youngdahl in the case of *Boudin v. Dulles* in the Federal District Court for the District of Columbia (Hennings Papers, Box 11, press release, November 25, 1955). In each of these cases, the court overturned the security decision because it was based on information whose source was kept secret by the agency involved. In each case, however, the appeal centered on a right (right to be a professional merchant seaman and the right to travel abroad) rather than the privilege of government employment.

cluded, was, "We will be walking in the footsteps of the Supreme Court and will be shielded by its majesty from political sharpshooting."[29]

Decisions of the lower federal courts provided hints to Hennings and the subcommittee of another approach to the security program. In *Schactman v. Dulles,* the Court of Appeals for the District of Columbia condemned the State Department's policy of arbitrarily denying passports to applicants it suspected of disloyalty. This willingness on the part of the courts to examine cases involving the *right* to a passport, coupled with their reluctance to interfere in cases concerned with the *privilege* of federal employment, suggested to Hennings that the security system was most vulnerable when the rationalization that government service is a *privilege* rather than a *right* became irrelevant. The security system, then, was most vulnerable when it touched applicants for passports, army draftees, and workers engaged in private industry. In the exciting days ahead, these two hints from the judiciary provided the Subcommittee on Constitutional Rights with the plan it needed for attacking the Eisenhower security program.[30]

[29] Hennings Papers, Box 160, memoranda from Ginzburg to Hennings, May 17, 1955; Ginzburg to Hennings, June 15, 1955; Ginzburg to Mac-Duffie, July 1, 1955. Peters v. Hobby, 349 U. S. 331 (1955).

[30] Schactman v. Dulles, 225 F. 2d 938 (D. C. Cir. 1955); Hennings Papers, Box 161, press release, June 27, 1955. The controlling decision that government service is a privilege and not a right is Bailey v. Richardson, 182 F. 2d 46 (1950). This decision of the Court of Appeals was affirmed by a divided Supreme Court, without an opinion, in Bailey v. Richardson, 341 U. S. 918 (1951). In the appellate decision, Judge Prettyman held that government service was not a right and dismissal was not a punishment; therefore, the government's dismissal procedure need not conform to the due process requirements of criminal law. In a dissent from this majority opinion, Judge Edgerton argued that "dismissal for disloyalty is a punishment and requires all the safeguards of a judicial trial." The rule of law emerging from this case is: "Government employment . . . is a privilege whose denial, at least when it is not arbitrarily effected, does not constitute punishment." (Ralph S. Brown, *Loyalty and Security,* 93.)

VI

Subcommittee on Constitutional Rights

T HE LONG-AWAITED INVESTIGATION of the security system began
on a theoretical plane, but it rapidly shifted to current practices.
In the first public session, on November 14, 1955, four legal
scholars discussed the extent to which they thought Congress, in
the interest of national security, could limit the First Amendment's
provisions for freedom of speech, of the press, and of assembly.
After this rather curt bow in the direction of theory, the hearings
concentrated on witnesses who were able to describe actual conditions. With Hennings in the chair and Hocker leading the questioning, a clear and frightening picture of administrative criminal
law began to emerge.[1]

The most obvious feature of the security program was its
tendency toward continual expansion. This growth frequently bore
little relationship to increased national security and at times even
lessened it. The Industrial Security Program, administered by the
Department of Defense, illustrated the point. Initiated in 1949,
this program attempted to protect government secrets in those
industries that held government contracts. With the cooperation
of employers, the Defense Department screened nearly three mil-

---

[1] The four scholars were: Alexander Meiklejohn, Zechariah Chafee,
Thomas I. Cook, and Morris L. Ernst. The speeches in the opening session
are in Senate, Committee on Judiciary, Subcommittee on Constitutional
Rights, *Hearings,* 84th Cong., 1st Sess., 1955 (henceforth, *Hennings Subcommittee Hearings*), Part 1, 1 ff.

lion workers in approximately 21,000 plants that used data classified as *confidential, secret,* or *top secret.* Testimony before the subcommittee indicated that while the Defense Department tended to expand the program at one end through overclassification of allegedly secret data, Congress promised similar expansion by extending the screening to every worker in every factory that was designated a defense plant. The latter effort, contained in a bill introduced in the previous session of Congress by Republican Senator John M. Butler of Maryland, would have extended the program to approximately seventeen million additional workers. In opposition to these tendencies, the subcommittee presented strong evidence that overclassification and extension of the screening process would not only endanger the rights of more workers but would substantially increase the danger of espionage by overburdening the persons responsible for surveillance.[2]

This same tendency toward expansion with little relation to national security appeared in testimony on the use of the Attorney General's list of subversive organizations. Arch Hindman, executive secretary of the Indiana State Athletic Commission, testified

[2] The conclusions of the Hennings Subcommittee can be gathered from Hennings' remarks during the November hearings and his press releases both during and after the hearings; Hennings Papers, Box 10, press release, November 2, 1955; Box 11, press releases, November 13 and 18, 1955; Box 161, press release, November 20, 1955; Box 11, press releases, November 23 and 25 and December 10, 1955 (most important); Box 5, press releases, January 27 and 29, 1956; Box 10, press releases, February 3 and 16, 1956; Box 11, press release, February 21, 1956; Box 12, press release, May 13, 1956; Box 10, remarks by Hennings at session of Subcommittee on Constitutional Rights, June 11, 1956; Box 12, press release, August 30, 1956. On the general program of industrial security: Brown, *Loyalty and Security,* 64, 246; Senate, Committee on Government Operations, Subcommittee on Reorganization, *Hearings,* 84th Cong., 1st Sess., 1955, 220 ff.; A. T. Morris, "A Trap for Labor," *Nation,* 181 (December 3, 1955), 471 ff.; "The Role of Employer Practices in the Federal Industrial Personnel Security Program—A Field Study," *Stanford Law Review,* 8 (March, 1956), 234 ff.; Benjamin D. Segal and Joyce L. Kornbluh, "Government Security and Private Industry," *Reporter,* 16 (May 2, 1957), 25 ff. For a discussion of Butler's bill: Industrial Relations Research Association, *Personnel Security Programs in U. S. Industry,* 18, 25, 75; *Saturday Evening Post,* 228 (July 23, 1955), 10. The Butler bill was Senate, 84th Cong., 1st Sess., 1955, S. 681. On Hennings' investigation: *Hennings Subcommittee Hearings,* Part 1, 534, 599. The Butler bill was reintroduced in the 85th Congress as S. 1140, but again no action was taken.

that his organization demanded that boxers applying for a license swear that they did not belong to any group listed by the Attorney General. Judge David W. Peck of the New York Supreme Court stated that he used the list as partial basis for excluding jurors. Similarly, Albert F. Jordon, superintendent of insurance for the District of Columbia, testified that he employed the list as a norm for denying licenses to sell insurance in the District of Columbia. Only the common sense of Captain Carl Lawrence, chief of the Bureau of Investigation for the State of Delaware, prevented enforcement of a state statute that directed the police to register members of listed organizations whenever they entered the state. Strict enforcement, said Captain Lawrence, would have required stopping every automobile that crossed the Delaware Memorial Bridge en route from Maryland to the Jersey Turnpike.[3]

The subcommittee called to the witness stand a victim of the security program, Clifford J. Hynning, to illustrate how an overzealous security system could lessen security and bring harm to the national interest. During his fifteen years of distinguished government service, Hynning had, among other laudable actions, played an outstanding role in opposing the Treasury Department's unfortunate policy, advised by Harry Dexter White, to allow inflation in Germany after World War II. Despite his long and devoted service, the "security bureaucracy at the Treasury" suspended him on the basis of vague charges of sympathy with subversive ideas and organizations. Since Hynning was not reinstated until he appeared before the Hennings Subcommittee and then promptly resigned his position as a lawyer for the Treasury Department, the government suffered the loss of his talented services. "The Hynning case," Hennings concluded, "teaches us that once we abandon the restraints of the Bill of Rights in our efforts to rid the government of Communists and engage in unrestrained herd-riding, the people who generally get hurt are not the Communists or the fellow-travelers but good, loyal, anti-Communist Americans."[4]

While the expanding security program frequently contributed

[3] *Hennings Subcommittee Hearings,* Part 1, 249, 348, 306, 296.
[4] *Hennings Subcommittee Hearings,* Part 1, 441, 701; Hennings Papers, Box 5, press release, January 27, 1956.

little to the nation's security, it sometimes caused immeasurable human suffering, as the subcommittee's presentation of the Foster case illustrated. The case involved a Negro couple from Seattle, Mr. and Mrs. William B. Foster, who were dismissed under the Army's Civilian Employee Security Program. Mr. Foster, a maintenance carpenter in a nonsensitive position, was suspended in May of 1953 on the basis of associations he had made in 1943. Since he had already received clearance on the same charges under the Truman loyalty program, Foster confidently went into his hearing without a lawyer and argued his own case. The hearing board split evenly in its decision, and Foster was dismissed as a security risk. Some time later his wife, who also worked for the Army, was suspended as a security risk because of the same associations. Wisely retaining a lawyer to argue her case, she was cleared and reinstated, on the ground that the charge was fully refuted. Despite his wife's clearance under the same charge, Foster had not been reinstated at the time he appeared before the Hennings Subcommittee. Hearing the recital of facts, Hennings concluded that "unless the national security is pictured as a capricious and fickle woman, it is hard to understand why national security should condemn the husband and clear the wife on the basis of the same facts." While Mr. Foster was reinstated in the summer of 1956, through the pressure of the Hennings Subcommittee, his three-year suspension constituted an untold amount of hardship.[5]

The subcommittee found that security officials at times violated the limited rules of fair procedure set down in their own department's regulations. The Treasury Department did this in the Hynning case, and the Interior Department made the same blunder in its dismissal of William Vitarelli as a security risk. In the latter case, the Department of the Interior failed to give Vitarelli a reasonable opportunity to answer the charges against him, even though its own regulations demanded this procedure. Realizing the error, the department changed the designation of Vitarelli's dismissal to suitability, which did not demand this procedure. In the wake of Vitarelli's appearance at the November

[5] *Hennings Subcommittee Hearings,* Part 1, 441; Hennings Papers, Box 11, press release, December 10, 1955; Box 12, press release, August 30, 1956.

hearings, the Supreme Court invalidated his dismissal, on the grounds that the Department of the Interior had not followed its own security regulations.[6]

It became clear to the Hennings group that, at times, a department's security regulations failed to square with the procedures outlined in the executive order on which they were based. Assistant Secretary of the Air Force David S. Smith admitted, under Hocker's questioning, that the Air Force's security regulations explicitly considered associations with individuals as grounds for an adverse security judgment, even though Executive Order 10450 mentioned only associations with organizations. The testimony of Joseph H. Sumners, Jr., dramatized a similar practice in the Navy. Sumners, a civilian employee of the Navy, was dismissed as a security risk in 1955, on the charge that he had associated with his mother, who allegedly belonged to an organization on the Attorney General's list. This "momism," as the *New Republic* labeled it, seemed to Hocker to go far beyond even the illiberal procedures of the Eisenhower executive order.[7]

The next logical step was for the Hennings Subcommittee to demonstrate that Executive Order 10450 went beyond the World War II "summary dismissal" statute on which it was based. This development, however, had to await the second session of public hearings the following June. Meanwhile, Hennings spent the remainder of the first session exploring the security system's most vulnerable areas, the control of passports and the policy of basing army discharges on pre-service behavior. In each case, the subcommittee drove home the point that, since applicants for passports and draftees seeking their discharges were exercising a right, not a privilege, the due process demanded by the Fifth Amendment protected them from arbitrary or unfair procedures.

Appearing for the State Department to answer the questions of Hennings and Hocker was its security officer, Scott McLeod. The subcommittee attempted to show that denials of passports violated

[6] *Hennings Subcommittee Hearings,* Part 1, 653, 679; Hennings Papers, Box 5, press release, January 27, 1956. Vitarelli v. Seaton, 359 U. S. 535 (1959).

[7] *Hennings Subcommittee Hearings,* Part 1, 507, 495, 462; "Follow that Mother!" *New Republic,* 133 (August 15, 1955), 4; (October 3, 1955), 18.

due process, since they were often based on secret information that the applicant had no chance to refute. From McLeod's testimony it became clear that the decision to deny a passport resulted solely from the uncontested evaluation of Mrs. Frances Knight, the director of the department's Passport Division. Applicants accused of being Communists received a hearing, but those whose foreign travel was vaguely alleged to be "not in the national interest" received neither a hearing nor any other measure of due process. The testimony of Dr. Linus Pauling, who sought a passport without success until he won the Nobel Prize in 1954 for scientific achievement, dramatized the practice. Hennings concluded that the Passport Division, by reasoning that refusal of a passport to a Nobel Prize honoree would do more harm than Pauling's possession of a passport, substituted its own arbitrary judgment for due process of law.[8]

Turning to the Defense Department's military security program, the subcommittee again concentrated on a right, not a privilege. To be drafted into the Army was not a privilege, though an enlistment might be so construed. With this in mind, the subcommittee concentrated on the treatment the Army accorded its draftees. As the story unfolded, officials of the Army admitted that there was no apparent authorization by Congress for a security practice developed as a result of Senator McCarthy's charging the Army with lax security policies in the summer of 1954. The central issue in this policy involved the Army's granting less than honorable discharges to draftees because of their pre-service activities or associations. Although a draftee's in-service record might be perfect, he was given at most a "General Discharge under Honorable Con-

---

[8] *Hennings Subcommittee Hearings,* Part 1, 85–216. The background of passports and the statutes governing their issuance may be found in: Reginald Parker, "The Right to Go Abroad," *Virginia Law Review,* 40 (November, 1954), 853 ff. The first case dealing with procedures of the Passport Division was Bauer v. Acheson, 106 F. Supp. 445 (D. D. C. 1952). That the Parker article was the basis for Hennings' investigation is clear from: CRS Files, 1955, letter from Hocker to Geoffrey F. Chew, October 20, 1955. Parker concluded that "at the present time there is no statute on the books that would allow the State Department to restrain citizens other than registered Communists from going abroad."

ditions" if the Army decided that his pre-service record made him a security risk. Hennings objected that, though the need of maintaining military discipline justified punishing in-service misconduct with less than honorable discharges, the Army had no right to punish pre-service behavior. In rebuttal, the Army argued that, since suspicious pre-service activity lessened a draftee's value by limiting his scope of activity, it had the right to place him on controlled duty during service and to refuse him an honorable discharge. Hennings replied that, if the Army felt it could not trust a draftee, it should not induct him.[9]

Just as the Army initiated its illiberal discharge policy during McCarthy's attack in 1954, its withdrawal from that policy began with Hennings' counterattack in 1955. In a directive of November 16, Secretary of Defense Charles Wilson promised that the Army would return to its pre-McCarthy policy of basing discharges solely on the character of military service. To accomplish this, Wilson directed that henceforth no draftee should be inducted until his security check was completed; if the security investigation indicated the draftee was not trustworthy, he would not be inducted. Although subsequent correspondence between Hennings and the departments of the Army and Defense indicated that this withdrawal was not complete, it began a trend that culminated in the 1958 case of *Harmon v. Brucker.* In that case, the Supreme Court settled two issues that had long bothered liberals. With only Justice Clark dissenting, the Court ruled that the Secretary of the Army exceeded his power if he based a discharge on anything other than the character of service rendered and that the federal

---

[9] On the miltary security program in general and its discharge policy: Brown, *Loyalty and Security,* 81, 465; "Follow that Mother!" *New Republic,* 133 (August 15, 1955), 4; "The Army Security Program," *Nation,* 181 (August 20, 1955), 147 ff.; the opinion of Judge Jerome Frank in Schustack v. Herren, 234 F. 2d 134 (2d Cir. 1956); Jacob K. Stein, "The Defense of Army Security Risk Cases," *St. Louis University Law Journal,* 4, 34 ff.; William K. Jones, "Jurisdiction of the Federal Courts to Review the Character of Military Administrative Discharges," *Columbia Law Review,* 57, 917 ff. On Hennings' investigation: *Hennings Subcommittee Hearings,* Part 1, 353–534. On the Army's reasoning in granting less-than-honorable discharges based on pre-service activity: *ibid.,* 472 ff.

courts had jurisdiction to review the fairness of military discharges.[10]

At least in part a product of the November hearings was another liberalization of the Army's security policy. In a memorandum of October 17, The Adjutant General of the Army cautioned security officers and boards to interpret derogatory security information in a common-sense manner, one faithful to "the spirit as well as the letter of existing instructions." This calm approach to derogatory information moved even the implacable Ginzburg to state that the memorandum "vindicates all the Committee's efforts at the hearings." He felt that the directive simply advised security officers not to "hold anybody to be a security risk unless there is real evidence that the man personally is subversive." To Ginzburg this meant "putting an end to the game of playing membership lists and coming out with security numbers." In April of the following year, Hennings urged Secretary Wilson to make these provisions standard policy for all Defense Department security programs. In 1957 the Department of Defense complied by enforcing the "common-sense principles" in all three military services. Continuing this cooperative spirit, the Army agreed to the subcommittee's suggestion that the new policies be made retroactive. The department reviewed all of the 730 security risk discharges given between November 10, 1948, and November 16, 1955, and upgraded 211 of them to honorable. Following the decision of the Supreme Court in the Harmon case, the Army informed Hennings that it had again reviewed the less-than-honorable discharges and had upgraded another 266 to honorable.[11]

[10] On this change: *Hennings Subcommittee Hearings,* Part 1, 423, 465, 470; Hennings Papers, Box 160, memorandum from Ginzburg to West, undated, but about November 17, 1955; Box 161, press release, November 18, 1955.

[11] On the interchanges between Hennings and Administration policymakers: *Hennings Subcommittee Hearings,* Part 1, 494; Hennings Papers, Box 161, press release, November 18, 1955; Box 136, letters from Hennings to Hugh Milton, II, assistant secretary of the Army, January 10, 13, and 16, 1956; Box 5, press release, January 29, 1956; Box 10, press release, February 3, 1956; Box 136, letter from Hennings to Hugh Milton, II, February 23, 1956; Box 160, letter from Hennings to Wilbur M. Brucker, February 24, 1956; letter from Mansfield D. Sprague, General Counsel of the Department of Defense, to Hennings, March 1, 1956; letter

This first session of the Hennings Subcommittee was hard-hitting and productive, but at the same time a model of fairness. The behavior of Hennings and Hocker accomplished as much by example as the previous movement for a code of fair committee procedure did by legislative effort. On one occasion, however, Hocker committed a breach of fairness, for which he immediately apologized. This occurred during the testimony of Civil Service Commissioner Philip Young, whom Hennings had invited to testify on his role as overseer of the Federal Employee Security Program. After Young was sworn, Hocker proceeded with a line of questioning that ultimately led to the "numbers game." Under the Chief Counsel's persistent queries, Young made the startling and erroneous assertion that he had never used the term "security risk" and that he had no idea what it meant. Pursuing the topic, Hocker precipitated the first public exposé of the mechanics of the "numbers game."

The source of the problem was Civil Service Form 77. Young sent this form to every executive agency as a means of computing the effectiveness of the Eisenhower security program. In reporting the volume of dismissals, the form directed agency heads to list the total number of employees dismissed under the criteria set down in Executive Order 10450. Then followed two subquestions, asking the agency head to break down the above total into those dismissed under the procedures of Executive Order 10450 or under other civil service procedures. Assuming that a strict definition of a security risk was an employee dismissed under both the

from Hennings to Hugh Milton, II, March 9, 1956; letters from Hennings to Charles E. Wilson, Secretary of Defense, February 1 and May 10, 1956; Box 12, press release, May 13, 1956. Harmon v. Brucker (Abramowitz v. Brucker), 355 U. S. 579 (1958). According to *The Nation,* the Army was evading the Harmon ruling by relating pre-service activities to in-service activities and then giving a less-than-honorable discharge (*Nation,* 187, October 11, 1958, 202). Hennings Papers, Box 160, memorandum from The Adjutant General, Department of the Army, to all Commanding Generals, October 17, 1955; CRS Files, 1956, memoranda from Ginzburg to Hennings, April 17 and May 2, 1956; Hennings Papers, Box 12, press release, May 13, 1956; Box 160, letter from Hennings to Charles E. Wilson, May 10, 1956. On the Army's review of less-than-honorable discharges: *Hennings Subcommittee Hearings,* Part 1, 494; *Congressional Record,* 85th Cong., 2d Sess., 1958, 104, A8082.

criteria and procedure of Executive Order 10450, Young's published figures were grossly misleading. Three-fourths of the security dismissals published by Young were employees separated in accord with normal civil service procedures. Their only connection with security came from the agency heads' mental determination that these employees came under the all-embracing criteria of Executive Order 10450, and Form 77 invited this determination by its confusing manner of questioning.[12]

When the meaning of Form 77 struck Hocker, he accused Young of purposely inflating the statistics on security risks. When Young replied that the remark was uncalled for, Hocker agreed and immediately tendered a complete apology. Some weeks later, in a return appearance before the Johnston Subcommittee, Young made an apology in turn. He confessed to the Johnston Subcommittee that he had, in fact, publicly used the term "security risk" on nine separate occasions.[13]

Apart from this single and understandable lapse on Hocker's part, the subcommittee's first public session moved smoothly and inexorably toward its goal. The countervailing force in defense of civil liberties had already made its presence felt. The State Department's Passport Division now had to contend with the Constitutional Rights Subcommittee in addition to the federal courts when refusing passports; the Army received regular communications from Hennings until it had completely reversed its discharge policy; the Supreme Court took its rationale from the November hearings in demanding that the Interior Department reinstate William Vitarelli. Individual victims of the security system sought and found redress through the Hennings Subcommittee. The subcommittee's staff prepared nearly one hundred cases for appeal either in public session or through private negotiation with the relevant department or agency, and approximately twenty of these led to a more favorable judgment for the victim. In none of the cases did Hennings attempt to adjudicate the facts. He continually insisted that, from the same set of facts that had been accepted as culpable by the government, he could reasonably deduce a contrary

12 *Hennings Subcommittee Hearings,* Part 1, 763, 797.
13 *Ibid.,* 812; *Johnston Subcommittee Hearings,* Part 2, 1306.

conclusion. Although the government was at the disadvantage of being unable to reveal all the facts at its disposal, Hennings nonetheless showed the futility of "total security," the futility of a democratic society's even attempting to achieve absolute certainty about the thoughts and motives of all its citizens.[14]

The first session of the subcommittee convinced Hennings that the system of administrative criminal law, so hazardous to civil liberties, was not essential to the national safety. He contended that the subcommittee's investigation had already proved that national security would actually be strengthened by arresting the spread of the security system and by diverting the nation's energy from "the persecution of loyal Americans who joined (or whose relatives joined) organizations that are not considered patriotic or acceptable today." In many instances, he said, individuals were asked to sacrifice their constitutional rights "not on the altar of national security but on the altar of bureaucratic authoritarianism." Exemplifying this, Hennings pointed to the case of William Foster, whose presence in the nonsensitive position of a civilian maintenance carpenter for the Army hardly threatened national security in the first place.[15]

While the Hennings Subcommittee had already made large inroads on the expanding security system, the *bête noire* of the program—Executive Order 10450—remained untouched at the close of the first session. It was not until the second session, in June of 1956, that Hennings attempted to demonstrate that Executive Order 10450 constituted an unlawful extension of the "summary dismissal" statute, Public Law 733, and was, therefore, an invalid use of executive power. But prior to the 1956 public hearings, Hennings had to hurdle several obstacles to the work of the sub-

[14] Hennings Papers, Box 11, press release, February 21, 1956. On the use of cases and their sources: *Hennings Subcommittee Hearings,* Part 1, 85. See the evaluation given by the right, the left, and the center, respectively, in: *National Review,* 1 (November 19, 1955), 12; (December 14, 1955), 12; (January 4, 1956), 4; (January 11, 1956), 15; Edgar Kemler, "Soft Impeachment," *Nation,* 181 (December 24, 1955), 556 ff.; Murrey Marder, *Washington Post,* February 12, 1956.

[15] Hennings Papers, Box 11, press releases, November 25 and December 10, 1955, and February 21, 1956; Box 12, press release, August 30, 1956.

committee, not the least of which was his own loss of enthusiasm. An untimely loss of interest in a project was not a rare occurrence in Hennings' senatorial career. The Senator had a persistent habit of wandering away from an issue when it ceased to challenge him. Unlike an earlier senator from Missouri, Harry S Truman, he normally acted in short bursts of brilliant effort in response to specific, even though unpublicized, events. The plodding, day-to-day committee work, so characteristic of Truman's senatorial career, repelled him. Basically, Hennings lacked the ambition needed for steady and continuous effort. Beyond satisfying his somewhat aristocratic tastes, wealth held no attraction for him. In fact, the idea that wealth constituted a symbol of status or of success annoyed him. When he ran for the Senate in 1950, for example, his private law practice was bringing him sizable fees for the first time in his life, yet he felt little compunction in giving it up. Similarly, political success offered him only the minimum amount of satisfaction and motivation. His decision to enter the race for the Senate resulted from an almost phlegmatic desire for the comfort of a Senate career and an opportunity to contribute to the national interest as he saw fit. The one incentive that consistently motivated him was a strong desire for the approval of certain persons whose ability and judgment he respected. Praise from his colleagues in the Senate, from legal scholars, and from journalists like Walter Lippmann, William S. White, Richard H. Rovere, and the staff of the *Post-Dispatch* greatly impressed and pleased Hennings. Hence, he was at his best when responding to a challenging issue, since this occasioned praise and approval from men he respected.[16]

Given this temperament, Hennings surprised few of his close associates when he brilliantly led every session of the November hearings and then did little for several months thereafter. The security problem had developed a noticeable staleness as a result of overexposure during 1955. Throughout that year, committee after committee examined every facet of the problem. The Humphrey and Johnston subcommittees, the special committee of

16 Interviews with former staff members, May and June, 1962; Eugene F. Schmidtlein, "Truman the Senator," unpublished doctoral dissertation, University of Missouri, *passim.*

the New York City Bar Association, and the Wright Commission preceded or accompanied the effort of the Constitutional Rights Subcommittee. Moreover, except for the Humphrey group, these investigations were scheduled to continue through 1956 or beyond. Thus, even though no group had as yet offered a solution to the fundamental problem, the impression grew that defects in the security program had been aired *ad nauseam*.[17]

Hennings' zeal declined further as the dimensions of the security problem decreased. Progressively fewer security cases appeared after March of 1955. To some extent, this decline followed from the lessened number of investigations undertaken within the Federal Employee Security Program. In accord with the terms of Eisenhower's 1953 executive order that established the program, heads of departments and agencies ran a post audit of all clearances granted under the Truman loyalty program. According to Civil Service Commissioner Philip Young, this review was nearly complete by the spring of 1955, and the system was functioning on a nearly current basis. Since only new applicants underwent clearance procedures thereafter, the number of controversial cases decreased proportionately.[18]

Some improvement in the methods of security officers and boards complemented this reduction in the number of investigations. The Attorney General's memorandum of March 4, 1955, stressing the need for greater caution in making security determinations, exerted a restraining influence on overzealous security personnel. As Brownell exercised his advisory power more vigorously, heads of departments and agencies became more amenable

---

[17] Subcommittee on Reorganization of the Senate Committee on Government Operations, Subcommittee to Investigate the Administration of the Federal Employee Security Program of the Senate Committee on Post Office and Civil Service, Special Committee on the Federal Loyalty-Security Program of the Association of the Bar of the City of New York, United States Commission on Government Security. The Humphrey Subcommittee ceased investigating the security program after its proposal to establish the Wright Commission passed the House and Senate. Indications that the security issue had become overexposed have come from: Interviews with former staff members, May, 1962, and the relative lack of interest on the part of the press that greeted the appearance of the reports of the New York City Bar Association and the Johnston Subcommittee in the summer of 1956.

[18] *Johnston Subcommittee Hearings,* Part 2, 1325–26.

to taking his advice. Investigations of specific cases by the Hennings and Johnston subcommittees as well as the adverse publicity given by the liberal press to unwise security decisions left their mark. After the Ladejinsky case, for example, there was less likelihood that Secretary of Agriculture Ezra Taft Benson would allow his security officers to refuse clearance without consulting the Internal Security Division of the Department of Justice. Even the harshest critics of the security program agreed that, although the system remained basically intact, its operation improved after the liberals' attack in 1955.[19]

The clearest indication of Hennings' lagging enthusiasm appeared in the shifting membership of his subcommittee's staff. Shortly after the November hearings, the subcommittee lost its chief hearings counsel and staff director, Lon Hocker. The St. Louisan shortened his six-month appointment by several weeks when the president of the Missouri Insurance Company died suddenly and the company's board elected Hocker to replace him. For five months after Hocker's departure, the subcommittee operated without a chief counsel. Research Director Benjamin Ginzburg, whose enthusiasm never lagged, served as acting staff director, but without permission to hold hearings. Finally, in May of 1956, Francis Smith, a former Missouri state senator from St. Joseph, began a brief term of two months as chief counsel. Several weeks after Smith returned to his private law practice, Hennings appointed Charles Slayman, from Senator Herbert Lehman's staff, as chief counsel and staff director. Such instability on the subcom-

[19] The memorandum from the Attorney General was contained in a letter from Attorney General Brownell to President Eisenhower on March 4, 1955 (*Johnston Subcommittee Hearings*, Part 1, 56–58); the response of the President, dated March 4, 1955 (*ibid.*, 58), directed that the memorandum be sent to all departments and agencies. Subsequent to this memorandum, the Internal Security Division of the Department of Justice was able to coordinate much more closely the security practices of individual departments and agencies. The "once burnt" attitude of Secretary Benson appeared in: *Johnston Subcommittee Hearings*, Part 1, 735–55. For evidence of general improvement in the security program: James Reston, *New York Times*, December 25, 1955, and January 31, 1956; Murrey Marder, *Washington Post*, February 12, 1956; Anthony Lewis, *New York Times*, July 30, 1956.

mittee's staff had no other explanation than that Hennings temporarily lost interest in pursuing the security investigation.[20]

In the midst of this staff shuffling, Senator McCarthy, undaunted by his censure fourteen months earlier, suddenly announced his intention to attack Hennings on the floor of the Senate for contributing to the collapse of the nation's antisubversive defenses. He warned the Senate that the attack would come when the Missourian made his request for his subcommittee's 1956 appropriation. While McCarthy's threat was sudden, it was not entirely unexpected, since both the Senator from Wisconsin and the conservative press had from the start taken a dim view of the Hennings Subcommittee. At first, the subcommittee's foremost critic was the syndicated columnist David Lawrence; the editor of *United States News and World Report,* whose column appeared regularly in the *St. Louis Globe-Democrat,* the *Kansas City Star,* and 198 other newspapers, opposed every project the subcommittee initiated. Following Lawrence were less influential columnists like John O'Donnell of the *New York Daily News,* Leon Racht of the *New York Journal American,* and Fulton Lewis, Jr., of King Features and the Mutual Broadcasting Company. As the November hearings began, the newly established *National Review,* a weekly journal edited by a McCarthy apologist, William Buckley, Jr., added its voice to the chorus of critics. Except for an unsuccessful attempt to soften the antagonism of Lawrence, Hennings initially dismissed this type of opposition as inevitable and continued his preparations for the November hearings.[21]

[20] Hennings Papers, Box 160, letter from Hennings to Robert A. Brenkworth, November 29, 1955; letter from Hennings to Senator Carl Hayden, January 13, 1956; memorandum from B. Ginzburg to Hennings, January 16, 1956; letter from Langdon C. West to Hocker, March 1, 1956; letter from Hennings to Senator James Eastland, May 14, 1956; Box 10, press release, May 1, 1956; CRS Files, 1956, letter from Hennings to Charles Slayman, July 2, 1956; Hennings Papers, Box 160, letter from Hennings to Senator James Eastland, July 12, 1956; memorandum from Francis Smith to Hennings, June 15, 1956.

[21] *Washington Star,* August 18 and September 13, 1955; *New York Daily News,* September 14, 1955; *Kansas City Star,* September 14, 1955; *St. Louis Globe-Democrat,* September 15, 1955; *New York Herald-*

(Continued on next page)

While the hearings were in progress, McCarthy added his inimitable bluntness to the criticism of the conservative press. In a press release of November 25, the Senator from Wisconsin called on the Democratic party to stop "the disgraceful and dangerous activities of the Democratic controlled committee under the chairmanship of Senator Hennings of Missouri." This committee, according to McCarthy, was waging "jungle warfare against the government security system on the argument that it is too tough on Communist suspects." Referring to the subcommittee as "a front for left wing organizations such as the Fund for the Republic and the ADA," the Wisconsin Republican charged that, since not one leader of the Democratic party had opposed Hennings, he could deduce only that Democrats were "as soft as ever on the Communist issue." In conclusion, he threatened that Communist subversion would be a major issue in the 1956 campaign unless Democrats withdrew support from Hennings.[22]

Hennings brushed McCarthy aside rather easily. In a brief statement, he quoted a portion of his recent speech to the St. Louis Lawyers Association, in which he had predicted such an attack. The unprecedented nature of the subcommittee's work and the controversial issues with which it dealt encouraged "extremists of all sorts and disgruntled individuals" to "do everything possible to frustrate and discredit" it. The Missourian believed it clear, however, to those "who had made any attempt to follow the course of these hearings with care," that the actions of the subcommittee represented no "attack on the security of the United States, but rather an effort to strengthen our security program by

Tribune, September 19, 1955; *St. Louis Globe-Democrat,* September 21, 1955; *Washington Star,* October 7, 1955; *New York Journal-American,* November 19, 1955; *Los Angeles Examiner,* November 22, 1955; *Washington Star,* November 28 and December 6, 1955; *National Review,* 1 (November 19, 1955), 12; (December 14, 1955), 12; (January 4, 1956), 4–5; (January 11, 1956), 15–17. The circulation of these columnists was: David Lawrence, 200 newspapers, Fulton Lewis, Jr., 100 newspapers, John O'Donnell, 16 newspapers (*Washington Star,* December 26, 1955). Evidence of attempts to silence the criticism of David Lawrence came from interviews with former staff members, May and June, 1962.

[22] Hennings Papers, Box 160, press release, November 25, 1955, from Office of Senator Joseph R. McCarthy.

protecting innocent and loyal men and women, and fully to safeguard the Bill of Rights and the Constitution of the United
States."[23]

Several days later McCarthy answered Hennings by observing
sarcastically that "the Sir Galahad pose you attempt to strike did
not quite come off." Turning to the speech the Missourian had
quoted, he charged that the reforms in security procedures that
Hennings demanded "would open the floodgates to wholesale
Communist infiltration of our government." Commenting on the
recent subcommittee hearings, the Senator from Wisconsin singled
out the effects they had on the Army's security policy. Specifically,
he accused Hennings of "daily browbeating of Army officials until
the Defense Department agreed not to draft security risks and
cease basing discharges on pre-service activities." The result of
this new policy, McCarthy concluded, was that "loyal American
youths must give several years of their lives to their country's
service, but Communists and Communist Party liners go scot-free
—neither drafted nor disgraced."[24]

A week later, in Tulsa, McCarthy continued his attack. Cynically
referring to Hennings as "Missouri's special contribution to the
left-wing bleeding hearts club," the Wisconsin Republican again
denounced the procedural reforms demanded by Hennings. He
claimed that the rejection of guilt by association and the use of
secret informers and the application of the "reasonable doubt"
security standard would effectively destroy the security system. He
denied the Senator from Missouri's charge that the government
based its security discharges on guilt by kinship, asserting that
family relationships constituted "just one of the factors taken into
account." Finally, he accused Hennings of playing politics by
making Republicans appear as enemies of civil liberties. To stop
this despicable tactic, he had addressed letters to the three leading
candidates for the Democratic presidential nomination—Adlai
Stevenson, Estes Kefauver, and Averell Harriman—asking them
to repudiate Hennings and his committee. If this failed, the Sena-

[23] Hennings Papers, Box 11, press release, November 25, 1955.
[24] Hennings Papers, Box 160, letter from McCarthy to Hennings,
November 29, 1955.

tor from Wisconsin told his audience, "we have our work cut out for us in 1956."[25]

Coinciding with McCarthy's attack, David Lawrence criticized Hennings from another angle. He charged that the effort of the subcommittee was unnecessary, since "there isn't a single question of constitutional rights before it on the 'security risk' problem that isn't being tackled now and cannot be solved by the Federal courts." Lawrence suggested that instead of wasting time on these cases, Hennings should tackle a real problem, such as "the right to work," the right of a worker to find employment without joining a union. After comparing the extent of the security problem with the labor problem, Lawrence concluded that there were "probably less than 100 'security cases' in America in which there is a serious question of mishandling, but there are millions of persons affected by the loss of the liberty known as 'the right to work.' "[26]

Adding to the difficulties created by McCarthy and the conservative press was the embarrassing treatment accorded Hennings by Communist groups. Alan Max, managing editor of the *Daily Worker,* repeatedly tried to induce Hennings to allow a representative of his newspaper to testify on freedom of the press before the subcommittee. Similarly, William Z. Foster, national chairman of the Communist party, attempted to bring a party representative before the subcommittee to comment on freedom of speech and of assembly. In each case, Hennings resisted the offer. Emphasizing further the good repute of the Senator from Missouri among Communists, Michael S. Russo, long identified as the Communist party's leader in New England, denounced the Massachusetts Commission on Communism and Subversive Activities for attack-

[25] Hennings Papers, Box 160, Address of Senator McCarthy, Tulsa, Oklahoma, December 7, 1955; letters from Langdon C. West to Averell Harriman and Adlai Stevenson, December 3, 1955; letter from Averell Harriman to Hennings, January 3, 1956; CRS Files, 1955, letter from Benjamin Ginzburg to George E. Sokolsky, December 12, 1955.

[26] *New York Herald-Tribune,* November 28, 1955. In this connection, note: Hennings Papers, Box 161, press release, November 25, 1955 (concerning Senator Carl T. Curtis); Box 159, letter from Hennings to Aaron Benesch, December 13, 1955. It is interesting to note that this criticism by Lawrence indicated already the alliance of business with the security-conscious which became so important in the Court fight of 1957–1958 (Chapter VII).

ing him and suggested that "it would be a good thing to have the Subcommittee of Sen. Thomas C. Hennings (D., Mo.) investigate the Commission." Most disconcerting of all, however, was the series of consistently friendly comments on Hennings and the subcommittee that appeared in the *Daily Worker*. The Senator was sufficiently concerned to request Benjamin Mandel, research director for the Internal Security Subcommittee, to make photostatic copies of all stories on the subcommittee that appeared in the *Daily Worker* during 1955. The result was a large collection of generous accolades out of which, Hennings realized, an unscrupulous political opponent could create some unpleasant impressions of him in the 1956 campaign.[27]

Hennings felt only minor concern over the criticisms from the right, especially since the press in his home state viewed the security probe with satisfaction. The *Post-Dispatch,* for example, regularly lauded the projects undertaken by the subcommittee and consistently praised the Chairman's principles of civil liberties. The nearest approach to criticism by a Missouri newspaper came on one occasion from the *Globe-Democrat.* Commenting on Hennings' speech before the St. Louis Lawyers Club that McCarthy found so objectionable, the *Globe* disagreed with Hennings in part, but it also judged his analysis "provocative and sincere." In a forceful display of its pro-Hennings bias, the *St. Joseph News-Press* responded to McCarthy's November 25 attack by defending Hennings and bitterly denouncing the Senator from Wisconsin.[28]

Assured by the support he was receiving from the press in

[27] Hennings Papers, Box 160, letters from Alan Max to Lon Hocker, November 21 and 28, 1955; letter from Hennings to Max, December 1, 1955; telegram from William Z. Foster to Hennings, November 10, 1955; telegram from Hennings to Foster, November 23, 1955; *New York Herald-Tribune,* December 8, 1955; Hennings Papers, Box 160, letter from Benjamin Mandel to Hennings, December 12, 1955. Dates of the New York *Daily Worker* were: July 27, August 2, 7, 8, 10, 15, and 22, September 9, 12, 19, 22, 23, 24, 25, and 26, October 3, 13, 17, and 19, November 13, 14, 15, 16, 18, 20, 21, 22, and 27, and December 2, 1955.

[28] *St. Louis Post-Dispatch,* May 15, September 16 and 17, and November 4, 19, and 23, 1955; *St. Louis Globe-Democrat,* November 6, 1955; *St. Joseph News-Press,* November 29, 1955. According to a close associate of Hennings, the Senator felt that the security issue would help him politically with the *Post-Dispatch* but would hurt him in the rural areas, and that the total effect would be slightly harmful (interview with former staff member, May, 1962).

Missouri, Hennings felt only minor alarm over McCarthy's threat to denounce him when he asked the Senate for additional funds for the Subcommittee on Constitutional Rights. Nonetheless, the Missourian recalled to Washington his long-time political adviser, St. Louis lawyer Thomas Guilfoil, to help parry the McCarthy threat. Under the handsome Guilfoil's counsel, Hennings decided to placate the Senator from Wisconsin, whose power in the Senate and grip on the nation were now rapidly slipping. Taking the floor to explain his request for funds, Hennings stated, for McCarthy's benefit, that the subcommittee had almost completed its work on the security program "because most agencies have revised and changed their programs." Equally soothing to McCarthy was Hennings' assertion that the next major investigation of his subcommittee would concern the Administration's practice of withholding information from congressional investigators, a subject that had long irritated the Senator from Wisconsin. When McCarthy took the floor, he accepted the olive branch Hennings had offered him. Leaving untouched on his desk the thick sheaf of papers that apparently was his anti-Hennings brief, McCarthy told the Missourian:

I should like to say to the Senator that I had prepared a rather extensive speech, but in view of the Senator's statement that he intends to investigate the question of government secrecy—keeping secret from the American people information which they should have, and will try to expose the facts and do something about it, and inasmuch as that is going to be one of his major aims, and because of his statement that he has practically finished the investigation of the security program, I shall desist from making the speech I had intended to make.[29]

After disposing of McCarthy and dispelling his own lethargy, Hennings moved on to the conclusion of the security probe, an analysis of Executive Order 10450 and its legislative base in Public Law 733. According to the original terms of Public Law 733, the "summary dismissal" statute, Congress gave to the heads of eleven departments and agencies the power to suspend and dismiss summarily employees they deemed security risks. In

[29] Hennings Papers, Box 11, press release, February 16, 1956; *Congressional Record*, 84th Cong., 2d Sess., 1956, 102, Part 3, 3005–11. On McCarthy's interest in the Eisenhower information policies: Clark R. Mollenhoff, *Washington Cover-Up*, 41–54, 210–11.

addition, the President received the right to extend this power to other departments and agencies as he "from time to time" saw fit. Hennings felt that Congress intended this summary power only for sensitive federal positions and that Eisenhower therefore went beyond congressional authorization when he made it the basis for a security program that blanketed the more than sixty departments and agencies of the civil service. He argued, moreover, that since most federal positions had little or nothing to do with the nation's vital secrets, this extension was unnecessarily wasteful in the costs of operation and the human suffering it inevitably inflicted.[30]

While paring the security program to its proper dimensions constituted Hennings' main objective, he hoped additionally to reform security procedures. He condemned the practice of immediately suspending employees when security investigation raised damaging evidence against them. Pending final determination of their cases, suspended employees often had to seek other employment immediately, since their financial reserves were insufficient to support the months of waiting for a final decision. As a result, the immediate suspension actually amounted to dismissal, even though the suspected employee was in no way a security risk. Hennings recommended, also, that every effort should be made to expedite final determinations, since the waiting period caused the suspects considerable mental anguish and lowered the morale of the federal service. The Missourian further proposed that in the trial-like security hearings at least a minimum amount of due process should be observed. This would include furnishing counsel to the accused, providing him with a full disclosure of the charges he had to refute, and granting him the right to subpoena witnesses in his own behalf. On the thorny question of the government's use of secret informers in arriving at security decisions, Hennings offered a compromise. He suggested allowing the government to protect the anonymity of informers who were *bona fide* undercover agents employed by the Justice Department, but "casual informers," as other anonymous witnesses were called, had to reveal themselves for cross-examination or retract their testimony. Finally, the Sena-

---

[30] Hennings Papers, Box 160, memorandum from Eleanor Bontecou to Langdon C. West, December 8, 1955; Box 161, letter from Francis Smith to Herbert Brownell, June 15, 1956; CRS Files, 1956, memorandum from James Caldwell to Francis Smith, June 7, 1956.

tor from Missouri proposed that the government discard entirely the Attorney General's list, unless it were revised so that security officers and boards could understand precisely why and for what period of time an organization was listed as subversive.[31]

With his reforms of security procedures clearly in mind, Hennings reasoned that the next step centered on forcing Attorney General Brownell to accept them or show cause for his refusal. The Attorney General, in Hennings' view, completely controlled the Eisenhower security program. According to the executive order that established the program, Brownell was to "render to the heads of departments and agencies such advice as may be requisite to enable them to establish and maintain an appropriate employee security program." Moreover, when the President circulated this executive order he noted that the Attorney General would furnish "sample instructions designed to establish minimum standards for the implementation of the security program under this order." In addition, Hennings' knowledgeable consultant on security matters Miss Eleanor Bontecou advised him that reliable reports indicated that not only the sample instructions but the executive order itself were composed in the Attorney General's office under the immediate supervision of Deputy Attorney General William Rogers. Hennings concluded, then, that no real changes in the security system would emerge without the Attorney General's approval, except in the unlikely circumstance of strong pressure from Congress.[32]

Assuming that Brownell would be the key witness, Hennings directed the subcommittee's staff to fix a date for the public hearings. When Francis Smith arrived on May 1 to replace the long-departed Hocker, he immediately invited the Attorney General to choose a date convenient to himself for testifying at the public session. Brownell delayed two weeks before answering and then refused to comply. Deputy Attorney General Rogers explained to Hennings that, since the Justice Department had already cooperated with the Humphrey and Johnston subcommittees and was, presently aiding the effort of the Wright Commission, he saw no

[31] See note 30.

[32] For the executive order, note, and sample instructions: *Johnston Subcommittee Hearings,* Part 1, 742, 746; Hennings Papers, Box 160, memorandum from Eleanor Bontecou to Langdon C. West, December 8, 1955.

reason for duplicating this testimony before the Constitutional Rights group.

Hennings answered Rogers by sending an angry telegram to Brownell, insisting that the Attorney General had an obligation to accede to a legitimate request from a Senate subcommittee and rejecting Rogers' offer to comment privately on the subcommittee's draft of a final report. At the conclusion of his telegram, the Senator made the threatening observation that "the position has often been taken that even though the Congress has a right to subpoena members of the Executive Branch of the government before it, yet that comity which should exist between the branches of government should not require such measures." A few days later Rogers called and arranged a meeting between Smith, Langdon C. West, and himself. Evidently more amenable now to testifying, Rogers asked Smith to outline the questions for which Hennings wanted answers. Smith described the questions the subcommittee felt important, and Hennings confirmed them in a lengthy letter on June 15. However, the Attorney General never replied, and Hennings sent him no more invitations. Chief Counsel Smith suggested that the Senator either subpoena Brownell, as a Senate subcommittee had done to Attorney General Harry M. Daugherty in 1927, or attempt to coerce him by bringing the matter to the floor of the Senate. Though he directed Smith to prepare a memorandum on the constitutionality of a subpoena, Hennings ultimately decided against either of these extremes. Instead, he confined himself to a severe but unproductive denunciation of Brownell's intransigence, when the Attorney General appeared before the full Judiciary Committee on another matter.[33]

In conjunction with preparation for the Brownell-oriented hearings Hennings had invited ex-Senator Harry P. Cain to testify also. He reasoned that, because of the protracted delay following the

[33] Hennings Papers, Box 160, memorandum from Smith to Hennings, May 4, 1956; Box 161, letter from Hennings to Brownell, May 11, 1956; Box 160, memoranda from Smith to Hennings, May 15, 17, and 24, 1956; Box 161, letter from Deputy Attorney General William Rogers to Hennings, May 28, 1956; letter from Hennings to Brownell, May 29, 1956; telegram from Hennings to Brownell, May 31, 1956; letter from Rogers to Hennings, June 1, 1956; Box 160, memoranda from Smith to Hennings, June 1 and 6, 1956; Box 161, letter from Hennings to Brownell, June 15, 1956.

November hearings, Cain's testimony could serve the purpose of recalling public attention to the evils surrounding security that needed correction. When Brownell refused to appear, Cain became the lone witness at the two-day hearing in mid-June.[34]

Harry P. Cain had remained at the center of the conflict over security since January of 1955. Between that date and his appearance before the Hennings Subcommittee, the Eisenhower appointee to the Subversive Activities Control Board had consistently belabored the Administration's handling of the internal security program. When he appeared before the Hennings Subcommittee his crusade was nearing its end, since no one, least of all Cain himself, expected the President to renew his appointment after it expired in August. Realizing this, Cain looked forward to his appearance before the subcommittee in June as an opportunity to summarize publicly his eighteen months of criticism.

Cain's summary differed little in essentials from Hennings' own conclusions, though the Missourian could scarcely match the intensity of Cain's presentation. The combination of Cain's decidedly ugly face and powerful, rasping voice alternately fascinated and irritated his listeners. His pithy and quotable frankness, faithfully relayed by the press, evoked a similar response from newspaper readers. In this instance, for example, the *Globe-Democrat,* in an editorial on the speech, remarked that Cain had finally "blown his stack." For two days he vividly described before the Hennings Subcommittee the suffering caused by the Eisenhower security system. Citing current security cases as evidence of distress inflicted by the system, Cain poignantly appealed to the Administration to halt this useless suffering and return to the traditional American respect for individual rights and freedom. He concluded his testimony by listing the reforms needed to prevent future injustices in the name of security. He charged that, since national secrets are both few in number and accessible to only a small group of federal employees, only a very limited security program is needed. Beyond this, the government should rely on the civil service's traditional suitability program, which eliminates employees whose lack of qualifications makes them a danger to

[34] Hennings Papers, Box 160, memorandum from Smith to Hennings, May 24, 1956.

the nation's security and yet does not stigmatize them as disloyal. As far as a loyalty program was concerned, Cain felt this was completely unnecessary, since disloyalty in the United States is a rarity. Neither the loyalty program of the Truman Administration nor the security system of Eisenhower, Cain concluded, had unearthed a single disloyal citizen.[35]

In the absence of Brownell, Cain at least kept the second session of the subcommittee's hearings from falling flat on its face. Nonetheless, Hennings was never able to reshape the security system in accord with the final recommendations he had prepared for the Attorney General. He even neglected to take a necessary step in that direction by failing to issue a report summarizing the entire security probe. After the Cain hearing, Smith and Ginzburg drafted such a report, but Hennings never issued it. When Smith left the subcommittee on July 1, his replacement Charles Slayman continued perfecting the document, but Hennings still resisted publishing it. The Senator's administrative assistant Langdon C. West explained Hennings' resistance in a letter to the departed Smith on September 10, 1956. Hennings, he wrote, feared that issuing a report during the 1956 campaign might invite a political opponent to lift parts of the material out of context and use them to distort the Senator's position on internal security.[36]

Passing over, for the moment, West's explanation, what was the position on internal security that Hennings feared would be distorted? Viewed by McCarthy from the right, it appeared dangerously radical; viewed from the left, by such liberals as Ginzburg or Columnist Edgar Kemler, it appeared too mild. According to Kemler, Hennings was too narrow and legalistic to cope with the heart of the security problem. While depicting the Missourian as "the best defender of constitutional rights the New Deal Demo-

[35] *St. Louis Globe-Democrat,* June 15, 1956; *Hennings Subcommittee Hearings,* Part 2.

[36] The Hennings Papers contain nothing but the title page of this draft. The title page is dated "July, 1956" (Hennings Papers, Box 160). The fact that it was drafted is clear from: Hennings Papers, Box 160, memorandum from Charles Slayman to Langdon C. West, July 24, 1956; CRS Files, 1956, memorandum from Ginzburg to Slayman, July 18, 1956; Hennings Papers, Box 160, letter from Langdon C. West to Francis Smith, September 10, 1956; Box 161, memorandum from Charles Slayman to Bernard Fensterwald, November 21, 1958.

crats have so far put forward," Kemler admitted that the legalistic approach brought a revolution in military security and was especially helpful in bringing relief to individual victims of the security program. Nonetheless, Kemler condemned the approach as superficial, and he warned Hennings and other Democrats that unless they themselves were "willing to take some of the chances that they would foist upon the security chieftains they are going to have to defend such victims for a long time to come." In short, Kemler felt that Hennings' proposals to pare down the size of the security program and to reform its procedural failings treated only the symptoms of the real evil. The radical solution consisted of scrapping the entire program and leaving the protection of the nation's secrets to the traditional elimination of undesirable employees through the suitability program.[37]

Whether or not he privately agreed with Kemler and Ginzburg, Hennings refused to take their position publicly. His solution, implicit in the recommendations proposed for Brownell, was "narrow and legalistic" in comparison. Hennings' view closely resembled the recommendations contained in the reports published by the New York City Bar Association and the Johnston Subcommittee. Both recommended reducing the scope of the security program. The New York lawyers suggested that Eisenhower accomplish this by amending his executive order, while the Senate group urged Congress to amend Public Law 733 for the same purpose. The bar association, in addition, made specific proposals, similar to Hennings', for reforming the procedures of the program.[38]

While the "narrow and legalistic" approach was moderate in comparison with that of Kemler and Ginzburg, it coincided with the solution that eventually became the law of the land. The decisive action came not from Eisenhower, as the New York bar hoped, nor from Congress, as the Johnston Subcommittee urged,

[37] Edgar Kemler, "Soft Impeachment," *Nation,* 181 (December 24, 1955), 556. For Ginzburg's view: CRS Files, 1956, memoranda from Ginzburg to Hennings, May 2, 1956, Ginzburg to Slayman, November 14 and December 12, 1956.

[38] According to the interviews I conducted with former staff members in May and June of 1962, Hennings even privately would not go as far as Ginzburg and Kemler. Association of the Bar of the City of New York, *Special Committee on the Federal Loyalty-Security Program, Report;* Senate, Committee on Post Office and Civil Service, 84th Cong., 2d Sess.,

but from the Supreme Court, as Hennings perhaps foresaw. The solution came in a 6 to 3 decision of the Warren Court, on June 11, 1956, in the case of *Cole v. Young.* The majority of the Court held that the Eisenhower security program exceeded the authority granted by Congress in Public Law 733. By that enactment in 1950, said the Court, Congress granted to the President the right to extend the exercise of the summary suspension and dismissal power only to federal employees in sensitive positions. Hence, subjecting all federal employees indiscriminately to the exercise of this power, as Eisenhower had done, was unlawful.[39]

This concurrence of the New York bar, the Johnston Subcommittee, and, most importantly, the Supreme Court in the same solution does more to explain Hennings' failure to issue a final report than the reason given by West. Hennings was an astute politician, capable of appreciating the political danger noted by West. At the same time, he showed unquestionable courage whenever an important issue called for it. West's explanation was correct, but only because Hennings no longer felt his recommendations were needed. It is significant that at the same time the Missourian was neglecting the issuance of his subcommittee's final report, he was alertly watching efforts in Congress to overturn the Cole decision. On July 5 he urged Chairman James Eastland of the Judiciary Committee to stop action on the three anti-Cole bills that the Subcommittee on Internal Security had favorably reported to the parent group. Whether or not he foresaw it at the time, blocking congressional attempts to overturn decisions like *Cole v. Young* was to occupy most of Hennings' energy during the next two years.[40]

1956, Report No. 2750. In contrast, the report of the Wright Commission recommended enlarging the security program: *United States Commission on Government Security, Report,* pursuant to Public Law 304, 84th Cong., as amended (Washington, 1957); Ralph S. Brown, "Regression in the Wright Report," *Bulletin of the Atomic Scientists,* 13 (September, 1957), 253.

[39] Cole v. Young, 351 U. S. 536 (1956). Subsequently, the Cole decision proved less important than first thought, although the security-conscious in Congress felt it was dangerous enough to overturn: Chapter VII; *Northwestern University Law Review,* 51 (January–February, 1957), 788 ff.

[40] Hennings Papers, Box 7, letter from Hennings to Eastland, July 5, 1956.

VII

The Warren Court on Trial

Attacking the Supreme Court is as much a part of American politics as criticizing umpires is a part of the national pastime. In each case, these arbiters of matters vital to Americans have come to expect controversy, and they maintain a stoical silence while more earthly men come to their defense. Such were the roles of the Warren Court and its critics during the Eighty-fifth Congress; leading its mundane defenders in 1957–1958 was Senator Hennings.

Perhaps no branch of the federal government can irritate Americans as acutely as the Supreme Court. Without warning, the nine appointed justices emerge from their sacrosanct isolation and flatten in minutes a congressional statute that took years to enact or condemn a practice dear to the heart of an executive department. Safe in their lifetime appointments, the justices are immune from the power of the ballot box and remain unbowed by criticism, save in the extraordinary event of impeachment.

In the verbal whipping that follows an unpopular decision, however, the Court's opponents have all the better of it. The power enjoyed by the Supreme Court of the United States is less a product of theory than of practice. Indeed, one can seriously question whether this power was ever intended by the framers of the Constitution. The basis of the Court's position is judicial review, the prerogative that allows it final authority not only to decide the meaning of statutes but also to pass judgment on whether they conform to the Constitution. The rationale underlying judicial review is itself undemocratic—the idea that the majority cannot always be trusted. This power, say its defenders, is necessary to prevent the Congress, representing the majority, from mistreating a minority. Such a rationale is hardly calculated to endear the Supreme Court to the majority at the very moment the "people's" will is called into question.

The Court's critics can cite noteworthy precedents also for attacking the judiciary. President Jefferson spared no rhetoric in slashing the Marshall Court for what he thought was overzealous concern for the property rights of the moneyed class. President Andrew Jackson did the same for supposedly the same reasons. The Abolitionists vigorously condemned the Taney Court for allegedly protecting slaveholders in the Dred Scott decision. Twentieth-century liberals attacked the Court for perpetuating the nineteenth-century liberalism so pleasing to the business class. President Franklin D. Roosevelt aimed broadsides at the Court for rejecting the reform legislation of the New Deal. In short, critics of the Warren Court could point to numerous American heroes in justification for their opposition to the high tribunal.

The chorus of critics of the Warren Court began assembling as early as May of 1954, when the Court condemned segregation in the public schools, in the decision in *Brown v. Board of Education of Topeka*. Subsequent decisions indicated that the Court would pursue desegregation as rapidly as a majority in the nation would allow. From that time on, an embittered South provided a base for any move to punish the Supreme Court or to restrict its activity.[1]

Closely associated with Southern antagonism against the Court, but for different reasons, was the enmity of the business community. The bond uniting the two groups was State rights, and the heaviest blow to State rights came in April of 1956, in the case of *Pennsylvania v. Nelson*. In that decision, the Warren majority

[1] Brown v. Topeka, 347 U. S. 483 (1954), 349 U. S. 294 (1955). For this entire chapter I have drawn heavily on the comprehensive treatment of the Court fight by Walter F. Murphy, *Congress and the Court,* and to a lesser extent on C. Herman Pritchett, *Congress Versus the Supreme Court.* On the reaction in the South: Murphy, 79 ff.

invalidated state sedition and antisubversive statutes on the ground
that federal laws had pre-empted the field. The business community interpreted federal pre-emption as a stiff blow because it had
found state governments more accessible and more sympathetic
to business interests than the federal government. Since the central threat to business was the union shop, fear of pre-emption
solidified when the Court, in the same term as *Pennsylvania v.
Nelson,* invalidated a Nebraska "right to work" law. As a result,
the pressure of powerful lobbies like the National Association of
Manufacturers, the Chamber of Commerce, and the American
Farm Bureau Federation added significant force to the anti-Court
feeling already boiling in the South.[2]

The third anti-Court force cut across regional and economic
lines. According to this group, the recent decisions of the liberals
on the Warren Court had progressively weakened the ability of
the government to resist internal subversion by Communists. The
trend began in 1955 when the Court, in *Peters v. Hobby,* invalidated a dismissal for reasons of security because the procedures
failed to conform to the provisions of President Truman's loyalty
program. Of greater importance, however, was the Warren Court's
crippling blow to the Eisenhower security program. In the 1956
case of *Cole v. Young,* the Court decided that the Administration's
security system had no congressional authorization to extend beyond a limited number of sensitive positions in the federal government. During the same term, the Warren majority, in addition to
destroying state antisubversion laws, reached a similar antisecurity
conclusion in the case of *Slochower v. Board of Higher Education
of New York City.* In that case, the Court held that New York
could not discharge a professor in a public college merely because
he had pleaded the protection of the Fifth Amendment before
a Senate investigating committee. The trend of the Court's decisions toward weakening the government's security system, critics
felt, was unmistakable.[3]

2 Pennsylvania v. Nelson, 350 U. S. 497 (1956). Railway Employees v.
Hanson, 351 U. S. 225 (1956). The participation of the business community in the Court fight comes from Murphy and is fully confirmed by
the Hennings Papers. Murphy, *Congress and the Court,* 89 ff.

3 Peters v. Hobby, 349 U. S. 331 (1955); Cole v. Young, 351, U. S. 536
(1956); Slochower v. Board, 350 U. S. 551 (1956). On the reaction:

By the end of 1956 the alliance of these three anti-Court groups was clear, but it was not yet dangerous to the Court. Their attacks thus far had centered on measures opposed to the Nelson decision that were pending in both houses of Congress and, to a lesser degree, on bills introduced in each chamber to combat the decision in Cole. Both houses held hearings on the anti-Nelson decision measures during 1956, but none reached the floor of Congress. The Senate Internal Security Subcommittee reported several anti-Cole decision bills to the parent Judiciary Committee, but Hennings and Senator Olin Johnston, Democrat from South Carolina, put pressure on Senator James Eastland, Democrat from Mississippi and chairman of the Judiciary Committee, to let them die in committee.[4]

While the ranks of the Court's critics formed, Hennings casually turned to an almost routine campaign for re-election to the Senate. In June of 1956, one of his staff, J. Delmas Escoe, reported that evidence gathered on a tour through Missouri indicated "overwhelming" acclaim of the Senator and his activities throughout the state and that all the Democratic factions in Kansas City, even the Pendergast group, had pledged their support to him. In July, Thomas Guilfoil announced from St. Louis that over a hundred Missouri newspapers had already endorsed Hennings and that there was no "organized opposition" to the incumbent senator. When the August primary arrived, only a single, obscure opponent, Thomas J. Gavin, appeared on the ballot with Hennings, and this Kansas City councilman stood so little chance of success

Senate, Judiciary Committee, Subcommittee on Internal Security, *Hearings,* 85th Cong., 1st Sess., 1957, *passim.* For a survey of Court cases: Murphy, *Congress and the Court,* 80–86, 97–109; Robert G. McCloskey, "The Supreme Court Finds a Role: Civil Liberties in the 1955 Term," "Useful Toil or the Paths of Glory? Civil Liberties in the 1956 Term of the Supreme Court," "Tools, Stumbling Blocks, and Stepping Stones: Civil Liberties in the 1957 Term of the Supreme Court," *Virginia Law Review,* 42 (October, 1956), 735; 43 (October, 1957), 803; 44 (November, 1958), 1029. For an analysis of the Warren Court's liberalism: Daniel M. Berman, "Constitutional Issues and the Warren Court," *American Political Science Review,* 53 (June, 1959), 500 ff.

4 On the Nelson measures: Murphy, *Congress and the Court,* 91 ff. On the Cole measures: Hennings Papers, Box 160, letter from Olin Johnston to Hennings, July 3, 1956; letter from Hennings to James Eastland, July 5, 1956; letter from Hennings to Olin Johnston, July 5, 1956.

that he withdrew from the race almost before the ink on the ballot was dry. The general election proved an even greater victory for Hennings than had been anticipated. His widespread support included even the *St. Louis Globe-Democrat,* a daily that was normally Republican and that supported the Republican nominees for President and Governor, but Hennings for the Senate. When the returns came in, Hennings led the Democratic ticket, defeating his Republican opponent, Neosho lawyer Herbert Douglas, by a margin of 230,898 in a total vote of 1,800,984.[5]

Shortly after Hennings' re-election, the Warren Court began grinding out the decision that unified the anti-Court bloc into a dangerous force in Congress. Early in the term, the Court stepped on the toes of the nation's lawyers by holding, in *Schware v. New Mexico,* that the New Mexico Board of Bar Examiners acted arbitrarily when they denied Schware a license to practice law. The FBI blinked in astonishment, a short time later, when the Warren majority overturned a conviction under the Smith Act because the accused was denied access to written statements given the government by adverse witnesses. The chagrin of the FBI increased when Justice Tom Clark, dissenting from the decision in *Jencks v. United States,* irresponsibly stated: "Unless the Congress changes the rule announced by the Court today, those intelligence agencies of our Government engaged in law enforcement may as well close up shop, for the Court has opened their files to the criminal and thus afforded him a Roman holiday for rummaging through confidential information as well as vital national secrets."[6]

On the heels of the decisions in the Schware and Jencks cases came the internal security decisions announced on June 17, 1957, the day labeled as "Red Monday" by foes of the Court. In *Watkins*

[5] CRS Files, 1956, memorandum from J. Delmas Escoe to Langdon C. West and Richard Brown, June 22, 1956; Hennings Papers, Box 12, press release, July 20, 1956. On Gavin's withdrawal: *St. Louis Globe-Democrat,* July 24, 1956. On the election results, see: *Official Manual of the State of Missouri, 1957–1958,* 980, 1103 (Stevenson defeated Eisenhower by a 3,984 margin, and James T. Blair, Jr., defeated Lon Hocker by 74,718 votes). *St. Louis Globe-Democrat,* October 4, 1956.

[6] Schware v. New Mexico, 353 U. S. 232 (1957); Jencks v. United States, 353 U. S. 657 (1957).

v. United States, the Warren Court invalidated a contempt of Congress citation issued against John T. Watkins for refusing to answer questions put to him by the House Un-American Activities Committee. A majority of the Court reasoned that Watkins had no obligation to answer the committee, since it had failed to show him that the questions were relevant to a legitimate legislative inquiry. In a companion case, the high tribunal struck down a similar contempt citation issued by the State of New Hampshire against Paul Sweezey, and then reversed fourteen more convictions under the Smith Act in *Yates v. United States.* With reasoning that foes of the Court termed sheer sophistry, Justice John Marshall Harlan, speaking for the majority in the Yates case, argued that the trial judge failed to instruct the jury to distinguish *abstract advocacy* to overthrow the government by force—which he said the Smith Act did not forbid—from *advocacy to action* and that the organizing of subversive groups, which the Smith Act prohibited, referred only to the initial establishment of such groups, not to their subsequent continuation.[7]

Another group that was calling for Warren's scalp was the District Police Department of Washington. In *Mallory v. United States,* the Court dismissed the conviction of a Negro boy who had confessed to raping a white woman in Washington, D. C. The Warren majority based its decision on the fact that law enforcement officers did not arraign Mallory until seven and one-half hours after his arrest, and during that delay they obtained a full confession through use of a lie detector on the mentally retarded youth. This case contained its own explosive overtones. The majority dismissed the case, not because the confession seemed unreliable, but to punish law enforcement officers by depriving them of the fruits of their violation of the federal criminal code that demanded arraignment "without unnecessary delay." Secondly, the problem arose in the District of Columbia, which Congress administered and which, because of its large Negro population, had delicate problems of race relations. Finally, the District's

[7] Watkins v. United States, 354 U. S. 178 (1957); Sweezy v. New Hampshire, 354 U. S. 234 (1957); Yates v. United States, 354 U. S. 298 (1957).

Chief of Police and one of its strongest newspapers spared no effort to prove that the Court's position had endangered law enforcement in the area.[8]

The opening salvo from the Court's enemies in Congress came abruptly in July of 1957. Throughout this first session of the Eighty-fifth Congress, the center of attention was not the Court but civil rights. By continuing efforts begun in the previous Congress, the Administration and liberals in Congress had pushed through the first Civil Rights Act since 1875. But near the end of the debate on civil rights, Senator Jenner unobtrusively introduced an omnibus anti-Court bill "to limit the appellate jurisdiction of the Supreme Court in certain cases." The "certain cases" referred to areas touched by the Court in the Nelson, Slochower, and Cole cases of 1956 and the Watkins and Schware cases of 1957. While all of these decisions touched internal security, Jenner's package contained something for nearly every critic of the Court. The South could find solace in condemning the anti-State rights implications of the Nelson and Slochower decisions; the Administration could rescue its security system by overturning the Cole decision; congressional investigators of subversion could feel more at ease in questioning witnesses if the Watkins decision were reversed; and the legal profession's interest in bar admissions could be protected if the Court were forbidden to interfere. Even the FBI and the police would find the Jenner bill psychologically rewarding and a boost to their own anti-Court proposals.[9]

As radical as the Jenner bill was, few doubted that in the wake of "Red Monday" it could well become law. The anti-Court bloc had leaders in Congress who had spent the previous session experimenting with this type of legislation. In the House, Howard W. Smith, Democrat from Virginia and chairman of the powerful Rules Committee, had championed an anti-Nelson decision measure throughout the previous Congress. In his bill, H.R. 3, he

[8] Mallory v. United States, 354 U. S. 449 (1957). CRS Files, 1958, memorandum from Maloney to Slayman, February 11, 1958; letter from Slayman to Edward Dumbauld, February 20, 1958. House, Judiciary Committee, Special Subcommittee to Study Decisions of the Supreme Court, *Hearings,* 85th Cong., 2d Sess., 1958, Part 1.

[9] Senate, 85th Cong., 1st Sess., 1957, S. 2646.

proposed that no federal pre-emption be assumed unless specifically stated by Congress or unless reconciliation between state and federal law was absolutely impossible. Hearings were held during 1956 on H.R. 3, as well as on a companion bill introduced by Senator Eastland, but neither reached the floor. In the same session, Eastland also introduced one of the three anti-Cole decision bills reported by the Senate Subcommittee on Internal Security, but squelched in the parent Judiciary Committee by Hennings. Aligned with Eastland on security matters were McCarthy, author of another bill opposing the Cole decision, Senators Jenner and John M. Butler, Republican from Maryland, and Francis Walter, Democrat from Pennsylvania, chairman of the House Un-American Activities Committee and author of the Lower Chamber's anti-Cole decision bill of 1956. With the common bond of concern over the Warren Court's alleged indifference to internal subversion, these six men formed a nucleus for the anti-Court bloc in Congress and the frightening possibility that the Jenner bill could become law.[10]

Many outside of Congress were also clamoring for a move against the Court. The FBI responded to Clark's dissent in the Jencks case with a well-organized program of grass-roots pressure from former members of the Bureau. Journalists were stirring up the nation to demand that the Warren Court be put in its place. Many lawyers, upset by the Schware decision and its companion, *Konigsberg v. California,* contributed legal respectability to the Jenner proposal. Even the Administration joined the outcry against the judiciary by supporting some anti-Court measures and exerting little pressure on Republicans in Congress to desist from pushing those it did not support. But the final blow came from Edward S. Corwin, professor emeritus at Princeton University and dean of American constitutional scholars, who announced that the time had

---

[10] Eastland's anti-Nelson bill was Senate, 84th Cong., 2d Sess., 1956, S. 3143. The anti-Cole bills were: Senate, 84th Cong., 2d Sess., 1956, S. 4050 (Eastland); S. 4051 (McCarthy); House, 84th Cong., 2d Sess., 1956, H.R. 11721 (Walter). The Cole decision actually proved less important than first thought: *Northwestern University Law Review,* 51 (January–February, 1957), 788 ff.

come for the Supreme Court to have its "nose well tweaked" for overstepping the boundaries of judicial restraint.[11]

Hennings caused little surprise when, shortly before Jenner's radical proposal, he appeared in the front ranks of the Court's defenders. His criticism of the security system, his defense of civil liberties, and his respect for the Supreme Court demanded that he come to its defense. Three years earlier, in 1954, he showed concern for the Supreme Court by helping to lessen the controversy surrounding Eisenhower's appointment of Chief Justice Warren while Congress was in recess. During 1955, when launching the Subcommittee on Constitutional Rights, he repeatedly promulgated the "call to arms" issued by Warren to arouse support for the Bill of Rights. In 1956, he publicly applauded the Court's ruling in the Cole case and put pressure on Eastland to stop action on three bills that, according to Benjamin Ginzburg, would have killed the Cole decision "by shooting, by drowning, or by asphyxiation." Finally, after announcement of the Watkins decision on "Red Monday," the Senator from Missouri again publicly congratulated the Court for its wisdom and courage.[12]

Among these indicators of pro-Court feeling in Hennings' past was an incident that took place in 1954 that, in retrospect, proved ironic. Inspired perhaps by gratitude toward the Court for blocking President Truman's seizure of the steel mills in 1952, Senator John M. Butler, Republican from Maryland, introduced a joint resolution to amend the Constitution by removing from Congress

11 On the FBI lobby: Murphy, *Congress and the Court,* 139 ff. For the reaction of lawyers: William H. Rehnquist, "The Bar Admission Cases: A Strange Judicial Aberration," *American Bar Association Journal,* 44 (March, 1958), 229 ff. For the press reaction: Murphy, 112 ff. The FBI lobby was strong in Missouri: Hennings Papers, Box 92, folder: 1957–FBI; Box 163, folder: Jencks. On the Administration's reaction: Murphy, 117, 213; Pritchett, *Congress Versus the Supreme Court,* 20, 120. *New York Times,* March 16, 1958.

12 Irving Dilliard, "Senator Thomas C. Hennings, Jr., and the Supreme Court," *Missouri Law Review,* 26 (November, 1961), 438–39. On the Cole decision: Hennings Papers, Box 12, press release, June 11, 1956; Box 160, memorandum from Benjamin Ginzburg to Francis Smith, June 29, 1956. On the Watkins decision: Hennings Papers, Box 163, press release, June, 1957.

its power to limit the appellate jurisdiction of the Supreme Court. In his debate on the issue with Butler on May 11, 1954—one week before the antisegregation decision—Hennings opposed the resolution because he felt it was unnecessary and, like other bills in the current epidemic of constitutional amendments, it lacked adequate study. The Missourian argued that, if the danger of tampering with the Court's jurisdiction arose, an "aroused public opinion" would deal with it promptly. Despite Hennings' opposition, the resolution passed the Senate by a 58 to 19 vote, though it ultimately died in the House. Four years later, with some embarrassment, Butler became coleader of a move to limit the jurisdiction of the Supreme Court and Hennings cosponsor of a constitutional amendment to outlaw congressional tampering with the Court's appellate jurisdiction.[13]

Hennings made every effort to create an "aroused public opinion" that would quash the anti-Court movement. On July 7, a few days before Jenner's radical proposal to punish the Court, Hennings aggressively attacked the foes of the Warren Court. He vigorously condemned the "growing tide of criticism" directed at the Court, "not only in the newspapers and over the air, but also in the halls of Congress." Attacks on the Court, he said, "ranged from carefully reasoned criticisms of what the Court has done and said, to malicious vilification of the justices themselves." While rejecting the various proposals for punishing the Court, he suggested that, although the high tribunal was not above criticism, "it should not be tampered with in a moment of passion or temporary pique." Analysis of the controversial decisions, he concluded, indicated that it was not the Supreme Court but "the unconstitutional and unlawful procedures which have been permitted

[13] The suggested relation between the steel seizure decision (Youngstown v. Sawyer, 343 U. S. 579, 1952) and the Butler resolution is from Murphy, *Congress and the Court,* 78. For the debate with Butler: *Congressional Record,* 83d Cong., 2d Sess., 1954, 100, Part 5, 6341 ff. Butler's role in the Court fight is treated below. The bill to outlaw tampering with the Court's jurisdiction was Senate, 85th Cong., 2d Sess., 1958, S. J. Res. 169. For a witty account of what he called the "amendment fever" of the Eighty-third Congress, see: Richard H. Rovere, *The Eisenhower Years,* 206 ff.

to develop in this country in recent years that should be criticized."[14]

While the liberal press paraded Hennings' statement, Jenner prepared to introduce his bill and push it swiftly through the Subcommittee on Internal Security. On August 7 the Indiana Republican joined Eastland in a nearly secret subcommittee hearing on the bill. The two senators gathered with the staff of the subcommittee at 2:35 P.M. The hearing ended twenty-five minutes later, after Jenner and a member of the staff testified in favor of S. 2646. On the basis of twenty-five minutes of testimony, the subcommittee coldly voted to strip the Supreme Court of appellate jurisdiction in cases involving the validity of: (1) the functions of congressional committees; (2) the security programs administered by the executive branch; (3) state laws and regulations dealing with subversion; (4) the acts and policies of boards of education designed to deal with subversion; (5) and the acts of state courts and boards of bar examiners concerning admissions to the practice of law in their states.[15]

Alerted by his staff that the Jenner bill would appear on the agenda of the Judiciary Committee for August 14, Hennings promptly halted action on the measure. He wrote Eastland that, even if his doctors should refuse to allow him to attend the meeting of the Judiciary Committee, he was vitally interested in the current question; he wanted it clearly understood that several other subcommittees, including his own, had an interest in the Jenner bill; in any event action on the bill should be withheld until the next session of Congress so full hearings on it could be held. On August 14 Hennings attended the meeting and, after eliciting from Eastland an accurate account of the twenty-five-minute hearing, moved to hold the measure until the next session of Congress. Jenner objected to the motion and moved to table it. With the fail-

<hr/>

14 Hennings Papers, Box 14, press release, July 8, 1957.
15 Examples of press reaction: Baltimore *Sun,* July 8, 1957, *New York Daily News,* July 8, 1957, *Minneapolis Star,* July 10, 1957, *St. Louis Post-Dispatch,* July 11, 1957. On Jenner's action: Senate, Judiciary Committee, Subcommittee on Internal Security, *Hearings,* 85th Cong., 1st Sess., 1957, Part 1.

ure of the tabling motion, Hennings had won for the liberals a breathing space of at least four months.[16]

During this session, however, Congress completed action on another anti-Court bill that was much less radical than Jenner's proposal. On August 31, 1957, the House gave final approval to a measure, inspired by the Jencks ruling, that the government must reveal to the accused in a criminal case the records of prior statements made by adverse witnesses. The final version of the bill passed the House unanimously and received only two dissenting votes in the Senate. To merit the approval of liberals, Senator Joseph O'Mahoney, who managed the bill in the Senate, cautiously stripped it of anti-Court overtones and shaped it into a slightly modified codification of the Court's ruling. Even though the bill was somewhat less liberal than the Jencks decision and despite the fact that he preferred letting the Court clarify its own rulings, Hennings voted for the O'Mahoney bill. He reasoned that, unless a liberal codification of the decision were enacted immediately, a conservative measure would eventually pass as a result of pressure generated by the frantic dissent of Justice Tom C. Clark, the urgent appeals of the Justice Department, and the fervent lobbying efforts of the FBI.[17]

With only the Jencks bill to mar the first session of the Eighty-fifth Congress, Hennings turned his attention during the recess to generating opposition to the Jenner bill. Fulfilling a commitment to address in September a meeting of the Interparliamentary Union in London, Hennings spoke primarily for the benefit of an audience on this side of the Atlantic. His topic was the Supreme

---

[16] Hennings Papers, Box 161, memorandum from Slayman to Caldwell, August 12, 1957; Box 163, letter from Hennings to Eastland, August 13, 1957. Murphy, *Congress and the Court,* 157 (Murphy had access to the minutes of the Senate Judiciary Committee).

[17] For a comprehensive treatment of the Jencks bill's developments: Murphy, *Congress and the Court,* Chap. 6. For Hennings' part in it: Hennings Papers, Box 163, correspondence on the Jencks bill, July, 1957; Box 39, memorandum from Bevan to Hennings, August 24, 1957; Box 92, letter from Hennings to W. W. Weinman, September 5, 1957. Thomas C. Hennings, Jr., "Equal Justice Under Law," *Georgetown Law Journal,* 46 (Fall, 1957), 13. The bill (S. 2377, 85th Cong., 1st Sess.) was approved on August 29, 1957, by a vote of 74 to 2.

Court of the United States. Cleverly placing the current bitterness toward the Court in the context of American history, he compared it with attacks on the independence of the judiciary in the past. He noted that the two most recent attacks on the Court—following the Civil War and during the New Deal—had resulted, interestingly, from the judiciary's efforts to protect the South and conservative Republicans, the two groups that were currently attacking the institution. But only once, Hennings pointed out, did opponents of the Court successfully chip away its jurisdiction and independence: Congress, in 1868, removed the appellate jurisdiction of the Court over habeas corpus appeals and thus prevented judicial review of Reconstruction legislation.[18]

Several weeks later, in a speech to the student body of Stanford University, Hennings stressed another danger in the Jenner bill. Safeguarding the independence of the judiciary, he said, ensured the nation's federal system of checks and balances. Since the founding of the United States, this delicate system of interaction between three equally powerful branches of the government had prevented power from being permanently lodged in any one branch and becoming unbridled. To limit the jurisdiction of the Supreme Court or to pursue other proposals aimed at lessening the Court's power or independence could permanently destroy the system under which the nation existed. Restraint of the judicial by the legislative or executive branches would permit such dominance by one or the other branch that it could institute a reign of tyranny by ignoring the provisions of the Constitution. The first victim of this power, Hennings concluded, would be individual rights, since their guardian, a judicial system that is relatively immune from political pressure and public upheaval, would be powerless to protect them.[19]

Besides placing the controversy over the Court in its historical and constitutional setting, Hennings pinpointed the immediate

[18] Hennings Papers, Box 14, press release, September 15, 1957. On the conflict over Reconstruction: Carl Brent Swisher, *American Constitutional Development,* 312 ff.; Murphy, *Congress and the Court,* 35 ff. On the 1937 conflict: Swisher, 920 ff.; Murphy, 53 ff. The Court decision accepting this limitation was *Ex parte* McCardle, 7 Wall. 566 (1869).

[19] Hennings Papers, Box 14, Address, November 6, 1957, Palo Alto, California.

cause of anti-Court bitterness. The Court's recent decisions had resulted from the nation's hysterical reaction to the dual threat of world communism and the super weapons of war. This threat created "a desire and fruitless search for complete, foolproof internal security." To achieve this objective, certain agencies of the government had developed practices and procedures that violated the safeguards in the Bill of Rights. "Foolproof internal security," Hennings stated, "can only be obtained (if at all) in a totalitarian police state." Although the reaction to fear of communism and the perils of modern warfare had begun shortly after World War II, the cases questioning the constitutionality of the security practices and procedures engendered by fear did not reach the Supreme Court in numbers until its 1956 term. After the high tribunal condemned these violations of the Bill of Rights, proponents of "foolproof security" accused the Supreme Court of usurping the power of Congress. In reality, the Warren Court did not indulge in "judicial pioneering," but merely exercised its traditional prerogative of compelling Congress and the Executive to abide by the Constitution. Criticism arose solely because the Court chose to ignore the political pressure which "a very vocal minority" had imposed upon some congressmen in an age of fear.[20]

Hennings' efforts during the recess period culminated in a long article, published in the November issue of the *Georgetown Law Journal*. After drawing heavily on his staff's research, he presented a full examination of the Court's controversial decisions and concluded that, although he did not agree with all of them, they were neither inconsistent with past decisions nor dangerous to the nation's security. He showed, further, that opponents of the Court had played on popular emotions by misconstruing or misrepresenting the rulings. Reactions to the Jencks case, for example, clearly illustrated their practice. Attorney General Brownell claimed that the Jencks opinion had created "a grave emergency in law enforcement," though the Warren majority merely insisted upon the traditional procedure of a criminal trial. The defendant in a criminal trial, said the Court, has a right to know an adverse witness's relevant prior statements in order to make his defense. This *right of*

[20] Hennings, "Equal Justice Under Law," *Georgetown Law Journal,* 13 ff.

discovery, as it is called, constitutes a significant element of due process, since it provides one of the most effective ways for a defendant to guard against perjured testimony. Moreover, in light of the government's current use of informers like Harvey Matusow, a self-confessed perjurer, in prosecuting cases of alleged Communist affiliations, the possibility of perjury was exceedingly real. Hennings further noted that, contrary to the frantic rhetoric of the Court's foes, the Jencks decision did not authorize "fishing expeditions" into the files of the FBI. The Warren majority specifically demanded only the disclosure of records made by an informer who was a witness and such disclosure to the extent only that the records contained the information on which he had testified. The Jencks decision, Hennings concluded, created "a grave emergency in law enforcement" only if law enforcement agencies had been completely dependent on the unconstitutional practice in the first place.[21]

Turning to Jenner's proposal for punishing the Court, the Senator from Missouri submitted an argument that ultimately proved fatal to the Jenner bill. If the provisions of that measure should become law, he argued, total confusion would result, since as many as fifty-nine different interpretations of due process could theoretically prevail in the five areas designated by Jenner; with the elimination of the Supreme Court as the ultimate arbiter and regulator of due process, each of the forty-eight state courts and eleven circuit courts could conceivably interpret it differently. The result would be that a citizen's right to due process, as guaranteed by the Fifth and Fourteenth amendments, would depend on the practices of the particular state in which he resided.

The efforts of Hennings and others during the recess period to allay the opposition to the Court proved insufficient. The anti-Court fever remained high, as the numerous anti-Court measures pending in both chambers of Congress indicated. In this second session, Hennings fixed his attention primarily on the Jenner bill, but two other issues concerning the Court also attracted his attention. In each of them, Hennings' involvement resulted from the fact that the continuing work of the Subcommittee on Constitu-

[21] *Ibid.*

tional Rights had conveniently anticipated movements ultimately involved in the attack on the Warren Court.[22]

The Subcommittee on Constitutional Rights was prepared in advance for the Mallory decision in June of 1957. The previous October, when the Court consented to hear the case, Chief Counsel Slayman saw the implications for civil liberties and immediately directed his staff to analyze the entire subject of confessions and police detention. As a result, when Justice Felix Frankfurter announced the unanimous opinion dismissing Mallory's confession of rape and a special subcommittee of the House instituted hearings weighted against the decision, Hennings was in a position for counterattack. Despite the fact that Eastland would probably refuse to refer anti-Mallory legislation to his subcommittee, the Missourian was able to hold hearings weighted in favor of the Court because he had beforehand placed the topic on the subcommittee's annual prospectus.[23]

The debate on the Mallory case centered on Rule 5(a) of the Federal Code of Criminal Procedure, which directs federal officers to arraign an arrested person before the nearest available magistrate "without unnecessary delay." The provision was intended to prevent violations of the accused's right to counsel, to assure his freedom from self-incrimination, and to protect his right to be arrested only for probable cause. In order to compel officers to follow this rule, the Supreme Court, in the 1943 case of *McNabb v. United States,* held that confessions obtained during a period of unnecessary delay were not admissible in federal courts. In the Mallory case, the Warren Court applied the 1943 ruling somewhat more stringently by terming "unnecessary" the seven and one-half hour delay permitted by officers who arrested Mallory. Moreover, Frankfurter, speaking for the Court, warned that Rule 5(a)

[22] For a summary of anti-Court proposals, see: Sheldon D. Elliott, "Court Curbing Proposals in Congress," *Notre Dame Lawyer,* 33 (August, 1958), 597.

[23] Hennings Papers, Box 161, memorandum from Slayman to West, November 30, 1956. Senate, Committee on Rules and Administration, 85th Cong., 1st Sess., 1957, Report No. 23, 3. House, Judiciary Committee, Special Subcommittee To Study Decisions of the Supreme Court, *Hearings,* 85th Cong., 2d Sess., 1958, Part 1. Senate, Judiciary Committee, Subcommittee on Constitutional Rights, *Hearings,* 85th Cong., 2d Sess., 1958.

"allows arresting officers little more leeway than the interval between arrest and the ordinary administrative steps required to bring a suspect before the nearest available magistrate."[24]

The anti-Court forces in Congress had a simple solution to the application to Mallory of the McNabb Rule. They suggested amending Rule 5(a) to read that no confession should be inadmissible solely because of delay in taking an arrested person before an arraigning officer. By this stratagem, the Court would be rendered powerless to punish violations, reducing enforcement of the McNabb Rule to the somewhat empty threat of prosecution by the Justice Department for violations of Rule 5(a). Hennings, recalling his experiences as a prosecuting attorney in St. Louis, knew that such an amendment would make Rule 5(a) impotent for protecting the rights of arrested persons. Moreover, having established a record in St. Louis for the highest percentage of convictions by a prosecuting attorney, he was convinced that such violations of individual rights were not at all essential to law enforcement.[25]

Liberals' hopes for blocking anti-Mallory legislation dimmed, however, after the Lower Chamber's special subcommittee assembled an impressive array of witnesses to testify that overturning the Mallory decision was an urgent necessity. Hennings responded by arranging his own hearings for March of 1958 to provide a forum for those who wished to leave the matter to the Court's decision. Though not all of the witnesses supported his position, the Senator's hearings enabled defenders of the Court to publicize—in the charged atmosphere of the District of Columbia—persuasive arguments that the McNabb-Mallory Rule would not upset law enforcement.[26]

[24] James E. Hogan and Joseph M. Snee, "The McNabb-Mallory Rule: Its Rise, Rationale and Rescue," *Georgetown Law Journal*, 47 (Fall, 1958), 1 ff.; Thomas C. Hennings, Jr., "Detention and Confessions: The Mallory Case," *Missouri Law Review*, 23 (January, 1958), 25; Alan Barth, *The Price of Liberty*, 3 ff.

[25] House, 85th Cong., 1st Sess., 1957, H.R. 8600. On Hennings' career as a prosecutor, see Chapter I. For Hennings' view: Hennings, "Detention and Confessions: The Mallory Case."

[26] Murphy, *Congress and the Court*, 177 ff. Murphy states that the Hennings hearings were of little impact, since they were not published

After the March hearings, Hennings watched helplessly as Eastland referred a House-passed anti-Mallory bill to O'Mahoney's Subcommittee on Improvements in the Federal Criminal Code. Under prodding from liberals in the Senate, such as John Carroll, Democrat from Colorado, O'Mahoney reported to the Judiciary Committee a surprisingly liberal version of a companion House measure. In fact, Hennings interpreted the confusing bill as being more liberal than the Court's ruling, since it added to the McNabb Rule the qualification that for any confession to be admissible in court the accused had to be informed beforehand of his constitutional right to silence. On the specific wording of Rule 5(a), the O'Mahoney bill, in effect, merely substituted "unreasonable delay" for "unnecessary delay." Though still preferring to pass no Mallory bill at all, Hennings withheld opposition in the Judiciary Committee to the liberalized measure. Thus, with only Senator William Langer of North Dakota dissenting, on the quite reasonable grounds that the bill as interpreted by liberals was unnecessary, the Judiciary Committee cleared the Mallory bill for action on the floor during the late August climax of the Court fight.[27]

The second anti-Court issue anticipated by the Constitutional Rights Subcommittee concerned the right of a citizen to a passport. This controversy arose initially during the subcommittee's study of the Administration's security program in November of 1955. At that time, Hennings criticized the State Department for violating freedom of speech and association by denying passports to

until December of 1958. The staff of the subcommittee, however, felt that press coverage during the hearings would counteract the furor created in the District of Columbia by, above all, a series of articles appearing in the *Washington Star* that attempted to show the absolute necessity of overturning the McNabb-Mallory Rule. This was the major goal of the hearing, not the publication of the record (CRS Files, 1958, memorandum from Maloney to Slayman, February 11, 1958; letter from Slayman to Edward Dumbauld, February 20, 1958). For press comment on the hearings: *Washington Post,* February 10, 1958; *Washington Star,* February 10 and March 10, 1958; *New York Times,* March 8, 1958.

[27] Murphy, *Congress and the Court,* 194 ff. CRS Files, 1958, memoranda from Slayman to Escoe and Maloney, June 2 and July 7, 1958; memorandum from Maloney to Dan Lynch (Senator Carroll's office), July 23, 1958; Hennings Papers, Box 161, Hennings to Senator O'Mahoney, July 18, 1958; Box 15, Address, October 10, 1958, St. Louis, Missouri. Senate, Judiciary Committee, 85th Cong., 2d Sess., 1958, Report No. 2252.

citizens whose views and associations made their foreign travel, in the opinion of the State Department, inimical to the national interest. In addition, he condemned as arbitrary and outside due process of law the Passport Division's manner of determining who could or could not leave the country. The issue erupted again late in 1956 when William Worthy, a foreign correspondent for the Baltimore *Afro-American,* and two reporters for *Look* magazine traveled to Communist China despite the prohibition of Secretary of State Dulles. In retaliation, Dulles refused to renew Worthy's passport after it expired early in 1957. Hennings promptly came to Worthy's aid by introducing a concurrent resolution, asserting that it was "the sense of the Congress that the passport application of Mr. William Worthy be acted upon favorably and without delay."[28]

Although the Worthy bill went to the Foreign Relations Committee, Hennings instituted hearings on the incident before his Constitutional Rights Subcommittee. He hoped to demonstrate that the State Department, in denying to Worthy and other newsmen the right to enter Red China, had violated freedom of the press, since travel is sometimes a prerequisite for gathering news. Moreover, not only the individual newsmen but the nation as a whole suffered, since it had no reliable means other than the news reports of calculating the behavior of Red China and the wisdom of the government's foreign policy toward it. Although Hennings' bill failed to gain support and Dulles refused to relent, the incident stimulated the Missourian's latent interest in exploring the whole subject of a citizen's right to travel.[29]

The villain in control over passports continued to be the State Department. Hennings objected both to the procedure by which the Secretary denied passports and the reasons on which he based

[28] CRS Files, 1957, memorandum from Caldwell to Slayman, March 20, 1957; Senate, Judiciary Committee, Subcommittee on Constitutional Rights, *Hearings,* 85th Cong., 1st Sess., 1957, Part 1, 24 ff. The Worthy bill was Senate, 85th Cong., 1st Sess., 1957, S. Con. Res. 21. Hennings Papers, Box 52, press release, March 12, 1957; Box 161, letter from Slayman to Hennings, March 16, 1957.

[29] Hennings Papers, Box 52, press release, March 12, 1957. Note, however, the subsequent action by the State Department: Richard Dudman, *St. Louis Post-Dispatch,* September 10, 1957.

such denials. The former violated a citizen's right to *procedural* due process, especially when the denial rested on evidence received from secret informers whom the applicant could not cross-examine; the latter violated *substantive* due process, when the basis of the denial was the applicant's beliefs or associations. Hennings argued, further, that only Congress could impose limitations on the right to travel and that Congress had never given the State Department the wide discretion it was exercising in denying passports. In response, the State Department reasoned that the broad power of the President and, therefore, his Secretary of State, to conduct foreign policy gave the secretary a free hand in regulating a citizen's foreign travel. Hennings retorted that travel was a right, not a privilege that the government could exploit as an instrument of foreign policy. Historically, he continued, a citizen obtained a passport as a convenience, not as a permit to leave the country. The notion that a passport constituted permission for travel arose only during World War I, and control of passports was fundamentally a wartime measure. Hence, except for the emergency of armed conflict, a passport was nothing more than a means of identification and a letter of introduction to a foreign government. Finally, the Missouri Democrat questioned the State Department's placing certain countries "off limits" even for citizens possessing a passport. If a citizen, at his own risk, wished to travel to an area where the government could not promise protection, that was his right so long as he knowingly waived his claim to the government's protection. The State Department took strong exception to Hennings' final point. The department objected that despite a waiver of protection the government still had an obligation, which it could never waive, of protecting its citizens.[30]

While Hennings traded blows with the State Department, the federal courts wrestled with the same issue. Appeals against pass-

[30] Hennings Papers, Box 14, press release, April 1, 1957; Hennings Missouri Press Report, April 10, 1957; Box 161, form letter sent to legal scholars, April 10, 1957; letter from Hennings to Dulles, April 23, 1957; Box 14, Address, June 29, 1957, Ithaca, New York; press release, October 25, 1957; Thomas C. Hennings, Jr., "The Right to Travel," *Coronet*, 43 (December, 1957), 133 ff.

port denials reached the courts after the Internal Security Act of 1950 specifically singled out Communists as ineligible for passports. In 1952 one of these cases reached the District of Columbia Circuit Court, which ruled that the State Department must provide minimum due process by establishing formal procedures for applicants to appeal denials. Subsequent cases, questioning both the procedural and substantive due process of State Department regulations, reached the same court in 1955–1957. When the circuit court denied relief to the disappointed applicants, the Supreme Court accepted the cases for argument in 1958.[31]

Several months before the Supreme Court accepted the passport cases, Hennings promised to introduce legislation aimed at clarifying the State Department's power to deny passports. Much to the surprise of the liberals, however, the complex bill that he introduced in February of 1958 allowed, however grudgingly, the very policies he had criticized. It authorized, in certain cases, the denial of a passport because of the applicant's beliefs or associations and supported the use of evidence obtained from secret informers. Explaining these provisions to the bill's fifteen liberal cosponsors, Hennings attributed the *faux pas* to inadequate draftsmanship by his staff and promised a substitute measure after the Supreme Court handed down its decision. The high court announced its opinion in June of 1958 and thereby added more fuel to the anti-Court fire. The Warren majority upheld the applicants' rights to receive passports, under the reasoning that the State Department had received no clear authorization from Congress to deny passports on the basis of an applicant's beliefs or associations. Speaking for the majority, Justice William O. Douglas stated, further, that foreign travel was a right, not a privilege; that denials

31 Testimony of Edward J. Ennis, General Counsel of the American Civil Liberties Union, Senate, Judiciary Committee, Subcommittee on Constitutional Rights, *Hearings,* 85th Cong., 1st Sess., 1957, Part 1, 2–13; *Freedom to Travel,* Report of the Special Committee to Study Passport Procedures, The Association of the Bar of the City of New York (New York, 1958), *passim.* (This report is a comprehensive treatment of passport matters up to and including the 1958 decisions. It also contains a complete bibliography.) The passport cases were: Bauer v. Acheson, 106 F. Supp. 445 (D. D. C. 1952), Briehl v. Dulles and Kent v. Dulles, 357 U. S. 116 (1958), Dayton v. Dulles, 357 U. S. 144 (1958).

were thus subject to the due process demands of the Fifth Amendment; that it was the province of Congress to determine the limitations on the right to travel; and that if Congress authorized denials because of the applicant's beliefs or associations, a grave constitutional problem would arise. Hence, by implication, the Court warned that it would probably declare unconstitutional any legislation as restrictive as Hennings' earlier passport bill.[32]

While Hennings labored to liberalize his passport bill, the Administration called on Congress to overturn the Warren Court's decisions regarding passports. Early in July, President Eisenhower sent a message to Congress asking for emergency legislation to allow the State Department to continue its policies concerning issuance of passports. The House acted first and passed a modified Administration bill during the hectic final week of the session. Later in the month, Hennings offered an extremely liberal bill, which Senator Hubert Humphrey, Democrat from Minnesota and a member of the Foreign Relations Committee, introduced and Hennings cosponsored. However, during the climactic struggle over the Court in the final days of the Eighty-fifth Congress, the Senate Foreign Relations Committee effectively prevented any

[32] For Hennings' promise: Hennings Papers, Box 14, press release, June 28 and October 25, 1957; Hennings, "The Right to Travel." The bill was Senate, 85th Cong., 2d Sess., 1958, S. 3344. The first indication that the bill was not liberal came from a story that Benjamin Ginzburg planted in *I. F. Stone's Weekly,* March 3, 1958. Then the *St. Louis Post-Dispatch,* March 5, 1958, picked it up and criticized Hennings gently, for which the *I. F. Stone's Weekly,* March 17, 1958, duly praised itself. On the reason for Hennings' illiberal passport bill, several opinions were given: (1) Inadequate drafting by his staff (*I. F. Stone's Weekly,* March 17, 1958; interviews with former staff members, May, 1962; Hennings Papers, Box 64, letter from Hennings to Senator Clark, March 19, 1958; Box 14, memorandum on S. 3344, undated, but about March 12, 1958); (2) pro-State Department bias of Fensterwald (*I. F. Stone's Weekly,* March 17, 1958; interviews with former staff members, May, 1962). Undoubtedly, there was a difference of opinion between Slayman, who wanted a bill that would simply state the liberal position succinctly, and Fensterwald, who wanted a bill that would fully solve the current passport problems (CRS Files, 1958, memorandum from Slayman to Fensterwald, December 9, 1957; *Labor's Daily,* March 20, 1958). Perhaps the best explanation of Hennings' confused bill was the difficulty of fitting the measure with a guess at what the Supreme Court would conclude on the passport cases it was then considering.

legislation concerning passports from entering the struggle on the Senate floor. The liberals realized that the Hennings-Humphrey bill had no chance of passing and that the Administration bill would only add more force to the attack on the Warren Court.[33]

Bills dealing with both the passport issue and the Mallory case figured prominently in the Court fight, but the main thrust of the anti-Court bloc was still the Jenner bill. Hennings' alert action that obstructed S. 2646 in the first session, together with his campaign in support of the Warren Court during the recess, failed to dampen Jenner's enthusiasm. In the 1958 session, Jenner, who had decided to retire from the Senate at the close of the Eighty-fifth Congress, renewed the battle once more and brought the Court fight to a climax in the Senate.

[33] *Congressional Record,* 85th Cong., 2d Sess., 1958, 104, Part 10, 13046; the House-passed passport bill was House, 85th Cong., 2d Sess., 1958, H.R. 13760; the Humphrey bill was Senate, 85th Cong., 2d Sess., 1958, S. 4137; on the outcome, see: Murphy, *Congress and the Court,* 192; Pritchett, *Congress Versus the Supreme Court,* 89–95.

VIII

Defense of the Warren Court

W HILE SENATOR JENNER viewed his anti-Court proposal as a fitting climax to his career in the Senate, Hennings had no intention of allowing S. 2646 to become anyone's epitaph. When, in close cooperation with Senator Eastland, Jenner placed his bill on the agenda of the Judiciary Committee's meeting scheduled for February 3, 1958, Hennings was prepared. As the meeting opened, the Missourian read a lengthy statement in which he insisted that full-scale hearings be held prior to committee voting and suggested that final action on the bill should be unfavorable. Chairman Eastland granted the first request and sent S. 2646 back to the Subcommittee on Internal Security with directions to hold hearings and report the bill back to the parent committee before March 10. With this preliminary skirmish the final round in the Court fight was under way.[1]

Hennings quickly began amassing authoritative opinion against the Jenner bill, to be inserted into the forthcoming hearings. He submitted his own name, along with those of six outstanding legal scholars, as witnesses, and sent a copy of S. 2646 to a hundred deans of law schools and fifty leading attorneys, soliciting their opinions and indicating his own. The replies overwhelmingly opposed the bill and went a long way toward redressing the

[1] Hennings Papers, Box 14, press release, February 3, 1958; Box 161, letter from Eastland to Hennings, February 3, 1958.

numerical superiority of persons and groups who appeared in its favor at the hearings. The opposition of the law school deans to the Jenner bill made an especially strong impression, which Hennings fully exploited by sending copies to the respective senators who represented the states in which the deans resided. Hennings' alert effort thus destroyed the legal respectability that some disgruntled law associations had accorded the anti-Court forces.[2]

Before the hearings on the Jenner bill had ended, it became clear that public sentiment had shifted. On the surface, the anti-Court group had the easier position to defend. Brent Bozell, editor of the *National Review,* made an impressive presentation of the case against the Court. He argued that the Warren Court, in each of its controversial decisions, had judged policy rather than law and that policy was the province of Congress or the President, who regularly submitted their decisions to the vote of the people; the Jenner bill, whose only defect was its failure to undo the Yates decision also, was wholly democratic, since the Constitution provides for the people to control the Court through congressional limitation of its jurisdiction. Bozell's logic, however, soon bogged down in the face of the pragmatic accomplishments of judicial review. Whether right or wrong in theory, judicial review gives final solution to otherwise insoluble conflicts of interest, and the nation has learned to acquiesce. This was a powerful argument, and it persuaded both liberals and conservatives. When the need to avoid nationwide legal confusion forced such institutions as the *Chicago Tribune,* the Justice Department, and the American Bar Association—none of which currently enjoyed a liberal reputation —into the anti-Jenner camp, even Senator Jenner saw his cause as hopeless.[3]

Senator John Marshall Butler, Republican from Maryland, a

[2] Hennings Papers, Box 161, letter from Hennings to Eastland, February 5, 1958; form letter, February 7, 1958; Senate, Judiciary Committee, Subcommittee on Internal Security, *Hearings,* 85th Cong., 2d Sess., 1958, Part 2, 393; Hennings Papers, Box 161, letter from Hennings to Senator Sam Ervin, February 23, 1958.

[3] Subcommittee on Internal Security, *Hearings,* Part 2, 637–59, 380–90. *Chicago Daily Tribune,* February 24, 1958. *Hearings, op. cit.,* Part 2, 370–77, 355–56, 241 (all on A.B.A.), 573–74 (Attorney General). Also, see the summary of testimony in Murphy, *Congress and the Court,* 157–63.

close associate of Jenner's, gave the first indication that the opponents of the Warren Court were in need of new strategy. During the hearings he introduced a bill to withdraw appellate jurisdiction from the Court only in cases involving the relationship of a state to the members of its own bar. In a dialogue with Hennings during the latter's testimony against the Jenner bill, Butler implied that his recent bill might serve as a compromise. Jenner confirmed the new approach by suggesting on the last day of the hearing that his bill was open to amendments. After the Subcommittee on Internal Security reported the bill to the parent committee, the new strategy began to emerge, with Butler in the role of chief strategist.[4]

The subsequent and much more dangerous attack on the Warren Court appeared in a new version of S.2646, known as the Jenner-Butler bill. Basically, the new approach substituted specific statutes for the unwieldy task of withdrawing the Court's appellate jurisdiction. In amending the Jenner bill, Butler retained only the original number and the single provision that coincided with his own proposal to overturn the Schware decision by withdrawing jurisdiction from the Court in cases concerning admission to state bars. To this he added Bozell's suggestion to undo the Yates decision. The Yates amendment broadened the term "organize" in the Smith Act and rejected the Court's distinction between "abstract advocacy" and "advocacy to action." To neutralize the Watkins decision, the Senator from Maryland proposed that the presiding officer of a congressional investigating committee be the final judge of the pertinency of questions that were asked witnesses. His amendment to void the Nelson decision provided that no act of Congress should be construed as pre-emptive unless specifically stated or unless the federal and state laws were positively irreconcilable. Finally, he proposed to nullify the Cole decision by extending the summary dismissal statute to all federal employees.[5]

---

[4] Subcommittee on Internal Security, *Hearings,* Part 2, 454–56, 694.

[5] Hennings Papers, Box 14, memorandum from Senator Butler, undated (issued on March 24, 1958). Walter F. Murphy made the acute observation that the statutory approach had been perfected shortly before the Court fight by the business community (*Congress and the Court,* 74–75).

Butler's amendments made the Jenner bill a much more dangerous instrument and seriously complicated the task of the Court's
defenders. All the testimony Hennings had amassed earlier and
that had seemed able to overwhelm Jenner and Butler now became
obsolete. Except for stripping the Court of jurisdiction in a narrow
area, the new version concentrated on rewriting the statutes involved in the controversial decisions. In most of these cases, the
Warren Court had reached its liberal rulings by construing, rather
than invalidating, congressional enactments. Though the justices
often "rattled the Bill of Rights" in profuse obiter dicta, the core
of the Court's decisions was generally an interpretation of congressional intent that stopped short of constitutional issues. The
practice implicitly invited Congress to clarify its intent by re-
phrasing its statutes. Butler accepted the invitation and made it
clear that the Warren majority had misconstrued the intentions of
Congress. As a result, the charge of legal confusion that had bur-
dened the original Jenner bill was useless against the multipronged
thrust of the Jenner-Butler bill.[6]

Hennings learned of the Butler amendments only in the last
days of March. Though his opposition was automatic, the time
factor made it difficult to block committee action, since the anti-
Court forces wanted an immediate vote and staunchly opposed
holding new hearings. With little chance of mobilizing legal
scholars in time, Hennings attacked the new amendments on the
Senate floor and promised a comprehensive memorandum to com-
pensate for the lack of adequate hearings. The memorandum appeared on April 7, two weeks before the Judiciary Committee began its deliberations. In general, Hennings based his objections on
the fact that the Butler amendments actually constituted a substitute bill whose various parts were totally unrelated and lacked
adequate study through hearings. The only relationship between
the individual provisions was that each stemmed from a recent
decision of the Supreme Court. Orderly and sound methods of

[6] It was significant that Erwin N. Griswold, Dean of the Harvard Law
School, suggested in a speech in October, 1958, that the Supreme Court's
indulgence in broad obiter dicta was an unfortunate source of its problems
(*Washington Post,* October 15, 1958). For a discussion of the various
ways Congress might attack the Court: Pritchett, *Congress Versus the
Supreme Court,* 26–31.

legislation demanded that each provision be introduced and considered separately on its own merits. He concluded with the statement that analysis of the specific amendments indicated that Butler's statutory revisions would do little more than confuse measures the Supreme Court had clarified.[7]

When the Easter recess delayed action in the Judiciary Committee, Hennings frantically roused some last-minute opposition to the Butler amendments. He sent his memorandum of April 7 and copies of the Butler amendments to deans of law schools, noted legal scholars, and heads of law associations for comment. He promptly turned on Butler again when the latter answered the memorandum of April 7 in a speech on the Senate floor. On one occasion he turned to the Court's advantage a clever maneuver by the anti-Court forces. In printing the record of the Jenner bill hearings, the Internal Security Subcommittee made a separate publication of testimony submitted by the "SPX Research Associates," an extreme right-wing organization, which described the Supreme Court as "an instrument of Communist global conquest." Printing this testimony separately enabled the subcommittee to distribute it on a wide scale and to imply approval of the fantastic thesis. Tipped off indirectly by his former administrative assistant Langdon West, Hennings exposed the maneuver and called for an investigation of the strangely-named organization. The resulting publicity cast the eerie light of fanaticism on the anti-Court move and pushed uncommitted congressmen closer to the liberals.[8]

Despite Hennings' feverish opposition, the Judiciary Committee acted favorably on all of Butler's amendments except the provision opposing the Cole decision. After the favorable vote, the Senator

[7] Hennings Papers, Box 32, press release, April 7, 1958.

[8] Hennings Papers, Box 161, unsigned memorandum indicating distribution of April 7 memorandum to nearly 700 persons associated with the defense of civil liberties, the legal profession, and the press. On the "SPX Research Associates," see: Hennings Papers, Box 15, press release, April 9, 1958; *Washington Daily News,* April 8, 1958; *Washington Post,* April 9, 1958; *New York Times,* April 9, 1958; *Kansas City Star,* April 10, 1958; *St. Louis Globe-Democrat,* April 10, 1958. West tried to bring the matter to Hennings' attention directly, and when this failed, he called it to the attention of Edward F. Woods of the *St. Louis Post-Dispatch* (April 8, 1958). On the subsequent debate between Butler and Hennings: *Congressional Record,* 85th Cong., 2d Sess., 1958, 104, Part 5, 6497 ff.; Hennings Papers, Box 15, press release, April 21, 1958.

from Missouri requested and received a two-week stay for preparing a minority report. At a press conference after the meeting, he pledged to wage a "bitter and prolonged fight" against the bill "every step of the way." Then he warned that if the bill should reach the Senate floor, "I will do everything in my power to make sure it is debated until every Senator and the public has complete understanding . . . even if it takes a month." To senators mindful of the unbending opposition Hennings gave year after year to various versions of the Bricker Amendment, this was no idle threat.[9]

While preparing his minority report, Hennings seized an opportunity to silence the most persuasive legal testimony presented by the Court's foes. At the time of the hearings on the Jenner bill, the highly respected circuit judge Learned Hand was delivering the Oliver Wendell Holmes Lectures at Harvard University. In the course of his analysis of the doctrine of judicial review, Hand unintentionally provided quotable authority for the Court's foes by questioning the theoretical basis of judicial review. As the fight progressed, the anti-Court forces made capital out of Hand's lectures. Early in May, Hennings sent copies of the Jenner-Butler bill to several legal scholars for comment. Among them was Hand, and in his reply the retired judge clarified his position by stating that, since judicial review had become a practical necessity, the Jenner-Butler bill "would be detrimental to the best interests of the United States."[10]

    [9] On the voting in the Judiciary Committee April 21 and 30, 1958, see: Murphy, *Congress and the Court,* 167 ff. On Hennings' request for two weeks to prepare a report: Hennings Papers, Box 161, letter from Hennings to Eastland, April 28, 1958. For Hennings' threats: Hennings Papers, Box 15, press release, April 30, 1958. It should be noted that the Judiciary Committee amended Butler's anti-Nelson bill so that it merely reinstated state laws against subversion. This was, in effect, the substitution of the Bridges bill (S. 654) for the McClellan bill (S. 337 or H. R. 3).
    [10] Hennings Papers, Box 161, letter from Hennings to Learned Hand, May 2, 1958; letter from Hand to Hennings, May 5, 1958. Hand's lectures have been published: Learned Hand, *The Bill of Rights* (Cambridge, 1958). For the exploitation of Hand's lectures: Senate, Judiciary Committee, Subcommittee on Internal Security, *Hearings,* 85th Cong., 2d Sess., 1958, Part 2, 46, 76, 77, 90, 91, 211, 219, 266, 267, 430, 534, 535, 545, 546, 573; *Wall Street Journal,* March 28, 1958; *Saturday Evening Post,* 230 (April 19, 1958), 10.

Shortly after Hennings filed his minority report, a lull occurred in the Court fight. When the inactivity continued through June, Hennings optimistically hoped the conflict was ended. The inactivity, however, lasted only as long as the Democratic Policy Committee and Majority Leader Lyndon B. Johnson were able to withstand pressure from anti-Court Democrats to schedule their bills for floor consideration. Hennings, from his position on the Policy Committee, supported Johnson and strengthened his position by supplying the Advisory Council of the Democratic National Committee with abundant propaganda against the bills and by soliciting from Adlai Stevenson a strong pro-Court statement. The Majority Leader himself had no use for the anti-Court measures, and in addition, he knew that debating them would surely split the Northern and Southern wings of the party. Nonetheless, since his success as majority leader resulted from giving due consideration to both sides of a question, on the insistence of the anti-Court bloc he called the issue to the floor.[11]

A flurry of activity in the House gave further indication that Hennings' optimism of June was mistaken. Early in July the House began grinding out piecemeal counterparts to the provisions of the Jenner-Butler bill and several other measures besides. On July 2 the Lower Chamber passed a restrictive Mallory bill and eight days later an anti-Cole measure similar to the Butler amendment that was earlier rejected by the Judiciary Committee. One week later, the House passed its major anti-Court bill, Howard Smith's broad anti-Nelson bill, H. R. 3. Its provisions not only

[11] On Hennings' optimism: Hennings Papers, Box 161, letter from Hennings to Erwin N. Griswold, June 2, 1958; letter from Hennings to Frank Wilkinson, June 12, 1958; letter from Hennings to Arthur J. Freund, June 27, 1958. On the role of Johnson: Murphy, *Congress and the Court,* 171; Anthony Lewis, *New York Times,* August 20, 21, 22, and 25, 1958; Joseph L. Rauh, Jr., "The Truth about Congress and the Court," *Progressive,* 22 (November, 1958), 30 ff. On Hennings' effort with the Advisory Council: Hennings Papers, Box 161, memorandum from Charles Tyroler, II, executive director of the Advisory Council (with copy of letter sent on May 20, 1958, to members of Advisory Council) to Hennings, May 20, 1958; letter from Hennings to Stevenson, May 19, 1958; letter from Stevenson to Hennings, May 22, 1958; letter from Hennings to Stevenson, May 23, 1958. On the pressure exerted on Johnson: Hennings Papers, Box 161, letter from Hennings to Frank Wilkinson, June 12, 1958; Murphy, 199 ff.

overturned the Nelson decision but, in Hennings' view, one hundred years of federal-state relations besides. Instead of simply reinstating the state antisubversion laws that the Nelson opinion voided, Smith's bill denied pre-emptive force to any congressional enactment unless explicitly stated or unless reconciliation with state laws was impossible. To complete the record of the Lower Chamber's anti-Court activity, on August 12 the House passed an anti-Yates bill and on August 23 a modified version of the Administration's bill to undo the recent passport decisions.[12]

In the first week of August, Eastland pressed the Judiciary Committee to equal the surge of House action. The committee responded by reporting, on August 4, a liberal version of the Mallory bill. On August 5 it acted favorably on a narrow anti-Nelson measure and, the following day, on a companion to H. R. 3, a broad anti-Nelson bill. Showing more restraint than the House, the fifteen-man group passed over bills to overturn the Yates decision and the passport cases. Still viable in conference, however, was an unintended companion to the Lower Chamber's anti-Cole bill. After the Senate, in 1957, passed a bill to liberalize the federal employee security program, the House appended to the bill an amendment to overturn the Cole decision. When the Senate conferees accepted the House version, the Upper Chamber unexpectedly received an anti-Cole bill.[13]

Amid this flurry of activity by the Judiciary Committee, anti-Court Democrats increased the pressure on the Majority Leader to bring some of this legislation to the floor. Unable to oppose his anti-Court wing any longer, Johnson agreed to call up several bills

[12] House, Judiciary Committee, 85th Cong., 2d Sess., 1958, H. Rept. 1815 to accompany H.R. 11477. House, Post Office and Civil Service Committee, 85th Cong., 1st Sess., 1957, H. Rept. 1201 to accompany S. 1411. House, Judiciary Committee, 85th Cong., 2d Sess., 1958, H. Rept. 1878 to accompany H.R. 3; H. Rept. 2495 to accompany H.R. 13272. House, Committee on Foreign Affairs, 85th Cong., 2d Sess., 1958, H. Rept. 2684 to accompany H.R. 13760.

[13] Senate, Judiciary Committee, 85th Cong., 2d Sess., 1958, Report No. 2252 to accompany H.R. 11477. S. 654 (no written report). Senate, Judiciary Committee, 85th Cong., 2d Sess., 1958, Report No. 2230 to accompany S. 337. House, Conference Report of Post Office and Civil Service Committee, 85th Cong., 2d Sess., 1958, Report No. 2687 to accompany S. 1411.

in the final week before the scheduled adjournment of Congress. Specifically, he agreed to schedule the Nelson and Mallory bills on the first day of debate. Anti-Court Republicans also wrung a promise from Johnson. When they threatened to offer the Jenner-Butler bill as an amendment to an unrelated bill, the Texas Democrat promised to allow Jenner opportunity to append his bill to an irrelevant measure that was scheduled to be called up on the first day of debate.[14]

Aware of the Majority Leader's pledge to their anti-Court colleagues, ten liberal Democrats forced Johnson to hedge on his promise. On August 12 Senator Humphrey personally delivered to Johnson a letter that he and nine other Democrats had signed and that outlined their intentions in the coming fight. Humphrey wasted no legal jargon on Johnson. His message was clear: The real motive of the anti-Court Democrats is to punish the Warren Court for its desegregation decision of 1954; we are perfectly willing to debate the merits of that decision, though the last week of the Congress is an unlikely time for the debate; since passage of any piece of anti-Court legislation would suit the symbolic purposes of the segregationists, we will oppose every anti-Court bill for the same symbolic purposes. To add force to Humphrey's threat, the liberals informed Johnson the next day that they would append to the Nelson bill a rider stating that the statute would not apply in states still maintaining segregation. Although the Democratic Policy Committee ratified Johnson's original pledge to the Court's foes, the Majority Leader prudently adjusted his strategy to the liberals' threat.[15]

Working closely with Hennings, Johnson decided to open the debate by calling up the least objectionable anti-Court measure, the Mallory bill. On August 19 the debate began, with O'Mahoney

[14] Murphy, *Congress and the Court,* 205, 207; Anthony Lewis, *New York Times,* August 20, 21, 22, and 25, 1958; Rauh, "The Truth about Congress and the Court." The vehicle for the Jenner-Butler bill was Senate, 85th Cong., 2d Sess., 1958, H.R. 6789.

[15] A copy of the Humphrey letter is in: Hennings Papers, Box 161, letter from Humphrey to Hennings with enclosure, August 13, 1958. The subsequent strategy is described in Murphy, *Congress and the Court,* 199–202; Rauh, "The Truth about Congress and the Court," and the series by Anthony Lewis, *op. cit.*

acting as floor manager for the bill and Hennings as spokesman for the opposition. After nine hours of debate, the liberal amendment worked out by O'Mahoney passed—in a close vote, 41 to 39 —and an hour later the amended version of the bill passed with a wide majority. This final vote gave some indication of the divisions in the liberal ranks. Among those unwilling to accept even an extremely liberal version of a symbolically anti-Court bill were all of the ten signers of the Humphrey letter except Hennings, Carroll, and John F. Kennedy. Aside from Kennedy, who had taken little active part in the defense of the Court, the acceptance by Hennings and Carroll of a thoroughly liberal bill, even though it implied a minimal symbolic attack on the Warren Court, indicated their closer agreement with Johnson—who did not favor imposing a complete shutout on the anti-Court wing—and their different brand of liberalism. Hennings, and perhaps Carroll also, felt no compulsion to oppose the segregationists when it served no apparent legislative purpose.[16]

The next day, August 20, Johnson opened the door for Jenner to offer his omnibus anti-Court bill. Certain that they had enough votes to defeat the measure, Johnson and Hennings agreed that the latter, after short debate, should move to table the bill. The Missourian's motion carried, 49 to 41, and provided the momentum Johnson hoped would defeat the most difficult of all anti-Court measures, the Nelson bill. The Majority Leader immediately called up the narrow Nelson bill, to which Senator John McClellan, Democrat from Arkansas, promptly appended the broad Nelson bill, the companion to H. R. 3. Lengthy debate followed until Hennings, at 11:00 P.M., again made the motion to table. Then followed a startling setback for the liberals, for Hennings' motion lost, 46 to 39. Johnson, who had promised the

16 *Congressional Record,* 85th Cong., 2d Sess., 1958, 104, Part 14, 18432– 521. The other seven signers of the Humphrey letter were: Humphrey, Douglas, Clark, McNamara, Neuberger, Morse, Proxmire. Carroll, four days later, went to great lengths to oppose the Mallory bill that came out of conference, but this bill was open to an illiberal interpretation (pp. 176–77, 179, 180, 181). That Johnson did not want a complete victory is based on the interpretations cited in note 11. This interpretation of Hennings' position is based partly on interviews with former staff members, May, 1962.

liberals enough votes to defeat H. R. 3 in return for their dropping the debate on segregation, had failed to fulfill his promise. Taken aback momentarily, the Majority Leader recovered sufficiently to move to adjourn for the night.[17]

Two factors apparently accounted for the Johnson-Hennings miscalculation of the votes against H. R. 3. On the one hand, the business bloc of the anti-Court alliance had been carrying on since midsummer a powerful lobbying effort in favor of H.R. 3. Especially effective was the subtle operation carried out by the National Association of Manufacturers in close cooperation with Senators John McClellan and Strom Thurmond, Democrat from South Carolina. This unpublicized effort escaped the notice of Johnson so that his view of anti-Nelson strength was distorted. In addition, Senator Paul Douglas, Democrat from Illinois, had interrupted the transition between tabling the Jenner-Butler bill and calling up H. R. 3. Douglas, in the same fashion as Jenner, introduced an amendment expressing full support and approval of the Supreme Court's "historic" decision outlawing segregation. In his speech in favor of the amendment, Douglas openly accused the anti-Court forces of desiring to punish the Court, primarily because of the segregation decision. A brief debate followed, and several liberals, including Carroll, joined the anti-Court forces in opposing the Douglas amendment. Quite possibly, this outburst by Douglas, which Journalist William S. White called "the other side of the Faubus coin," accounted in part for the failure of Hennings' motion to table H. R. 3.[18]

---

[17] *Congressional Record,* 85th Cong., 2d Sess., 1958, 104, Part 14, 18687, 18748, 18750. Walter F. Murphy notes that "a leader of the Southern Conservatives" quietly approached Johnson and apparently helped him regain control by suggesting that he move to adjourn (*Congress and the Court,* 211).

[18] Murphy, *Congress and the Court,* 208 ff.; Anthony Lewis, *New York Times,* August 25, 1958; Rauh, "The Truth about Congress and the Court." Murphy attributed Johnson's miscalculation to the quietness of the NAM campaign and the ultimate victory to Johnson's ability and the lobbying efforts of labor. The same author feels that the move by Douglas was not responsible, since it gained Republican votes (by stating the segregation issue so boldly) to offset Southern antagonism. Rauh claimed Hennings' move to table H. R. 3 was "unscrutable" since it was known that

(Continued on next page)

Between adjournment and 5:00 P.M. the next evening Johnson
gathered enough votes to defeat H. R. 3 and, by a clever
maneuver, the narrow Nelson bill also. As soon as he was certain
of the necessary votes, Johnson directed Carroll to move to recommit H. R. 3, and the motion carried, 41 to 40. Prior to the resumed
debate, Hennings and Carroll cautioned their liberal colleagues not
to extend the debate after it was clear that the needed votes were
available and not to mention the narrow Nelson bill to which
H. R. 3 was appended. As a result, when the Senate voted to
recommit H. R. 3, the narrow Nelson bill—which most likely
would have passed by itself—went with it.[19]

The victory over the anti-Court forces became complete when
the Mallory bill, passed on August 19, died on a technicality as
the Eighty-fifth Congress adjourned sine die at 4:11 A.M. on
August 24. Since O'Mahoney's liberal version of the bill differed
from the conservative House measure the bill went to conference
after passing. Following several days of discussion with the House
conferees, O'Mahoney agreed to a compromise amendment whose
confusing terminology left the bill open to a conservative interpretation. On Saturday night, August 23, the House passed the
conference bill, and later that night O'Mahoney presented it to
the Senate. Carroll, a conferee with O'Mahoney, refused to accept
the compromise and determined to prevent passage. In collusion
with Senators Wayne Morse, Democrat from Oregon, and Jacob
Javits, Republican from New York, Carroll carried out a two-
pronged plan that defeated the bill. Morse supplied the threat of
a filibuster to prevent adjournment, and a member of Javits' staff
provided a technicality as a graceful alternative to the filibuster.
Rule 27 of the Senate Rules forbids conferees to add material that

he did not have the votes to defeat it. Lewis seemed to imply that Hennings did not know there were not enough votes and that the Douglas
move broke the psychology of victory built on the prior defeat of S. 2646.
The quotation from White is from Rauh, who referred to White as Johnson's spokesman. The Hennings Papers do not solve the problem entirely,
but Hennings later referred to the defeat as a "test vote" (Hennings
Papers, Box 65, letter from Hennings to Irving Dilliard, November 6,
1958).
    [19] *Congressional Record,* 85th Cong., 2d Sess., 1958, 104, Part 15, 18928.
Hennings Papers, Box 65, letter from Hennings to Irving Dilliard, November 6, 1958.

is in neither the House nor Senate versions of a bill. The conferees violated this rule by adding a short sentence of new material. Faced with Morse's threat of a filibuster, the Democratic Policy Committee agreed to allow defeat of the bill on a point of order based on Rule 27. Early Sunday morning Hennings dutifully questioned O'Mahoney who, by prearrangement, admitted that there was new material in the conference bill. Carroll then raised the point of order, and Vice-President Nixon, who was presiding, upheld it. Because adjournment was at hand, another conference was impossible, so the Mallory bill perished. Since Johnson called up none of the remaining anti-Court bills, the victory of the Court's defenders in the Eighty-fifth Congress was complete.[20]

Renewed assault on the Warren Court was attempted in the next Congress, but the greatly diminished force of the anti-Court drive made it anticlimactic. The first hint that the anti-Court mood still existed came at the very moment liberals were nailing down their victories in the Eighty-fifth Congress. On August 20, 1958, the Conference of State Chief Justices received from its Committee on Federal-State Relations as Affected by Judicial Decisions a startling report that vigorously condemned the Warren Court's lack of restraint in exercising its policy-making powers. Significantly, only three of the ten chief justices who signed the unanimous report represented southern states, and the document itself explicitly excepted from its criticism the decision on segregation. Three days later, the conference approved its committee's report 36 to 8, with two chief justices abstaining and four absent. This well-publicized

[20] This account is taken from Murphy, *Congress and the Court,* 219-23, and is partially confirmed by *Congressional Quarterly Almanac,* 14, 297. The account, as far as I know, is the product of original research, since it contradicts the account given by Hennings (Hennings Papers, Box 15, Speech, October 10, 1958, St. Louis, Missouri) and his staff (interviews with former staff members, May, 1962). Murphy's account rings true, and the misinformation by Hennings' staff was due either to the fact that they did not know of the "deal" or were not at liberty to reveal it. Senator O'Mahoney (interview, May, 1962) said nothing either, though his physical condition in May of 1962 was precarious, and I did not press the point. The explanation given by Hennings and his staff is as follows: In questioning O'Mahoney, Hennings was building a legislative history to ensure a liberal interpretation of the Mallory bill when he "stumbled on" the point of order possibility, and Carroll, working with him, picked it up from there.

rebuke of the Court destroyed the hopes of its defenders that the assault on the high tribunal had ended.[21]

After the Eighty-sixth Congress assembled, a second conclave of legal minds, echoing the spirit of the state chief justices' report, further invigorated the foes of the Court. The American Bar Association, at its meeting in February of 1959, unexpectedly approved the anti-Court resolutions of its Special Committee on Communist Tactics, Strategy and Objectives. While this committee opposed legislative efforts to limit the jurisdiction of the Supreme Court, it urgently recommended that Congress remedy the Court-created gaps in the nation's security system. Specifically, the committee demanded laws to undo the effects of: *Pennsylvania v. Nelson, Cole v. Young, Slochower v. Board, Watkins v. United States, Sweezy v. New Hampshire,* and *Yates v. United States.* On February 24, 1959, the ABA's House of Delegates approved the resolutions and thereby assured another Court fight.[22]

The third major stimulus to the assault on the judiciary in 1959 came several months later from the Court itself, when it overturned another Eisenhower antisubversive system. The victim was the Industrial Personnel Security Program of the Defense Department. In the case of *Greene v. McElroy,* an 8 to 1 vote held that Congress had not given the President power to refuse security clearance to employees of defense plants without granting them the right to confront and cross-examine adverse witnesses. Following its familiar tactic, the Court chose to evade the constitutional question whether Congress could have authorized dismissal without confrontation and cross-examination, concluding, simply, that it had not done so.[23]

Backed by the impressive authority of the state chief justices and the American Bar Association, congressional critics of the Court quickly introduced remedial legislation in both houses. Unlike the measures introduced in the previous Congress, the new bills at-

[21] *New York Times,* August 21, 1958; *Congressional Record,* 85th Cong., 2d Sess., 1958, 104, A7782–88.
[22] For an analysis of the ABA action: Roy M. Cohn and Thomas A. Bolan, "The Supreme Court and the A.B.A. Report and Resolutions," *Fordham Law Review,* 28 (Summer, 1959), 233 ff. For the report itself: *Congressional Record,* 86th Cong., 1st Sess., 1959, 105, Part 3, 3362.
[23] Greene v. McElroy, 360 U. S. 474 (1959).

tempted to overturn the liberal decisions through case-by-case legislation rather than by limiting the Court's jurisdiction as the original Jenner bill proposed. Moreover, until late in the first session, no omnibus measure akin to the Jenner-Butler bill appeared. Instead, the critics proposed a series of narrow bills methodically aimed at refuting the unwelcome constructions the Warren Court had repeatedly placed on congressional statutes.

As in the previous Congress, however, progress on the anti-Court legislation came initially from the House. On March 2, 1959, the Lower Chamber passed an anti-Yates decision bill to overturn the interpretation the Warren majority gave to the Smith Act's prohibition against *organizing* subversive groups. While the House continued to approve anti-Court bills, the Senate Subcommittee on Internal Security arranged what Hennings called an "omnibus hearing" on twelve measures introduced by Senator Eastland in compliance with the ABA's resolution. With newly elected Senator Thomas J. Dodd, Democrat from Connecticut, replacing Eastland as acting chairman, the group heard testimony during April and May of 1959. Hennings submitted a lengthy statement to the subcommittee in which he objected to the procedure of lumping a "basketfull of bills" in one hearing and opposing each measure individually. After the hearing, Dodd sent the bills to the parent Judiciary Committee for favorable action.[24]

Fearing committee approval of at least some of the bills, Hennings promptly prepared his defense. In mid-May he sent copies of the twelve bills, as well as a new anti-Mallory measure, to deans of law schools and presidents of law associations for comments he hoped would neutralize the authority of the ABA and the state chief justices. Shrewdly anticipating the decision in *Greene v. McElroy,* he announced that the Subcommittee on Constitutional Rights would soon examine the fairness of procedures employed in the federal loyalty-security programs, "particularly the Industrial Personnel Security Review Program." Hennings, accurately predicting both the Greene decision and the reaction in Congress, hoped to sidetrack anti-Greene decision bills from the Subcommit-

[24] House, 86th Cong., 1st Sess., 1959, H.R. 2369; Senate, Judiciary Committee, Subcommittee on Internal Security, *Hearings,* 86th Cong., 1st Sess., 1959. Hennings Papers, Box 16, press release, May 8, 1959.

tee on Internal Security. In an effort to take the offensive against the Court's foes, he testified before the Subcommittee on Constitutional Amendments in support of a joint resolution he had co-sponsored to outlaw future congressional tampering with the jurisdiction of the Supreme Court. Finally, he tried in vain to obtain from FBI Director J. Edgar Hoover an admission that anti-Nelson bills were unnecessary, since the federal government could give the nation adequate protection against internal subversion. As May ended, Hennings felt satisfied that he had provided the groundwork for blocking any move against the Warren Court.[25]

During June and July the House continued the anti-Court movement by passing the familiar and dangerous pre-emption bill, still numbered H. R. 3, and an anti-Mallory measure. In addition, Representative Francis Walter introduced H. R. 8121, designed to overthrow the Greene decision and force a ruling on the constitutional issue of confrontation. After surveying these developments, Hennings chose to concentrate on blocking the Mallory and Greene bills, which he felt had the greatest likelihood of receiving favorable action. He scheduled hearings on the Industrial Security Program for early July and invited the Secretary of Defense and two known supporters of the Greene decision to testify. The Secretary begged off, explaining that he was preparing a new program for industrial security, but the two liberals testified as expected. Meanwhile, the Mallory bill had been referred to Senator O'Mahoney's Subcommittee on Improvements in the Federal Criminal Code. Exploiting his membership on the parent Judiciary Committee, Hennings requested that the subcommittee chairman hold hearings on the Mallory bill prior to committee action. Chagrined at his request, but reluctant to violate senatorial courtesy, the Senator from Wyoming complied. Since a hearings delay so late in the year made approval by the parent group un-

[25] Hennings Papers, Box 164, letters to law school deans, May 14, 1959; letters to presidents of bar associations, May 18, 1959; Box 16, press release, May 25, 1959; Box 132, statement by Hennings before Subcommittee on Constitutional Amendments, May 28, 1959; Box 164, letter from J. Edgar Hoover to Hennings, June 2, 1959.

likely, O'Mahoney dropped the Mallory bill for the remainder of the first session.[26]

Late in the session, several additional attempts to reverse Warren Court decisions ended in failure. A joint resolution to amend the Constitution to forbid federal interference with a state's administration of its educational system—the so-called Talmadge Amendment—failed to pass the Subcommittee on Constitutional Amendments. Hennings helped assure defeat when, alerted by Senator Estes Kefauver, he publicized the fact that the bill was not pro-education but anti-integration. In the final days of the first session, too late for the Senate to consider it, the House passed a moderate bill to qualify the passport decisions of 1958.[27]

Despite the surplus of bills and the aggressive action in the House, none of the anti-Court measures received approval during the first session of the Eighty-sixth Congress. In fact, not a single bill cleared the Senate Judiciary Committee. Upset by this failure, Senators Dodd and Kenneth Keating, Republican from New York, reverted to the omnibus approach. Unobtrusively, they introduced on September 7, 1959, a four-part measure "to strengthen the internal security of the United States." The first two sections of the bill were unrelated to Court decisions, but the third contained an anti-Yates provision, and the fourth overruled the passport decisions of 1958. The Dodd-Keating bill received little notice until midway through the second session, when it became the final effort of the collapsing attack on the Court.[28]

[26] House, 86th Cong., 1st Sess., 1959, H. R. 3 and H. R. 4957. On the Greene bills: Hennings Papers, Box 16, press release, June 25, 1959; Box 162, press release, office of Subcommittee on Constitutional Rights, January 22, 1960; Senate, Judiciary Committee, Subcommittee on Constitutional Rights, *Hearings,* 86th Cong., 1st Sess., 1959, Part 3. On the Mallory bill: Hennings Papers, Box 16, press release, July 22, 1959; Box 130, copy of letter from Senator O'Mahoney to Senator Eastland, July 23, 1959.

[27] Congress, 86th Cong., 1st Sess., 1959, S. J. Res. 32. Hennings Papers, Box 16, press release, August 4, 1959. House, 86th Cong., 1st Sess., 1959, H. R. 9069.

[28] The Dodd-Keating bill was Senate, 86th Cong., 1st Sess., 1959, S. 2652. The Subcommittee on Constitutional Rights noticed the bill immediately and analyzed its provisions (Hennings Papers, Box 164, memorandum from William Patton to Charles Slayman, September 11, 1959).

Before the Dodd-Keating bill became an issue, however, the House added to the four anti-Court bills awaiting the Senate's approval in the second session when Walter's anti-Greene measure passed unnoticed on the Lower Chamber's Consent Calendar of February 2, 1960. The bill had received neither public hearing nor comment from the Administration prior to passage. Its unnoticed presence on the Consent Calendar and the absence of opposition resulted from Walter's earlier assurance that the measure was useless, since the Administration had prepared a new executive order to adjust the industrial security program to the Greene decision. Hennings, who had also learned of the new executive order, demanded that the Secretary of Defense consult with the Subcommittee on Constitutional Rights before issuing it. But the Secretary ignored the demand, and a few weeks after the Walter bill passed, the President issued Executive Order 10865, reinstituting the program invalidated by *Greene v. McElroy*.[29]

The new executive order, of course, rendered Walter's anti-Greene bill obsolete. The Senate Judiciary Committee ignored the bill along with the other anti-Court measures passed by the House. Instead, the committee, on June 30, 1960, favorably reported the Dodd-Keating bill. Because of illness, Hennings was absent from this judiciary meeting, but he later directed his staff to prepare a minority report and to reach liberals on the committee to organize concerted opposition. The minority report appeared in August, but it proved unnecessary. The Dodd-Keating bill failed to reach the Senate floor primarily because Senator William Fulbright, Democrat from Arkansas and chairman of the Foreign Relations Committee, threatened to recommit the bill unless his group held hearings on the passport section. Balked a final time, congressional

[29] Hennings Papers, Box 162, memorandum from Slayman to Hennings, February 2, 1960; Murphy, *Congress and the Court,* 241; Hennings Papers, Box 17, press release, January 22, 1960. The first indication that the new executive order was imminent came from Anthony Lewis, *New York Times,* January 17, 1960. A copy of Executive Order 10865 (February 20, 1960) can be found in: Senate, Judiciary Committee, Subcommittee on Constitutional Rights, *Hearings,* 86th Cong., 1st Sess., 1959, Part 3, Appendix, 1920.

critics of the Warren Court quietly surrendered the fight over the Court.[30]

The abortive anti-Court movement in the Eighty-sixth Congress failed for several reasons. The threat of continuing opposition on the part of the Court's defenders like Hennings made passage of punitive legislation difficult, especially in the more deliberate Upper Chamber. The efforts of the Court's defenders, however, seemed less important in the Eighty-sixth than in the previous Congress. Pressure against the Court during 1959–1960 lacked the force of the earlier attack, partly because of the change in the personnel of Congress. Seven Republican senators who had supported one or more of the anti-Court proposals in the Eighty-fifth Congress did not return: the leading critic of the Warren Court, Senator William Jenner, retired, and the other six failed to survive the 1958 elections. The Supreme Court itself helped to deflate the opposition by moderating its views concerning civil liberties in the Barenblatt and Uphaus cases of 1959. In *Barenblatt v. United States,* Justices Harlan and Frankfurter deserted the four liberals— Warren, Douglas, Black, and Brennan—to uphold a contempt citation issued by the House Un-American Activities Committee against a college professor who refused to answer questions regarding possible Communist activity at the University of Michigan. In the companion case *Uphaus v. Wyman,* the same majority upheld a similar contempt citation issued by the State of New Hampshire against Willard Uphaus for refusing to surrender the guest list of a camp suspected of being a meeting-place for Communists. The two rulings neatly calmed congressional critics of the 1957 Watkins and Sweezy decisions.[31]

---

[30] Senate, Judiciary Committee, 86th Cong., 2d Sess., 1960, Report No. 1811, Part 1; Hennings Papers, Box 164, memorandum from Bevan to Hennings, June 30, 1960; letters from Hennings to Senators John A. Carroll, Philip A. Hart, Estes Kefauver, July 8, 1960; Report No. 1811, Part 2; Murphy, *Congress and the Court,* 241.

[31] Murphy, *Congress and the Court,* 237 ff.; letter from Walter F. Murphy to me, February 24, 1963. Barenblatt v. United States, 360 U. S. 109 (1959); Uphaus v. Wyman, 360 U. S. 72 (1959). The other senators, in addition to William Jenner, were: Bricker of Ohio, Thye of Minnesota, Watkins of Utah, Revercomb and Hoblitzell of West Virginia.

In addition, the longer the nation found it could stay afloat despite the controversial decisions of the Warren Court during the period 1955 to 1958, the less enthusiasm it had for undoing them. The real crisis, then, in the defense of the Court had occurred in the previous Congress, when its antagonists had their greatest chance of success. Commenting later on that critical struggle in 1958, Hennings observed that the victory was "a cooperative affair, and, for once, the 'liberals' pulled together." Singling out individuals, he indicated that Johnson was a key man in the struggle, and he stressed that in his opinion "one of the Senators who deserves an extra amount of credit is John Carroll, who did a fine job throughout the year on that issue."[32]

Hennings, too, had done a "fine job throughout the year" on the Court issue. In the front ranks of the Court's defenders from beginning to end, his greatest contributions had been made in the early stages of the conflict. The Supreme Court, Hennings stated on occasion, had no public relations department, so the defense of its actions fell to members of the legislative and executive branches of the government. Hennings took this obligation seriously. Since Chief Justice Warren's speech in 1955 in which he depicted an erosion of the Bill of Rights, Hennings cultivated the public image of the Supreme Court as the one institution capable of defending individual rights threatened by the emphasis on internal security brought about by the tensions of the Cold War. As the Court began fulfilling this image—in the Peters case of 1955, the Nelson and Cole cases of 1956, and dramatically on "Red Monday" in 1957—Hennings publicly applauded and explained the decisions.[33]

But the Senator from Missouri gave more than moral support to the Warren Court. After the high tribunal's decisions had irritated large segments of the population in June of 1957, Hennings began the crucial task of clarifying the decisions in order to counteract the frantic shouts of alarm emitted by the Court's own dissenters and by the conservatives in Congress and the press. In

---

[32] Hennings Papers, Box 65, letter from Hennings to Irving Dilliard, November 6, 1958; interviews with former staff members, May, 1962.
[33] Hennings, "Equal Justice Under Law," 20.

speeches and articles he consistently debunked the vivid exaggerations of future dangers to internal security and law enforcement inherent in the Court's decisions. Since much of the support for the move against the Court resulted from these exaggerations, Hennings' clarifications had an incalculable effect in deflating critics of the Court.

When legislative action against the Warren Court became likely, Hennings almost singlehandedly built a countervailing force to block it. Through his own staff and that of the Constitutional Rights Subcommittee, he conducted a one-man lobby to swing the nation's legal community behind the Court. Outstanding lawyers, deans of law schools, and law associations received regular communications from him, informing them of the latest anti-Court proposals and subtly soliciting their opposition. Hennings consistently pleaded that even though no one agreed with every ruling of the Court, it would be disastrous to "kill the umpire" because of disagreements with some of them.[34]

Hennings' legal homework exerted an influence on fellow legislators also. His arguments often reappeared in the pro-Court speeches of legislators on both sides of the Capitol and on both sides of the aisle. When, for example, Republican Congressman Kenneth Keating filed his minority view against H. R. 3, he displayed, in slightly modified form, Hennings' assertion that the measure was one hundred years too late. Similarly, when the Court fight moved into the final stages, the point at which Majority Leader Lyndon Johnson became the key figure, Hennings' legal briefs gave Johnson a solid platform for opposing the wishes of the Southern wing of his party. Without this sound legal posi-

---

[34] The record of the American Bar Association in the Court fight is confusing, due in some measure to the number of voices speaking in its name. The ABA had supported the Supreme Court in 1937 and had composed the Butler Amendment passed by the Senate in 1954. In 1957–1959, the position of the ABA fluctuated from one of its committees to the other. Daniel M. Berman, "Voice of the American Bar," *Nation,* 188 (March 21, 1959), 247 ff.; Murphy, *Congress and the Court,* 78, 94–95, 118–19, 164–65, 177, 224–27, 237, 255; Philip B. Kurland, "The Supreme Court and its Judicial Critics," *Utah Law Review,* 6 (Fall, 1959), 457 ff.; Robert B. McKay, "The Supreme Court and its Lawyer Critics," *Fordham Law Review,* 28 (Winter, 1959–1960), 615 ff.

tion, the Majority Leader would have experienced difficulty in holding down the punish-the-Court aspirations of powerful Democrats like Richard Russell of Georgia, James Eastland, John McClellan, and Strom Thurmond.[35]

As the conflict reached the final stage, which was complicated by an intraparty clash between two groups of Democrats, Hennings' effort merged with Johnson's strategy. At this point, the work of the Court's defenders was necessarily a group endeavor in which cooperation rather than individual brilliance was needed for success. Though Hennings remained the spokesman for the liberal bloc, he contributed no more to the group effort than, for example, Carroll, Humphrey, Douglas, Morse, or Joseph Clark, Democrat from Pennsylvania.[36]

In looking back on the Court fight, some observers questioned the sincerity of the attitudes that were expressed both for and against the Supreme Court. With the utmost cynicism, Fred Rodell, a professor of law, denied that sincerity existed on either side:

It is utterly absurd to praise or damn the Supreme Court—or to damn those who damn it or damn those who praise it—on such esoteric highfalutin' grounds as the sanctity of the Court or the desecration of precedent by the present Court or such abstractions of governmental theory . . . which belong only in Ph.D. theses—"judicial supremacy," "states' rights," "federal supremacy," and all the rest. . . . Max Lerner cares no more about Court sanctity or supremacy than does David Lawrence; if you don't believe it, look at what both of them were writing about the Court back in 1937 as compared with what they are saying today—and laugh.[37]

A fact that was forgotten or unknown by even his closest associ-

---

[35] House, Judiciary Committee, 85th Cong., 2d Sess., 1958, Report No. 1878; Hennings Papers, Box 32, press release, April 7, 1958; interviews with former staff members, May, 1962.

[36] The pro-Court bloc among Democrats included, in general, the ten liberals who signed the Humphrey letter (see note 16). To these should be added a number of liberal Republicans, such as Javits, Wiley, and Cooper.

[37] Fred Rodell, "Conflict over the Court," *Progressive*, 22 (December, 1958), 11–13.

ates remains: Hennings, as the Representative of Missouri's Eleventh District, had supported President Roosevelt's Court-packing plan in 1937. Fortunately for his later defense of the Warren Court, this inconsistency was well hidden. During the debate over Roosevelt's plan Hennings repeatedly refused to publicize his position, and yet he privately attempted to mitigate the vigorous opposition Senator Bennett Clark, Democrat from Missouri, gave to Roosevelt's move against the Court. Since the Administration's proposal died in the Senate, Hennings' only publicized view consisted of a belated admission to the press that he would probably support a compromise measure. Uneasy about his semisecret inconsistency and taking no chance of jogging long memories, Hennings refrained during the current conflict from mentioning his 1937 position.[38]

Hennings, then, verified Rodell's charge that in defending or opposing the Supreme Court much depended on whose ox was gored. Both sides were *result-oriented*—to use a term Anthony Lewis reserved for the Court's critics—and the results protected by the Court's defenders held great significance for civil liberties. Along with the censure of McCarthy and the attack made on the Administration's security program during the Eighty-fourth Congress, they constituted a turning point in the defense of individual rights that were threatened during the Cold War. What the earlier two episodes accomplished by moral pressure, the Warren Court enacted into law and the Court's defenders enforced. Specifically, the total victory of congressional liberals in 1958 provided a period of time in which Congress and the nation could discover that concern for civil liberties need not compromise internal security. Slowly, the security-conscious legislators in Congress, the

[38] Franklin D. Roosevelt Papers, P.P.F. 5807, memorandum from S.T.E. to General Watson, August 17, 1940; memorandum from S.T.E. to Mr. Hassett, December 19, 1940; OF 300–Missouri, unsigned memorandum on Thomas C. Hennings, Jr., as appointee to U. S. Senate from Missouri, January 15, 1945. According to these sources, Hennings supported the President's court reorganization plan in opposition to Missouri Senator Bennett Clark. On Hennings' public statements: *St. Louis Post-Dispatch,* February 26 and May 16, 1937; *St. Louis Globe-Democrat,* March 14, 1937; *St. Louis Star-Times,* March 29 and April 21 and 22, 1937.

Administration, and the nation began to realize that henceforth
the search for subversives must be conducted, at least on the
surface, with traditional respect for the rights of the individual.[39]

[39] Anthony Lewis, "The Supreme Court and its Critics," *Minnesota Law
Review*, 45 (January, 1961), 305–32. Lewis, who is a feature writer for
the *New York Times*, places critics of the Supreme Court in three cate-
gories: the *result-oriented*, which embraces the security-conscious and the
segregationists; *opponents of judicial review*, which contains, above all,
Learned Hand; and *academic critics*, which includes those law professors
who regularly scrutinize and evaluate the work of the Supreme Court. This
latter group, Lewis claims, is growing rapidly.

IX

Unfinished Business

THE CRUSADE that Thomas Hennings led in behalf of individual liberties ended in no climactic battle. In the Eighty-sixth Congress, his last, he achieved only minor success in several long-range projects touching on civil liberties. To some extent this failure to pursue a more aggressive course reflected Hennings' belief that the nation's impatience with constitutional rights had abated, leaving fewer and less urgent problems. Moreover, the drawn-out debate over the Civil Rights Act of 1960 dissipated much of the energy that might otherwise have been devoted to civil liberties. Then, early in that same year, the ultimately fatal abdominal cancer appeared, forcing Hennings to spend the remaining months of his life being shunted to and from the hospital. As the disease followed its inevitable course, the senior Senator from Missouri closed his ten-year defense of individual rights by publicly urging his state's Democrats, during the Kennedy campaign of 1960, to remain faithful to the constitutional guarantee of religious liberty. He never lived to see the effects of this sick-bed appeal, for two months before the November election Hennings was dead and the nation had lost one of its ablest defenders of civil liberties.

The most publicized problem Hennings left unresolved concerned the Eisenhower Administration's policy of withholding information from Congress and the press. Hennings joined the "Freedom of Information" crusade during 1956, in muted concert with, of all people, Senator McCarthy of Wisconsin. The latter's interest in freedom of information had begun two years earlier during his subcommittee's investigation of the Army's security program. At the height of this inquiry, the Army's counsel John Adams balked at revealing information that McCarthy felt was crucial to the investigation. The information concerned conversations at a Justice Department meeting, called to find ways of curbing McCarthy's investigation of the Defense Department's loyalty-security program. President Eisenhower now stepped into the conflict and supported Adams and his superiors in the Defense Department by appealing to *executive privilege* which, he said, gave executive departments and agencies the right to withhold information from Congress whenever they deemed such information confidential or its disclosure incompatible with the public interest. In this specific situation Eisenhower gave the Secretary of Defense, in a now famous letter of May 17, 1954, this advice:

Because it is essential to efficient and effective administration that employees of the executive branch be in a position to be completely candid in advising with each other on official matters, and because it is not in the public interest that any of their conversations or communications, or any documents or reproductions, concerning such advice be disclosed, you will instruct employees of your Department that in all of their appearances before the subcommittee of the Senate Committee on Government Operations regarding the inquiry now before it they are not to testify to any such conversations or communications or to produce any such documents or reproductions.[1]

In February of 1956, when McCarthy threatened to attack Hennings because of the latter's criticism of the loyalty-security program, the Senator from Missouri, combining his own interest in the Freedom of Information crusade with a desire to mollify McCarthy, placed the topic of government secrecy on the agenda of the Constitutional Rights Subcommittee. By this time, however, the criticism of government secrecy was already far advanced, so Hennings' belated entry evoked little enthusiasm from the leaders of the movement. Journalists who had been advocating a halt to government secrecy politely advised Hennings that his Constitu-

[1] Clark R. Mollenhoff, *Washington Cover-Up*, 41–54, 210–11.

tional Rights Subcommittee would do more harm than good by duplicating the well-established efforts of a special subcommittee of the House. The House group, led by Representative John E. Moss, Democrat from California, jealously guarded its leading role and forced Hennings to limit his 1956 study of government secrecy to a relatively unimportant investigation of the Administration's withholding of plans for maintaining civil liberties during a nuclear attack on the United States.[2]

When Hennings' interest in the matter persisted into 1957, Moss gradually agreed to a cooperative effort. From a series of meetings between the staffs of the two subcommittees a tacit agreement emerged: The House group would concentrate on withholding of information from the public by the executive branch, while the Hennings Subcommittee would examine similar withholding from Congress. When either group introduced legislation, the other would be welcome to introduce a companion bill. With this foothold, Hennings rapidly rose to a position rivaling Moss for leadership of the movement.[3]

As Hennings' prominence in the investigation of government secrecy grew, he constructed an elaborate rationale for his criticism. A democratic people, he reasoned, possessed a constitutional right to know everything its elected officials did or did not do in their capacity as representatives of the people. The public's "right to know" stemmed by implication from the sovereignty of the people, since the people could not retain control of a government whose activities remained secret. The First Amendment's insistence on freedom of the press and of assembly—the media of information—confirmed the fact, in Hennings' view, that a close relation-

---

[2] *Congressional Record,* 84th Cong., 2d Sess., 1956, 102, Part 3, 3010. Hennings Papers, Box 161, memorandum from Mary A. Irwin, William D. Patton, and Richard L. Carp to Francis Smith, May 14, 1956; memorandum from Francis Smith to Hennings, May 14, 1956; CRS Files, 1956, memorandum from Smith to Hennings, May 22 and July 2, 1956; Hennings Papers, Box 10, press releases, July 19 and 21, 1956.

[3] CRS Files, 1956, memorandum from Irwin to Slayman, November 1, 1956; memorandum from Slayman to Raymond, Patton, and Irwin, December 20, 1956; Hennings Papers, Box 161, memorandum from Slayman to Hennings, January 8, 1957; CRS Files, 1957, memorandum from Irwin to Slayman, February 27, 1957; Hennings Papers, Box 161, memorandum from Slayman to Hennings, March 16, 1957.

ship existed between the sovereignty of the people and the free flow of information about government activity or inactivity. Because of this constitutional right to know, government officials had no power to withhold information from the people except as a consequence of some other grant of power whose exercise demanded it. The President, for example, had the power to conduct international relations and, as a consequence, to keep secret some of his negotiations with foreign powers. Therefore, the right to withhold information depended on some other grant of power and extended only as far as the exercise of that power required. Moreover, this right existed only when revealing information would constitute a "clear and present danger" to the national security or the public welfare. Hence, a basic presumption against secrecy always existed and forced government officials to bear the burden of proving the existence of a "clear and present danger" in each instance of withholding information.[4]

While his reasoning applied equally to the legislative and executive branches, Hennings focused his attention on the latter. He expressed alarm over the current increase in the amount of information executive departments and agencies withheld from Congress and the press. At times this withholding resulted from a real need to protect national secrets or was the product of honest mistakes. At other times, however, it constituted little more than a deliberate attempt at personal and political gain or avoidance of personal and political embarrassment. Executive officials, said Hennings, indulged in a variety of secretive maneuvers. In some cases they simply suppressed information, but on other occasions they either delayed, or distorted, or colored the facts in order to obtain the effect that best served their interests.

During the Eighty-fifth Congress Hennings and Moss attempted to lift government secrecy through legislation. Their investigations indicated that executive officials based withholding policies

4 Thomas C. Hennings, Jr.: "The Executive Privilege and the People's Right to Know," *Federal Bar Journal*, 19 (January, 1959), 1; "A Legislative Measure to Augment the Free Flow of Public Information," *American University Law Review*, 8 (January, 1959), 19; "Secrecy—Threat to Freedom," *Progressive*, 22 (April, 1959), 21; "The People's Right to Know," *American Bar Association Journal*, 45 (July, 1959), 667.

on three alleged sources of authority. Most often cited was the broad claim of executive privilege, exemplified by Eisenhower's letter of May 17, 1954, to the Secretary of Defense. The President based this privilege on the doctrine of 'separation of powers,' which entitled the executive branch to check invasions of its power by Congress. This reasoning contained far-reaching implications, since it enabled an executive official to withhold whatever information the national interest, in his unilateral judgment, demanded be kept secret. Congress and the public had no assurance, apart from the official's word, that such secrecy was serving anything other than self-interest.[5]

Two other frequently cited sources of authority were specific statutes. One was a law passed in the First Congress of 1789, which gives executive departments authority to prescribe regulations for the "custody, use, and preservation of the records, papers, and property" pertaining to their departments. The other was the public information section of the Administrative Procedure Act of 1946, which directs executive departments and agencies to make their records public except "to the extent that there is involved (1) any function of the United States requiring secrecy in the public interest or (2) any matter relating solely to the internal management of an agency."[6]

Opposition to executive privilege came first from the Moss Subcommittee, which challenged both the constitutionality of the claim and its broad application. In June of 1956, Deputy Attorney General William Rogers answered Moss's challenge with a long memorandum in which he traced the dubious history of executive privilege and asserted, in effect, that the President and department heads could withhold information whenever they felt it necessary. Uncertain whether the memorandum—a thinly disguised version of a series of articles published by a Justice Department official in 1949—reflected official policy, Hennings asked the Attorney Gen-

[5] Senate, Judiciary Committee, Subcommittee on Constitutional Rights, *Hearings,* 85th Cong., 2d Sess., 1958, Part 1, 287–428 (surveys conducted by subcommittee in 1956 and 1957); House, Committee on Government Operations, 84th Cong., 2d Sess., 1956, Report No. 2947.

[6] Hennings, "A Legislative Measure to Augment the Free Flow of Public Information."

eral in March of 1957 to clarify his department's view of the constitutional basis for executive privilege. Rogers again replied for
the Attorney General, asserting that the memorandum constituted
the official view and observing that Eisenhower's letter of May 17
validly reflected that view. Early in 1958, following Rogers' nomination as attorney general, Hennings invited the new head of the
Justice Department to defend his thesis before the Subcommittee
on Constitutional Rights. Rogers accepted, and in his testimony
he extended the application of executive privilege to include, in
addition to the President and heads of departments, the heads of
independent agencies as well. Executive departments and agencies,
he said, had the right to maintain their independence from Congress by refusing at their discretion to divulge intradepartmental
matters even to a congressional committee. Hennings objected,
but Rogers replied with another memorandum in defense of his
position. Completely frustrated, Hennings conceded nothing, but
he confessed that "it almost seems as though the Attorney General is attempting to amend the Constitution by writing mem-
orandums."[7]

The antisecrecy movement made greater progress in attacking
the specific statutory authority cited by executive branch officials.
During the Eighty-fifth Congress, Moss and Hennings introduced
companion bills to prevent misconstruction of the 1789 statute and
to amend the Administrative Procedure Act. The first bill added
a single sentence to the 1789 law—which the Missourian termed
nothing more than a "housekeeping statute"—stating that the law
did not authorize "withholding information from the public or
limiting the availability of records to the public." The second bill

[7] Hennings Papers, Box 161, letter from Hennings to Attorney General
Brownell, March 13, 1957; letter from Deputy Attorney General Rogers
to Hennings, April 11, 1957; letter from Hennings to Attorney General
Rogers, November 19, 1957; letter from Attorney General Rogers to Hennings, January 29, 1958; letter from Slayman to Rogers, February 14,
1958; Box 14, press release, March 3, 1958; Senate, Judiciary Committee,
Subcommittee on Constitutional Rights, *Hearings,* 85th Cong., 2d Sess.,
1958, Part 1, 1 ff.; Hennings Papers, Box 15, press release, February 2,
1959. The 1949 articles and the Attorney General's memorandum are
reprinted in: Senate, Judiciary Committee, Subcommittee on Constitutional
Rights, *Hearings,* 85th Cong., 2d Sess., 1958, Part 1, 147–270, 63–146.

attempted to rewrite the loose language of the public information
section of the 1946 Act so as to delineate the limited areas in
which information could be withheld. Hennings argued that the
legislative history of the Act indicated that Congress had intended
the public information section to increase rather than restrict the
free flow of information. To ensure this original intent, his bill
permitted withholding information only (1) when national security demanded it, (2) when a specific statement allowed it, or (3)
when disclosure constituted a "clearly unwarranted invasion of
personal privacy."[8]

Subsequent to hearings held by both subcommittees, the first
Hennings-Moss bill passed Congress and was signed by the President on August 12, 1958. The second bill received little attention
in the Eighty-fifth Congress. Nonetheless, the press optimistically
hailed the passage of the first "freedom of information" measure
as a major step in rolling back the cover of government secrecy.
Eisenhower was more realistic. In placing his signature on the
Hennings-Moss bill he observed that the measure in no way
lessened the force of executive privilege.[9]

From this three-year interest in freedom of information, Hennings emerged as a leading critic in Congress of government
secrecy. As the first session of the Eighty-sixth Congress opened,
he indicated plans to enlarge the drive against secrecy by giving
the problem top priority on the agenda for 1959 of the Subcommittee on Constitutional Rights and by reintroducing his bill to
amend the Administrative Procedure Act. He reviewed the obstacles to a free flow of government information and presented
a four-point program for the current Congress: (1) Enactment
of his second "freedom of information" bill; (2) creation of a
"Code on Executive Privilege" to prescribe the circumstances
under which the President and executive officials could withhold

[8] The first Hennings-Moss bill was 85th Cong., 1st Sess., S. 921 and
H. R. 2767. The second bill was 85th Cong., 1st Sess., S. 2148 and H. R.
7174. Hennings Papers, Box 14, press release, April 24, 1957.

[9] Senate, Judiciary Committee, 85th Cong., 2d Sess., 1958, Report No.
1621. White House press release, August 12, 1958 (quoted in Hennings,
"The Executive Privilege and the People's Right to Know"). The bill
eventually passed was the House version, H. R. 2767.

information from Congress; (3) preparation of a federal records law defining which government papers were open to public inspection; and (4) continued surveillance of information practices throughout the federal government to protect the constitutional right to know.[10]

Hennings' generous proposals contrasted sharply with the meager accomplishments that followed. Despite considerable effort, his bill failed to reach the Senate floor. After hearings during the first session, he revised it and, with the approval of the nine-man Subcommittee on Constitutional Rights, sent it to the parent Judiciary Committee. However, before the committee could act, Hennings' cancer struck, and the bill gathered dust until Congress adjourned. Similarly, Hennings failed to develop a "Code on Executive Privilege" or a federal records law, although his collection of state laws indicated some progress toward achieving the latter. Early in 1960 he introduced a third antisecrecy bill, but he failed to pursue it. The measure would have withdrawn from federal judges their discretion to keep secret the details of civil suits. This bill, which was stimulated by a controversy between federal judges and a Detroit newspaper, failed in the face of immediate opposition from both the legal community and the American Civil Liberties Union.[11]

[10] Senate, Committee on Rules and Administration, 86th Cong., 1st Sess., 1959, Report No. 31, 3; S. 186. Hennings, "The Executive Privilege and the People's Right to Know," and "A Legislative Measure to Augment the Free Flow of Public Information"; Hennings Papers, Box 15, press release, January 11, 1959. The second bill was 86th Cong., 1st Sess., 1959, S. 186.

[11] Hennings Papers, Box 17, press release, January 6, 1960. Senate, 86th Cong., 2d Sess., 1960, S. 2780. *Congressional Record,* 86th Cong., 2d Sess., 1960, 106, Part 1, 196–97. For the collection of state records laws: Senate, Judiciary Committee, Subcommittee on Constitutional Rights, *Background Materials on a Comprehensive Federal Public Records Law—State Public Records Statutes and Notes on Related Court Decisions Compiled by the Constitutional Rights Subcommittee,* Committee Print, 86th Cong., 2d Sess., 1960. The third antisecrecy bill was 86th Cong., 2d Sess., 1960, S. 3183, and its relation to the Detroit incident is analyzed in *Detroit News,* March 20, 1960. For reactions to the bill: Hennings Papers, Box 162, memorandum from Slayman to John Brannon and Robert Bevan, May 23, 1960; memorandum from Slayman to Hennings, July 7, 1960.

The lone antisecrecy bill Hennings promoted successfully in the Eighty-sixth Congress was a measure unexpectedly forced on him by an energetic reporter who exposed a questionable policy of secrecy within the Senate itself. The controversy over senatorial secrecy arose when Vance Trimble, reporter for the Scripps-Howard newspapers, began examining the payrolls of House members of the Eighty-sixth Congress. On January 5, 1959, he published in the nineteen newspapers of the Scripps-Howard chain the interesting fact that freshman Congressman Steven Carter, Democrat from Iowa, had made his nineteen-year-old son the highest paid member of his staff, at a salary of $11,081 per year. As Trimble continued his research, he unearthed more strange practices by members of Congress. He discovered, for example, that another freshman representative was using the front porch of his home in Indiana as an office, at a rental to the taxpayers of $100 per month. In the midst of these revelations, observers recalled that, unlike the members of the Lower Chamber, senators had been withholding information concerning their office payrolls since 1948. Hennings, the Senate's leading critic of secrecy in the executive branch, realized the inconsistency, but said nothing. When the controversy failed to abate, Hennings reluctantly announced that while he personally favored disclosing the payrolls, he would not invite invidious comparisons with other senators by unilaterally revealing his own staff's salaries. Several days later, newsmen discovered that Hennings and sixteen other senators employed relatives on their staffs. The Missourian's step-daughter Mrs. Sue McCandless worked for the Subcommittee on Constitutional Rights. Hennings explained that Mrs. McCandless was the first relative he had ever hired, that she began working for the subcommittee eighteen months earlier, that her assignment was menial, and that her salary was in line with her assignment. In the wake of these disclosures, Trimble filed suit against the Senate, demanding access to payrolls. Simultaneously, Senator Wayne Morse, Democrat from Oregon, showed his maverick character by introducing a bill to force his colleagues to publicize their payrolls. Now Hennings had to act. As chairman of the Rules Committee, he drafted a bill to publish payrolls five times each year, and the Upper Chamber promptly passed the measure by a voice vote.[12]

Though the controversy over Senate payrolls was unimportant in itself, it illustrated the artificiality of Hennings' drive against secrecy in the government. While he felt that entirely too much government information was being stamped as confidential, partisan politics provided as much motivation for his interest as did the dangers of secrecy. During the first two years of his career in the Senate he had denied the existence of any serious amount of secrecy. He chided the press for its criticism of the Democratic Administration's information policies, especially as contained in Truman's 1951 executive order giving heads of departments and agencies the right to classify data as confidential. When the press objected, Hennings assured them that he saw no real danger then or in the foreseeable future that the American press could be muzzled. Yet four years later, when a Republican was in the White House, he saw secrecy in the government as a major threat to American democracy, and he promised McCarthy that he would investigate it. When leaders of the antisecrecy drive advised him either to forget his promise or restrict his effort to secrecy in Congress, Hennings did neither. Instead, he pursued a course that eventually established him as the Senate's leading critic of secrecy in the executive branch. Finally, when obvious examples of unwarranted secrecy appeared in the Senate itself, he acted only after Trimble's suit and Morse's resolution forced his hand.[13]

[12] "Digger on Capitol Hill," *Time,* 73 (March 6, 1959), 74; *Washington Daily News,* January 5, 1959; *New York Times,* February 20, 1959; *Tampa Tribune,* February 27, 1959; *St. Louis Post-Dispatch,* February 28, 1959. Hennings Papers, Box 132, memorandum from Kitty Frank, undated (about March 1, 1959); memorandum from Slayman to Kitty Frank, March 5, 1959. *Kansas City Star,* April 7, 1959. On the Trimble suit: *New York Times,* April 2 and June 3, 1959. The Morse bill was 86th Cong., 1st Sess., 1959, S. Res. 99. On Hennings' bill: Hennings Papers, Box 16, press release, June 10, 1959; Senate, Committee on Rules and Administration, 86th Cong., 1st Sess., 1959, Report No. 429; *Congressional Record,* 86th Cong., 1st Sess., 1959, 105, Part 9, 11951–53.

[13] Hennings Papers, Box 132, letter from Clarence Cannon to Hennings, July 1, 1959; Box 3, Address to B'nai B'rith, November 5, 1951, Mt. Vernon, New York; Address to Women's National Democratic Club, March 17, 1952, Washington, D. C. The directive of President Truman was Executive Order 10290, September 24, 1951 (*New York Times,* October 5, 1951).

ᴋ The results of Hennings' five-year interest in the secrecy issue were mostly political. He successfully mollified McCarthy; he regularly tagged the Administration as bumbling and inept and intent on hiding its failures through secrecy; he obtained widespread publicity from a press whose support for attacks on government secrecy was constant, exuberant, unthinking, and deplorably one-sided. Apart from these obvious political gains, there is little evidence that Hennings increased the flow of information from the executive branch. Administration officials even continued to cite the amended 1789 statute as authority for withholding information, leading the Moss Subcommittee to admit in 1960 that it detected no improvement in the Eisenhower Administration's policies concerning secrecy.[14]

In addition to the investigation of government secrecy, the senior Senator from Missouri gave considerable attention in the Eighty-sixth Congress to another controversial project affecting civil liberties, the problem of wire tapping. Hennings' initial interest arose in December of 1957 following the Supreme Court's decision, in *Benanti v. United States,* outlawing the use in federal courts of evidence produced by wire tapping, though state officers applied the device. This ruling from the high tribunal came as the public's growing awareness of the capability and sophistication of scientific listening devices reached a climax and moved Hennings to direct the Subcommittee on Constitutional Rights to study the implications for civil liberties.[15]

The subcommittee's comprehensive investigation began with an exposition of the frightening variety of tools available for elec-

[14] In this regard, it is significant that Senator Hennings possessed a copy of a speech given by Paul M. Butler, chairman of the Democratic Committee, to a state convention of Young Democrats on May 6, 1955, in New London, Connecticut, harshly condemning the secrecy policies of the Eisenhower Administration (Hennings Papers, Box 5). On the results of the Hennings-Moss bill: Hennings Papers, Box 162, memorandum from Marcia MacNaughton to Slayman, February 12, 1959; House, Committee on Government Operations, 86th Cong., 2d Sess., 1960, Report No. 2207, 5.
[15] Benanti v. United States, 355 U. S. 96 (1957). On the growth of public awareness of the wire-tapping problem: Alan F. Westin, "Wiretapping: The Quiet Revolution," *Commentary,* 29 (April, 1960), 333 ff. For a brief summary of the history of wire tapping, from the viewpoint of an opponent of the practice: Alan Barth, *The Price of Liberty,* Chap. VII.

tronic eavesdropping. The group found that developments in electronics had provided such sensitive devices for eavesdropping that, as a newsman in the nation's capital phrased it, "The only way to have a really private conversation with someone is to put on skindiving equipment, get underneath the water in the Potomac and communicate in sign language." At one of its hearings, the subcommittee allowed a witness to "bug" the hearing room by means of a recording device concealed in a shoulder holster and then play back to the startled audience a record of the entire proceedings. This incident and the subsequent testimony caught the attention of the press and further educated the nation to the potential invasions of privacy such instruments implied.[16]

The subcommittee next attempted to ascertain the extent to which public and private investigators employed such devices. The most significant evidence in this phase of the study came from *The Eavesdroppers,* a report published in 1959 on a survey conducted by the Pennsylvania Bar Association Endowment under a grant from the ubiquitous Fund for the Republic. Led by a former prosecuting attorney, Samuel Dash, the investigators concluded that electronic invasions of privacy occurred on a large scale, especially in New York City. According to the hotly challenged survey, the police in New York City applied anywhere from 13,000 to 26,000 wire taps annually.[17]

The final and most confusing phase of the Hennings investigation centered on the legal status of wire tapping and the use in court of evidence that resulted from it. The legal status of wire tapping—as distinct from the more recent practice of electronic eavesdropping—was established in the case of *Olmstead v. United*

---

[16] Hennings Papers, Box 162, copy of radio newscast of Bill Sprague, December 15, 1959. The fact that the subcommittee knew in advance of this demonstration is clear from: Hennings Papers, Box 162, memorandum from Charles Slayman to Robert Bevan, December 4, 1959. Senate, Judiciary Committee, Subcommittee on Constitutional Rights, *Hearings,* 85th Cong., 2d Sess., 1958, Parts 1 and 2.

[17] Samuel Dash, Richard F. Schwartz, and Robert E. Knowlton, *The Eavesdroppers,* and the testimony of Dash in: Senate, Judiciary Committee, Subcommittee on Constitutional Rights, *Hearings,* 86th Cong., 1st Sess., 1959, Part 3, 503 ff. The strongest challenge to Dash came from: Edward S. Silver, "The Wiretapping-Eavesdropping Problem: A Prosecutor's View," *Minnesota Law Review,* 44 (April, 1960), 835.

States in 1928. The efforts of law enforcement agents to halt the traffic in alcohol during the prohibition era had at this time brought the wire tap into use as an investigative tool. In the Olmstead case, the majority on the Court concluded that wire tapping did not violate the Fourth Amendment's prohibition against unreasonable search and seizure, and that evidence so produced was valid in court. Of more importance for the future, however, was the oft-quoted dissent of Justice Oliver Wendell Holmes, who described wire tapping as a "dirty business," contrary to the Fourth Amendment and unbecoming a democratic government. Six years later, Congress inserted into the Federal Communications Act of 1934 an unnoticed provision—Section 605—that followed Holmes's dissent by forbidding any person to intercept and divulge the contents of any interstate or foreign communication "by wire or radio." The Supreme Court subsequently developed a case-by-case interpretation of Section 605 governing the introduction of wire-tap evidence in a criminal prosecution. Two professors of law, Edwin J. Bradley and James E. Hogan, following the Benanti ruling, neatly summarized these rules:

A single sentence can now tell us what the law concerning wiretapping is: on timely motion by a defendant who was party to the call, a federal court will suppress the contents, and evidence derived therefrom, of any interstate or intrastate telephone communication overheard by any person, whether a private citizen or state agent, if the listening in is without the permission of the other party to the call.[18]

Despite the prohibitions of both Congress and the Court, federal and state investigators continued tapping telephones. "The reaction of law officers across the country to the wiretap ban," observed Bradley and Hogan, "resembles the response of the vast majority of our nation's fun-loving populace to Prohibition. The latter was, and the former is, honored more in the breach than in the observance." J. Edgar Hoover, chief of the FBI, admitted that federal agents, with the permission in each instance of the Attor-

---

[18] Olmstead v. United States, 277 U. S. 438 (1928). The legal development of wire-tapping law is ably presented in: Edwin J. Bradley and James E. Hogan, "Wiretapping: From Nardone to Benanti and Rathbun," *Georgetown Law Journal,* 46 (Spring, 1958), 418 ff.

ney General, continued to tap telephones in cases of kidnapping or threats against internal security. The Justice Department has countenanced these violations of Section 605 by reasoning that the statute forbids intercepting and divulging communications only, not interceptions alone. And since the federal government constitutes a single person, divulging the contents of a wire tap within that body did not violate Section 605. Thus, the federal government has continued applying wire taps, although it cannot introduce the contents as evidence in a federal court.[19]

State investigators labored under fewer restrictions, since the Supreme Court did not ban from state courts evidence resulting from wire tapping if the state permitted it. In 1958 six states explicitly allowed their police to tap telephones, five demanding a court order beforehand and one, Louisiana, making no such qualification. Thirty-three states explicitly prohibited wire tapping, while eleven had no statutes bearing on the matter. Hence, despite a congressional statute forbidding wire tapping, the investigative technique enjoyed widespread use at both the state and federal levels.[20]

The law governing electronic eavesdropping had a much shorter history that, in the absence of legislation, came entirely from the Supreme Court. The high tribunal, in the 1942 case of *Goldman v. United States,* ruled that eavesdropping with a stethoscope-type device from an adjoining hotel room did not violate the Fourth Amendment and that the resulting evidence could be introduced into federal court. Ten years later, the Court upheld the validity of testimony gained by listening to the conversation of a suspect by means of a microphone concealed on the person of a would-be conspirator. Shortly after Hennings' death, the Court indicated some limits to electronic eavesdropping, set by the Fourth Amendment, by disallowing evidence gained by inserting a "spike mike"

[19] Edwin J. Bradley and James E. Hogan, "Wiretapping: From Nardone to Benanti and Rathbun." On Hoover's views: Barth, *The Price of Liberty,* 130–33. On Department of Justice view: Herbert Brownell, "Public Security and Wire Tapping," *Cornell Law Quarterly,* 39 (Winter, 1954), 195, and Senate, Judiciary Committee, Subcommittee on Constitutional Rights, *Hearings,* 86th Cong., 1st Sess., 1959, Part 4, 1037.

[20] Hennings Papers, Box 162, memorandum from Slayman to Robert Bevan, May 25, 1960.

into the wall of the suspect's home. Without overruling Goldman, the Court stated that by penetrating the victim's home with the spike, the eavesdroppers had violated the Fourth Amendment.[21]

After exploring this legal maze, the Hennings Subcommittee found that three viewpoints prevailed. Some insisted that wire tapping should never be allowed for any reason. While admitting that the practice facilitated law enforcement, they believed that the potential invasions of privacy suffered by innocent persons outweighed the benefits. They denied that the practice could be controlled through court orders, as in the case of search warrants, because the wire tap by its nature perdured for an unspecified time and because the victim, unaware of its existence, had no chance to object to its validity. At the other extreme were those who felt that wire tapping should be allowed even in private investigations. This group, consisting mostly of private investigators, believed the practice a necessary investigative technique to protect innocent persons whose property, reputation, or freedom were threatened by criminals. Between the two extremes was a large majority of the nation's law enforcement officials who felt that government officers should be allowed to keep pace with the sophisticated techniques of the criminal by employing wire taps, under judicial control, in the investigation of certain types of crimes. They reasoned that denying scientific advances to the police reflected a naïve approach to the conflict with criminals and a view that police work is a game in which it is better to lose honorably than to win by resorting to the "dirty business" of wire tapping.[22]

While Hennings insisted that he would not take sides until he had studied the need for wire tapping, his public statements showed that he favored complete elimination of the practice. This

[21] Goldman v. United States, 316 U. S. 129 (1942); On Lee v. United States, 343 U. S. 747 (1952); Silverman v. United States, 365 U. S. 505 (1961). In a subsequent case, Lopez v. United States, 373 U. S. 427 (1963), the Court intimated that it would soon overturn On Lee.

[22] Hennings Papers, Box 16, press release, Subcommittee on Constitutional Rights, December 15, 1959; Senate, Judiciary Committee, Subcommittee on Constitutional Rights, *Hearings,* 85th Cong., 2d Sess., 1958, Part 1, 20–28; Part 2, 259–65; Part 3, 532–66. Harold K. Lipset, "The Wiretapping-Eavesdropping Problem: A Private Investigator's View," *Minnesota Law Review,* 44 (April, 1960), 873 ff. Barth, *The Price of Liberty,* 144–45.

opposition became clearer during a move in 1960 by the New York police to protect their wire-tapping practices against the adverse reaction generated by the Benanti decision. The city's law enforcement officers put pressure on their congressmen and senators to introduce a statute that would exempt the states from Section 605 of the Federal Communications Act. To obtain national support for the move, Edward S. Silver, district attorney for Kings County, New York, and president of the National Association of County and Prosecuting Attorneys, obtained the support of the group he headed. Silver, in a symposium on wire tapping published in a prominent law journal, took special exception to the charges Samuel Dash made about wire-tapping practices in New York. The Dash report, claimed Silver, relied on vague sources for conclusions that were little more than guesswork. In response to pressure from New York's enforcement officers, Kenneth Keating, the state's Republican senator, introduced the desired bill, and it made steady progress in the second session of the Eighty-sixth Congress. The measure would have legalized wire tapping in states allowing it, provided the practice remained under court control. Hennings promptly opposed the bill because he felt law enforcement officers had failed to prove the need for wire tapping. In June of 1960 the Keating bill passed the Judiciary Committee, so the Subcommittee on Constitutional Rights began preparing a minority report, but Hennings was too ill to pursue the issue. The opposition proved unnecessary, however, for the Senate passed over the Keating bill, and the proponents of wire tapping in the six states that allowed it had to remain on the defensive.[23]

23 For Hennings' apparent neutralism: Hennings Papers, Box 16, press release, Subcommittee on Constitutional Rights, December 15, 1959. On the New York development: "Criminal Procedure—Admissibility of Wiretap Evidence in State Courts," *De Paul Law Review*, 12 (Autumn–Winter, 1962), 159 ff.; Hennings Papers, Box 162, memorandum from Slayman to Hennings, April 7, May 3, and June 28, 1960; Alan F. Westin, "Wiretapping: The Quiet Revolution." The symposium is contained in *Minnesota Law Review*, 44 (April, 1960). The Keating-Cellar bill was Senate, 86th Cong., 2d Sess., 1960, S. 3340. Thomas C. Hennings, Jr., "The Wiretapping-Eavesdropping Problem: A Legislator's View," *Minnesota Law Review*, 44 (April, 1960), 833–34. *Congressional Record*, 86th Cong., 2d Sess., 1960, 106, Part 11, 14143 and 14689; *ibid.*, Part 13, 16750. Hennings

Although wire tapping and government secrecy received the largest measure of Hennings' attention in the Eighty-sixth Congress, a variety of projects bearing on civil liberties also attracted him. The right to counsel for indigents, the rights of the mentally ill, and censorship by the Post Office were recurring topics on the agenda of the Constitutional Rights Subcommittee. Hennings' illness, which eventuated in his death, accounted in part for the subcommittee's failure to pursue them. At the same time, this wide variety of projects, coupled with the lack of urgency in pursuing them, illustrated Hennings' belief that in 1960 no serious dangers threatened the Bill of Rights. Optimism of this kind pervaded a speech he delivered in March of 1960 at the fortieth anniversary meeting of the American Civil Liberties Union. Having reflected on the past decade, Hennings expressed satisfaction that individual rights had weathered the difficulties of the Cold War. In the coming decade he saw only minor problems, left over from the fear that dominated the 1950's—the deplorable practice, for example, of requiring loyalty oaths from scientists, scholars, and students receiving fellowships and loans under the National Science Foundation Acts or the National Defense Education Act. "The most disturbing aspect of these requirements," he observed, "is that they imply that our most intelligent and educated citizens, our greatest potential leaders, are most vulnerable to Communist subversion." Hennings expressed satisfaction that, apart from these absurd "doubts as to democracy's vigor and appeal," the Cold War's invasions of civil liberties had nearly ended by 1960.[24]

While not all defenders of civil liberties agreed with this optimistic appraisal, Hennings' sense of satisfaction was understandable. In his ten-year career in the Senate he had repeatedly fought

Papers, Box 162, memorandum from Slayman to Hennings, June 28, 1960; Slayman to John Brannon and Robert Bevan, August 11, 1960; Slayman to Brannon, August 23, 1960.

[24] Senate, Committee on Rules and Administration, 85th Cong., 1st Sess., 1957, Report No. 23; 85th Cong., 2d Sess., 1958, Report No. 1203; 86th Cong., 1st Sess., 1959, Report No. 31; Hennings Papers, Box 162, memorandum from Slayman to Hennings, January 5, 1960; Box 17, press release, Subcommittee on Constitutional Rights, February 9, 1960; Box 162, memorandum from Slayman to Hennings, April 13, 1960; Box 17, Speech to American Civil Liberties Union, March 8, 1960, New York City.

and overcome freedom's greatest enemy, "the fear which burgeons into panic." This fear, Hennings said, "dissolves the bonds of a free society; reason gives way to distrust and suspicion; democratic processes disappear in a welter of social and political restrictions." Such fear, he concluded, would have left the nation in a pitiable state, except that "our vigorous democratic heritage and our long experience with constitutional government sustained us."

The two phrases—"vigorous democratic heritage" and "long experience with constitutional government"—neatly summarize the basic sources of Hennings' political philosophy. The former characterized him as a liberal at a time when many sincerely doubted that the imperatives of individual freedom were relevant in a struggle for survival in a cold war; the latter characterized him as conservative in an era when Congress was eager to amend the Constitution on the slightest provocation and to abolish the traditional system of checks and balances whenever the executive or judicial branches opposed its will.

Both as a liberal and as a conservative, Hennings' greatest contributions to civil liberties were made in his role as an imposing and articulate obstructionist. His efforts aimed less at passing laws than at blocking them, less at initiating policies than at eradicating them. His obstructionist tactics operated outside the Senate chamber and within. As member and then chairman of the Subcommittee on Privileges and Elections, he led a drive to break the hold of Senator McCarthy on the nation and on the legislators in the Upper Chamber. Through public speeches he helped provoke a mounting antipathy toward the unfair procedures of congressional investigating committees that prosecuted, judged, and punished by exposure citizens who held unorthodox thoughts or opinions. After establishing the novel Subcommittee on Constitutional Rights, whose procedures were a model of fairness, he forced security chiefs of the executive branch to reform their caricature of due process in the ever-expanding network of loyalty-security programs. Through learned statements in floor debate and in the privacy of the Judiciary Committee, he proved a constant and effective defense against a flood of reactionary legislation that sought to cancel the liberal decisions of the Warren Court. To the cries of the nation's law enforcement officers that the high tribunal had handicapped the detection and prevention of crime, Hennings drew on his long experience as a prosecuting attorney to deny that effective crime prevention requires the abolition of civil liberties.

The "fear burgeoning into panic" that Hennings fought stemmed almost invariably from a fear of communism. The major dangers to civil liberties in the 1950's arose from the nation's effort to defend itself against Communist-inspired subversion. Fear of internal subversion made possible the excesses of McCarthy, the unfair practices of congressional investigating committees, the impatience with due process in the loyalty-security programs, and the repeated efforts by Congress to overturn decisions of the Warren Court. Like a thread the security problem knit together the conflicts between liberal and conservative legislators during the Eighty-second and Eighty-third congresses; between the Eisenhower Administration and the Democratic-controlled Eighty-fourth Congress; and between the legislative branch and the Warren Court during the Eighty-fifth and Eighty-sixth congresses. Problems emerging from the need to control crime, differences over civil rights following the decision on integration in 1954, and the normal tactics of partisan politics affected these conflicts, but the basic tension between internal security and individual rights always dominated.

Hennings' reaction to fear-inspired hesitations over the wisdom of individual freedom and the pertinency of the Bill of Rights was prompt, consistent, and automatic. From the start of his 1950 campaign to his untimely death in 1960, he firmly maintained that a democratic nation was not worth saving from communism if in the process it lost the principles that made it democratic. Moreover, as a lifelong student of history, he believed that democratic principles constituted the means rather than the price of victory over communism. He admitted that following democratic principles involved a gamble that frightened the faint-hearted in times of crisis, but he insisted that history shows that a democracy enjoys more favorable odds than any other system. Through reasoning that was old-fashioned and not at all sophisticated, Hennings arrived at a faith in democracy that was refreshing and childlike in its simplicity.[25]

Apart from his faith in democracy, many of Hennings' closest associates and admirers claimed, the Senator possessed no consistent philosophy—an opinion that developed from his pragmatic approach to the problems of government. This verdict is both understandable and erroneous, resembling the judgment some historians have made of Hennings' constant idol, Thomas Jefferson. The conclusion is understandable because, as had Jefferson, Hennings allowed a pervasive pragmatism over means to govern his political thought and action; it is erroneous because, again as had Jefferson, Hennings consistently pursued certain fundamental goals without deviation.[26]

Hennings' political philosophy came from two main sources. The first was the native American theory of democracy as contained in the writings of Jefferson. As he understood Jefferson, the fundamental purpose of government consists of providing an environment in which the individual can freely develop his personality through the widest possible exercise of his intellectual faculties. This development flows from the free inquiry into every facet of life and the opportunity to live in accord with one's conscience. From this environment a nation has built a culture, the greatest achievement of a civilization, and has enlarged its freedom, since freedom increases true knowledge and true knowledge in turn increases a nation's freedom. Thus, for Hennings, the essence of democracy was freedom of thought and communication.[27]

[25] Hennings Papers, Box 3, Speech, Jackson Day Banquet, January 12, 1952, Springfield, Missouri; Speech, Women's National Democratic Club, March 17, 1952, Washington, D. C.; Speech, Jefferson-Jackson Day Dinner, April 13, 1953, Pittsburgh, Pennsylvania; Box 20, Speech, Economics Club of New York City, January 19, 1954; Box 18, Speech, Trinity College, May 8, 1954, Hartford, Connecticut; Speech, Central College, May 30, 1954, Fayette, Missouri; Box 19, Speech, Law Club of Chicago, March 25, 1955.

[26] Interviews with former staff members, May, 1962. For the various estimates of Jefferson, see: Merrill D. Peterson, *The Jefferson Image in the American Mind.*

[27] Hennings Papers, Box 20, Speech, Economic Club of New York City, January 19, 1954; Box 18, Speech, Haverford College, May 4, 1954,

The second major source of Hennings' political philosophy was law. From the legal tradition he derived his second fundamental goal, negative in character and intimately bound up with the development of personality. Closely related to individual freedom, said Hennings, is the right of a citizen to receive fair treatment at the lowest level of contact with his government, the police level. Without assurance of fair treatment in this encounter, a citizen lacks the security needed to develop his personality and capabilities. This minimal guarantee of justice comes from the procedural rights of orderly arrest, habeas corpus, speedy trial, right to counsel, full disclosure of charges, confrontation of adverse witnesses, and compulsory process for one's own witnesses. In short, justice consists of due process in the relationship of a citizen with the police power of his government. As in his definition of freedom, Hennings here again emphasized human rights rather than economic rights. Without denying the latter, he seldom spoke of them with the fervor reserved for the former. His notion of justice stressed criminal justice, the protection of a citizen from restrictions on his person that result from an unjust conviction of crime. Such an emphasis enabled Hennings to spot the dangers inherent in the growth of administrative criminal law in the security program, but would not likely have inspired him, for example, to produce minimum wage laws.[28]

Uncompromising in his defense of intellectual freedom and criminal justice, Hennings was in other respects openly pragmatic.

Haverford, Pennsylvania; Box 19, Speech, Law Club of Chicago, March 25, 1955; Speech, Washington University, May 4, 1955, St. Louis, Missouri; Speech, William Woods College, May 29, 1955, Fulton, Missouri; Box 10, Speech, B'nai B'rith, October 16, 1955, St. Louis, Missouri.

[28] Hennings Papers, Box 18, Speech, Washington University (St. Louis) alumni, May 20, 1954, Washington, D. C.; Box 19, Speech, Lawyers Association of St. Louis, December 13, 1954, St. Louis, Missouri; Speech, Law Club of Chicago, March 25, 1955; Box 161, Speech, Lawyers Association of St. Louis, November 3, 1955, St. Louis, Missouri; Box 5, press release, Speech, meeting of Interparliamentary Union, November 23, 1956, Bangkok, Thailand. This is not to imply that Hennings opposed labor legislation. On the contrary, he viewed Jefferson as a potential New Dealer, in line with the thesis of Charles M. Wiltse, *Jeffersonian Democracy in the American Tradition,* as is seen from: Hennings Papers, Box 11, Introduction by Hennings of Robert F. Wagner, Jr., Jefferson–Jackson Day meeting, December 14, 1955.

Except for the Bill of Rights, which embodies basic goals, he approached the Constitution as a practical means for assuring freedom and justice in a sometimes repressive society. Because it is only a means, he believed it can and should be changed to keep pace with the times. Yet, because it is a proven means, he was slow to favor constitutional changes or to upset its gradual development by the Supreme Court. While admitting a theoretical need for changes, he confessed a reluctance to make them unless the innovator could show sufficient cause. He was willing to tamper with the Constitution, but only after long study and factual evidence should indicate an existing inadequacy. In 1953 and 1954, for example, he opposed the many attempts to amend the Constitution, which included a resolution to withdraw from Congress the power to determine the jurisdiction of the Supreme Court. Four years later, in the wake of the Jenner bill, he favored a similar resolution. This pragmatic but reluctant view of change appeared again in 1956. At that time he favored an amendment to abolish the electoral college, reasoning that direct election of the President and Vice-President would be "the one change in our basic election law which is most in keeping with the spirit of our times and the democratic temper of our people."[29]

The basis of Hennings' legal conservatism was a scholarly knowledge of the Constitution and its history. He often admitted his fascination with the simple but rather astounding fact that the Constitution had lasted so long. The Founding Fathers, he felt, had built exceedingly well. In combining contemporary political theories with colonial experience they erected a dynamic system whose realism and flexibility have kept it functioning for the protection of liberty and justice. The key to its success is the system of checks and balances, which prevents any one branch from gaining

---

[29] On Hennings' view of the need to change the Constitution but his reluctance to do so: Hennings Papers, Box 4, press release, June 14, 1953; Box 19, press release, January 9, 1955; Speech, Law Club of Chicago, March 25, 1955; Speech, Washington University, May 4, 1955, St. Louis, Missouri; Box 161, Speech, Lawyers Association of St. Louis, November 3, 1955; Box 14, Speech, Missouri Order of the Coif, April 27, 1957; *Congressional Record,* 83d Cong., 2d Sess., 1954, 100, Part 5, 6341–46, 6967–68. On the direct election of the President and Vice-President: Hennings Papers, Box 12, press release, March 30, 1956.

enough permanent power to violate democratic principles for an indefinite period. Inevitably, one branch enjoys dominance for a period, but as long as the power of the other branches remains structurally intact they eventually check the unbalance.[30]

In most cases Hennings acted in accord with this evaluation of checks and balances. During the conflict over the Bricker Amendment he struggled against heavy odds to defend from congressional attack the power of the President over foreign affairs. He consented to the President's nominations more readily than did the members of Eisenhower's own party. He objected to the executive branch's invasions of congressional power in controlling the loyalty-security programs. Most vehemently of all, Hennings defended the power and independence of the judiciary from a dissatisfied Congress. Of the three branches, he felt that the judiciary played a special role in protecting civil liberties. While moments of panic could frighten the legislative and executive branches into violating civil liberties, the judiciary branch would always remain the protector of individual freedom and justice. But despite this intimate relationship that Hennings saw between the Supreme Court and civil liberties, he was prepared, on one occasion early in his political career, to participate in an attack on the Court's independence. When President Roosevelt attempted to force the judiciary into approving New Deal legislation, Hennings almost surreptitiously cooperated in the ill-fated scheme.

While Hennings lived by a philosophy, he was not a philosopher but a politician, and a superb one. His accomplishments proceeded from his excellent grasp of the American political process. His political style, however, was unusual. He consistently violated the common rules for elected officials, yet seldom suffered

[30] Hennings Papers, Box 4, press release, June 14, 1953; Box 18, Speech, Washington University (St. Louis) alumni, May 20, 1954, Washington, D. C.; Speech, Judge Advocates Association, August 17, 1954, Chicago, Illinois; Box 19, press release, January 9, 1955; Speech, Law Club of Chicago, March 25, 1955; Speech, Washington University, May 4, 1955, St. Louis, Missouri; Box 161, undelivered speech, meeting of Interparliamentary Union, August 31, 1955; Box 10, Speech, B'nai B'rith, October 16, 1955, St. Louis; Box 161, Speech, Lawyers Association of St. Louis, November 3, 1955; Box 12, press release, March 30, 1956; Speech, Interparliamentary Union, November 23, 1956, Bangkok, Thailand.

as a result. He spent little time with constituents, yet retained their votes. He hated campaigning, yet never lost an election. He gave little concern to press relations, yet received the adulation of most newsmen. Constituents received little attention from the easily bored Hennings. He saw them only by appointment—and carefully instructed his staff not to make appointments. He lacked the desire, and probably the ability, to cultivate notice of his activities by the press. He was friendly to reporters, but highly inaccessible. One journalist, a friend and admirer of Hennings, said that he found it easier to see the President of the United States than the senior Senator from Missouri. On one occasion, several reporters, expecting a long interview, met Hennings by prearrangement as he left the Senate floor following his dramatic defeat of the Bricker Amendment. The Missourian chatted affably about other matters on the five-minute walk to the elevator where, to the astonishment of the newsmen, the interview suddenly ended as the Senator graciously excused himself.[31]

Hennings retained the support of constituents and the press for many of the same reasons his fellow legislators supported him. They liked him as a person and respected his talents. In his role as a statesman Hennings modeled his conduct after Lincoln. When defining leadership he inevitably recalled the Republican President and pointed to his power of moral persuasion and his modesty, "the key that opened the heart of man to his sincerity, honesty, and his deep understanding of the political exigencies of his epoch." The bases of leadership, said Hennings, were "the gift of intuitive penetration into things encountered along the path of life" and "the extraordinary ability to size up people and happenings quickly and correctly." Having this gift and this ability, a leader's success depended, further, on the "content" and "intent" of his ideas and the ability of his followers "to rise to the understanding of the leader's ideas."[32]

To a great extent Hennings' definition of leadership explained

[31] Interviews with former staff members, May and June, 1962. On Hennings' political skill: Hennings Papers, Box 73, letter from Richard H. Brown to Hennings, December 25, 1956; Box 65, memorandum from Robert L. Bevan regarding Allen Drury's interview on August 13, 1959; *Washington Post,* November 7, 1959.

[32] Interviews with former staff members, May, 1962; Hennings Papers, Box 3, Speech, Delta Kappa Epsilon, December 30, 1952, Washington,

his own success. Moral persuasion, rather than the commands or coercion he despised, accounted for the size and enthusiasm of his following. He possessed a remarkable ability to penetrate issues and expose their inner meaning or contradiction in clear, articulate, and logical argument. With this ability he often made a favorable cause out of unpopular issues. The Washington press referred to him as "the golden boy" because of his ability to enhance his reputation by undertaking an unpopular cause. When he touched it, the cause turned into political gold. In defending his position he relied on a quick, retentive mind, cultivated by wide reading in law and history, and the practiced skill of an old-fashioned trial lawyer. Dressed always in a dark suit with an out-of-style vest laced across by an antiquated gold watch-chain, the tall and handsome senator confidently defended his position with an up-to-date realism that belied his dress and courtly manner.[33]

Courtesy enhanced Hennings' skill in debate. His fluent speech seldom became caustic, even in heated argument, and he exploited an easy flow of rhetoric on numerous occasions. His favorite tactic in floor debate consisted of heaping effusive praise on an opponent he suspected was readying a loaded question. Soundly flattered, the opponent usually rephrased the intended question. On one occasion, Hennings even bested the Senate's master of rhetoric, Everett Dirksen of Illinois. After Hennings thoroughly flustered the Republican by referring to the latter's speech as exceedingly glib and adroit, Dirksen objected to the characterization. Hennings promptly replied that he would gladly retract the statement and henceforth insist that the Senator from Illinois was neither glib nor adroit. The usually fluent Dirksen had no rejoinder.[34]

Gentle jibes were the extent of Hennings' personal attacks on opponents. He seldom allowed ideological conflicts to become personal, preferring to retain the friendship of his fiercest oppo-

D. C.; Box 19, Speech, Washington University, May 4, 1955, St. Louis, Missouri.

[33] Interviews with former staff members, May and June, 1962; *Thomas C. Hennings, Jr., Memorial Services; Los Angeles Times,* November 18, 1959; Max Freedman, *Manchester Guardian* (reprinted in *Washington Post,* November 7, 1959); "American Survey," *Economist* (March 19, 1960).

[34] Interviews with former staff members, May and June, 1962. The Dirksen incident is related in *Reporter,* 22 (February 18, 1960), 6.

nents. Even McCarthy retained a liking for the Senator from Missouri despite their harsh conflicts. As an early member of the "Senate Club," Hennings remained acceptable to his Southern colleagues in spite of his persistent pressure for meaningful civil rights legislation. He accepted realistically the facts of life in Southern constituencies, and, while laboring against the tide, he felt no need to make the conflict a personal one.[35]

Realism was a constant facet of Hennings' political philosophy. He illustrated this in 1959, when Democratic National Chairman Paul M. Butler publicly questioned the compromising tendencies of the Democratic leadership in Congress over civil rights legislation. Asked by Robert G. Spivak, Washington correspondent of the *New York Post,* to comment on Butler's observations, Hennings stated:

Most Democrats are aware that the Party Platform is a goal, a target at which their congressional leadership can aim. It is not always possible to attain fulfillment of the platform under the present circumstances. ... The present congressional leadership has two choices it might make: one positive, one negative. It can pass needed legislation or it can, by insisting on the unattainable, bring our legislative process to a halt. I feel it philosophically and politically wise to accomplish whatever is possible. This course of action will benefit the American people and the Democratic Party.[36]

Not all of Hennings' habits, of course, were political virtues. His closest associates unanimously agreed on two conclusions: The senior Senator from Missouri was the acknowledged leader and spokesman for civil liberties in the Upper Chamber during the 1950's; he possessed the position and the talent to have accomplished more than he actually did. Assuming that more was attainable, why did Hennings fail to attain it? Part of the explanation lay in the Missourian's personal habits, especially his frequent lapses into lethargy or boredom, and his periodic bouts with alcoholism. Inattention to the task at hand accounted in part for his

35 Interviews with former staff members, May and June, 1962; *Congressional Record,* 86th Cong., 1st Sess., 1959, 105, Part 14, 17926. On Hennings' civil rights effort, see: Wayne Morse, "Senator Thomas C. Hennings, Jr., and Civil Rights," *Missouri Law Review,* 26 (November, 1961), 420–28.
36 Hennings Papers, Box 16, press release, July 14, 1959.

failure to complete his criticism of the Eisenhower security program and for his illiberal passport bill of 1958, which embarrassed his liberal cosponsors and weakened their confidence in his leadership. Perhaps his failures derived also from a too-ready admission that a goal was realistically unattainable, the hazard of the political realist. Of the two suggested explanations of Hennings' failures, the first seems more likely and more difficult to fathom, involving as it does the hidden drives of the inner man.

But despite his shortcomings, Hennings' death on September 13, 1960, constituted a distinct loss for the cause of individual rights in a nation still involved in a cold war. At the time of his death a new but temporary facet of infringements on individual rights was tempting the American people. The nation was preparing to elect the first Catholic President in its history, and Hennings characteristically recalled the relevant constitutional admonitions for the situation. In a letter to John W. Inglish, Democratic chairman for Missouri, the senior Senator suggested that the party remember the proper relationship between religion and public life in American democratic theory. He recalled Jefferson's statement, "The opinions of men are not the object of civil government," and the Virginian's draft of a bill for establishing religious freedom:

the proscribing any citizen as unworthy the public confidence by laying upon him an incapacity of being called to offices of trust and emolument, unless he profess or renounce this or that religious opinion, is depriving him injuriously of those privileges and advantages to which, in common with his fellow citizens, he has a natural right.

After citing the authority of Jefferson, Hennings concluded his letter by appealing to the principle of religious freedom as guaranteed by the First Amendment and to the prohibition against a religious test for officeholders contained in Article VI of the Constitution. This final defense of individual rights, based on the authority of Jefferson, the Bill of Rights, and the Constitution, provided a fitting epitaph for Senator Thomas C. Hennings, Jr., as death closed for him a decade of effort in support of civil liberties.[37]

37 Hennings Papers, Box 17, press release, September 13, 1960.

Bibliography

BOOKS

Acheson, Dean, *A Democrat Looks at His Party*. New York, 1955.

Adams, Sherman, *Firsthand Report; the Story of the Eisenhower Administration*. New York, 1961.

Agar, Herbert, *The Price of Power; America since 1945*. Chicago, 1957.

American Civil Liberties Union, *Annual Reports*, 1947–1960.

Anderson, Jack, and Ronald W. May, *McCarthy, the Man, the Senator, the "Ism."* Boston, 1952.

Andrews, Bert, *Washington Witch Hunt*. New York, 1948.

Association of the Bar of the City of New York, *Report of Special Committee on the Federal Loyalty-Security Program*. New York, 1962.

——, *Freedom to Travel*, Report of the Special Committee to Study Passport Procedures. New York, 1958.

——, *Report of Special Committee to Study Committee Procedures*. Ithaca, 1962.

Barth, Alan, *Government by Investigation*. New York, 1955.

——, *The Price of Liberty*. New York, 1961.

Bentley, Elizabeth, *Out of Bondage*. New York, 1951.

Blanshard, Paul, *God and Man in Washington*. Boston, 1960.

Bontecou, Eleanor, *The Federal Loyalty-Security Program*. Ithaca, 1953.

Bowers, Claude G., *Jefferson and Hamilton: The Struggle for Democracy in America*. Boston, 1925.

Brock, Clifton, *Americans for Democratic Action*. Washington, 1962.

Brown, Ralph S., *Loyalty and Security Employment Tests in the United States.* New Haven, 1958.

Buckley, William F., and Brent Bozell, *McCarthy and His Enemies.* Chicago, 1954.

——, and the editors of *National Review, The Committee and Its Critics; A Calm Review of the House Committee on Un-American Activities.* New York, 1962.

Carr, Robert K., *The House Committee on Un-American Activities, 1945–1950.* Ithaca, 1952.

Caughey, John W., *In Clear and Present Danger: The Crucial State of our Freedoms.* Chicago, 1958.

Chafee, Zechariah, Jr., *Free Speech in the United States.* Cambridge, 1942.

Cogley, John, *Report on Blacklisting: Radio.* New York, 1956.

——, *Report on Blacklisting: Movies.* New York, 1956.

Cross, Harold L., *The People's Right to Know.* New York, 1953.

Cushman, Robert E., *Civil Liberties in the United States.* Ithaca, 1956.

Dash, Samuel, Richard F. Schwartz, and Robert E. Knowlton, *The Eavesdroppers.* New Brunswick, 1959.

Davis, Elmer, *But We Were Born Free.* Garden City, 1954.

Donovan, Robert J., *Eisenhower: The Inside Story.* New York, 1956.

Geiger, Louis G., *Joseph W. Folk of Missouri.* Columbia, 1953.

Gellhorn, Walter, *Security, Loyalty, and Science.* Ithaca, 1950.

——, *The States and Subversion.* Ithaca, 1952.

——, *Individual Freedom and Governmental Restraints.* Baton Rouge, 1956.

——, *American Rights,* New York, 1960.

Ginzburg, Benjamin, *Rededication to Freedom.* New York, 1959.

Goldman, Eric F., *The Crucial Decade—and After, America 1945–1960.* New York, 1961.

Griswold, Erwin N., *The Fifth Amendment Today.* Cambridge, 1955.

Hand, Learned, *The Bill of Rights.* Cambridge, 1958.

Hook, Sidney, *Common Sense and the Fifth Amendment.* New York, 1957.

Hyde, William, and Howard L. Conard, *Encyclopedia of the History of St. Louis.* St. Louis, 1899.

Industrial Relations Research Association, *Personnel Security Programs in U. S. Industry.* 1955.

Jackson, Robert H., *The Supreme Court in the American System of Government.* Cambridge, 1955.

Johnson, Walter, *1600 Pennsylvania Avenue; Presidents and the People, 1929–1959.* Boston, 1960.

Knauff, Ellen R., *The Ellen Knauff Story.* New York, 1952.

Konvitz, Milton R., *Civil Rights in Immigration.* Ithaca, 1953.

————, *Fundamental Liberties of a Free People: Religion, Speech, Press, Assembly.* Ithaca, 1957.

————, *Bill of Rights Reader.* Ithaca, 1960.

————, ed., with Clinton Rossiter, *Aspects of Liberty.* Ithaca, 1958.

Lattimore, Owen, *Ordeal by Slander.* Boston, 1950.

Leonard, John W., ed., *The Book of St. Louisans.* St. Louis, 1906.

Levy, Leonard W., *Legacy of Suppression: Freedom of Speech and Press in Early American History.* Cambridge, 1960.

Longaker, Richard P., *The Presidency and Individual Liberties.* Ithaca, 1961.

McCarthy, Joseph R., *McCarthyism, The Fight for America.* New York, 1952.

McCloskey, Robert J., *The American Supreme Court.* Chicago, 1960.

MacDuffie, Marshall, *The Red Carpet.* New York, 1955.

Madison, Charles A., *American Labor Leaders.* New York, 1950.

Mason, Alpheus T., *The Supreme Court from Taft to Warren.* Baton Rouge, 1958.

Matthews, Donald R., *U. S. Senators and Their World.* Chapel Hill, 1960.

Matusow, Harvey, *False Witness.* New York, 1955.

Meiklejohn, Alexander, *Political Freedom: The Constitutional Powers of the People.* New York, 1960.

Miller, Merle, *The Judges and the Judged.* New York, 1952.

Missouri Association for Criminal Justice, *The Missouri Crime Survey.* New York, 1926.

Mollenhoff, Clark R., *Washington Cover-Up.* Garden City, 1962.

Murphy, Walter F., *Congress and the Court.* Chicago, 1962.

O'Brian, John Lord, *National Security and Individual Freedom.* Cambridge, 1955.

Ogden, August Raymond, *The Dies Committee.* Washington, 1945.

Peterson, Merrill D., *The Jefferson Image in the American Mind.* New York, 1960.

Pritchett, C. Herman, *The Roosevelt Court, A Study in Judicial Politics and Values, 1937–1947.* New York, 1948.

————, *Civil Liberties and the Vinson Court.* Chicago, 1954.

————, *Congress Versus the Supreme Court.* Minneapolis, 1961.

Reddig, William M., *Tom's Town.* New York, 1947.

Rorty, James, and Moshe Decter, *McCarthy and the Communists*. New York, 1954.

Rovere, Richard H., *The Eisenhower Years*. New York, 1956.

————, *Senator Joe McCarthy*. New York, 1959.

————, *The American Establishment and Other Reports, Opinions, and Speculations*. New York, 1962.

Schaar, John H., *Loyalty in America*. Berkeley, 1957.

Shils, Edward, *The Torment of Secrecy*. Glencoe, Illinois, 1956.

Stouffer, Samuel A., *Communism, Conformity and Civil Liberties*. New York, 1955.

Straight, Michael, *Trial by Television*. Boston, 1955.

Swisher, Carl Brent, *American Constitutional Development*. Cambridge, 1954.

Taylor, Telford, *Grand Inquest, the Story of Congressional Investigations*. New York, 1955.

Thomas C. Hennings, Jr., Memorial Services. Washington, 1961.

Tugwell, Rexford G., *The Stricken Land, the Story of Puerto Rico*. New York, 1947.

Watts, Rowland, *The Draftee and Internal Security*. New York, 1955.

Wechsler, Herbert, *Principles, Politics, and Fundamental Law*. Cambridge, 1961.

Weinstein, Sandra, *Personnel Security Programs of the Federal Government*. New York, 1954.

White, Nathan, *Harry Dexter White: Loyal American*. Waban, Mass., 1956.

White, William S., *Citadel*. New York, 1956.

Who's Who in America, 21 (Chicago, 1940).

Williams, Edward Bennett, *One Man's Freedom*. New York, 1962.

Wiltse, Charles M., *Jeffersonian Democracy in the American Tradition*. Chapel Hill, 1935.

Yarmolinsky, Adam, *Case Studies in Personnel Security*. Washington, 1955.

ARTICLES

Arendt, Hannah, "The Ex-Communists." *Commonweal,* 57 (March 20, 1953), 595.

Aron, Raymond, "Realism and Common Sense in Security Policy." *Bulletin of the Atomic Scientists,* 11 (April, 1955), 110.

Ascoli, Max, "The Jurisprudence of Security." *Reporter,* 11 (July 6, 1954), 8.

Baldinger, Wilbur H., "Faceless Talebearers and the Right to Travel." *Progressive,* 20 (April, 1956), 17.

Begeman, Jean, "What Ellen Knauff Won." *New Republic,* 126 (January 7, 1951), 14.

Berman, Daniel M., "Voice of the American Bar." *Nation,* 188 (March 21, 1959), 247.

————, "Constitutional Issues and the Warren Court." *American Political Science Review,* 53 (June, 1959), 500.

Bontecou, Eleanor, "President Eisenhower's 'Security' Program." *Bulletin of the Atomic Scientists,* 9 (July, 1953), 215.

————, "Due Process in Security Dismissals." *Annals of the American Academy of Political and Social Science,* 300 (July, 1955), 102.

Bradley, Edwin J., and James E. Hogan, "Wiretapping: From Nardone to Benanti and Rathbun." *Georgetown Law Journal,* 46 (Spring, 1958), 418.

Brown, Ralph S., "6,000,000 Second-Class Citizens." *Nation,* 174 (June 28, 1952), 644.

————, "Loyalty-Security Measures and Employment Opportunities." *Bulletin of the Atomic Scientists,* 11 (April, 1955), 113.

————, "Personnel Security." *Annals of the American Academy of Political and Social Sciences,* 290 (November, 1953), 100.

————, "The Operation of Personnel Security Programs." *Annals of the American Academy of Political and Social Science,* 300 (July, 1955), 94.

————, "Regression in the Wright Report." *Bulletin of the Atomic Scientists,* 13 (September, 1957), 253.

————, and John D. Fassett, "Security Tests for Maritime Workers: Due Process Under the Port Security Program." *Yale Law Journal,* 62 (July, 1953), 1163.

Brown, Ray A., "Administrative Commissions and the Judicial Power." *Minnesota Law Review,* 19 (February, 1935), 261.

Brownell, Herbert, "Public Security and Wire Tapping." *Cornell Law Quarterly,* 39 (Winter, 1954), 195.

Buckley, William F., Jr., "The 'Times' Slays a Dragon." *National Review,* 1 (January 25, 1956), 11.

Burkhart, James A., "Hennings of Missouri." *Frontier,* 8 (April, 1957), 13.

T.R.B., "Washington Wire." *New Republic,* 128 (January 12, 1953), 3.

Cain, Harry P., "I Could Not Remain Silent." *Coronet,* 39 (November, 1955), 29.

Cater, Douglass, "Is McCarthy Slipping?" *Reporter,* 5 (September 18, 1951), 25.

———, "How the Senate Passed the Civil-Rights Bill." *Reporter*, 17 (September 5, 1957), 9.

Chase, Harold W., "The Warren Court and Congress." *Minnesota Law Review*, 44 (March, 1960), 595.

Cohn, Roy M., and Thomas A. Bolan, "The Supreme Court and the A.B.A. Report and Resolutions." *Fordham Law Review*, 28 (Summer, 1959), 233.

Crawford, John D., "Free Speech and the Internal Security Act of 1950." *Georgetown Law Journal*, 39 (March, 1951), 440.

Davis, Kenneth, "The Requirement of a Trial-Type Hearing." *Harvard Law Review*, 70 (December, 1956), 193.

Dilliard, Irving, "Senator Thomas C. Hennings, Jr., and the Supreme Court." *Missouri Law Review*, 26 (November, 1961), 438.

Dotson, Arch, "The Emerging Doctrine of Privilege in Public Employment." *Public Administration Review*, 15 (Spring, 1955), 77.

Edwards, Willard, "The Reformation of Harry Cain." *American Mercury*, 81 (October, 1955), 39.

Elliott, Sheldon D., "Court Curbing Proposals in Congress." *Notre Dame Lawyer*, 33 (August, 1958), 597.

Fellman, David, "The Loyalty Defendants." *Wisconsin Law Review* (January, 1957), 4.

Fleeson, Doris, *St. Louis Post-Dispatch*, March 18, 1953.

Fleming, Robert H., "Can McCarthy Win Again?" *Nation*, 175 (August 16, 1952), 147.

Gilbert, Brian, "Judge Youngdahl Wins His Fight." *New Republic*, 133 (July 11, 1955), 5.

Ginzburg, Benjamin, "Loyalty, Suspicion and the Tightening Chain." *Reporter*, 11 (July 6, 1954), 10.

Goudsmit, S. A., "The Task of the Security Officer." *Bulletin of the Atomic Scientists*, 11 (April, 1955), 145.

Green, Harold, "The Unsystematic Security System." *Bulletin of the Atomic Scientists*, 11 (April, 1955), 118.

Green, John Raeburn. *Virginia Law Review*, 42 (January, 1956), 123.

Halper, Sam, "New York: Mud-Slinging Derby." *Newsweek*, 36 (October 30, 1950), 17.

Heffron, Edward F., "McCarthy: the Case for Him." *Commonweal*, 57 (October 31, 1952), 87.

Hennessy, Bernard, "The Chance of McCarthy's Defeat." *New Republic*, 127 (August 18, 1952), 14.

Hennings, Thomas C., Jr., "Equal Justice Under Law." *Georgetown Law Journal*, 46 (Fall, 1957), 13.

————, "The Right to Travel." *Coronet,* 43 (December, 1957), 133.

————, "Detention and Confessions: The Mallory Case." *Missouri Law Review,* 23 (January, 1958), 25.

————, "A Legislative Measure to Augment the Free Flow of Public Information." *American University Law Review,* 8 (January, 1959), 19.

————, "The Executive Privilege and the People's Right to Know." *Federal Bar Journal,* 19 (January, 1959), 1.

————, "Secrecy—Threat to Freedom." *Progressive,* 22 (April, 1959), 21.

————, "The People's Right to Know." *American Bar Association Journal,* 45 (July, 1959), 667.

————, "The Wiretapping-Eavesdropping Problem: A Legislator's View." *Minnesota Law Review,* 44 (April, 1960), 833.

Hennings, Thomas C., Sr., "The Greatest Father in the World." *Trust Companies,* 53 (October, 1924), 449.

Hoffman, Paul G., "To Insure the End of Our Hysteria." *New York Times Magazine* (November 14, 1954), 9.

Hogan, James E., and Joseph M. Snee, "The McNabb-Mallory Rule: Its Rise, Rationale and Rescue." *Georgetown Law Journal,* 47 (Fall, 1958), 1.

Horn, Robert A., "The Protection of Internal Security." *Public Administration Review,* 16 (Winter, 1956), 40.

————, "The Warren Court and the Discretionary Power of the Executive." *Minnesota Law Review,* 44 (March, 1960), 639.

Hovey, Graham, "McCarthy Faces the Voters." *New Republic,* 125 (December 3, 1951), 15.

Jaffe, Louis L., "Right to Travel." *Foreign Affairs,* 35 (October, 1956), 17.

Jones, William K., "Jurisdiction of the Federal Courts to Review the Character of Military Administrative Discharges." *Columbia Law Review,* 57 (November, 1957), 917.

Kemler, Edgar, "Soft Impeachment." *Nation,* 181 (December 24, 1955), 556.

Kirschten, Ernest, "Donnell Luck and Missouri Scandal." *Nation,* 171 (October 14, 1950), 332.

Knowles, Clayton, *New York Times,* January 17 and May 18, 1952.

Kramer, Robert, and Herman Marcuse, "Executive Privilege—A Study of the Period 1953–1960." *George Washington Law Review,* 29 (April and June, 1961), parts 1 and 2.

Krasnowiecki, Jan Z., "Confrontation by Witnesses in Government

Employee Security Proceedings." *Notre Dame Lawyer,* 33 (March, 1958), 180.

Kurland, Philip B., "The Supreme Court and its Judicial Critics." *Utah Law Review,* 6 (Fall, 1959), 457.

Lewis, Anthony, "What Happens to a Victim of Nameless Accusers." *Reporter,* 10 (March 2, 1954), 10.

————, "Security: Interim Reports." *Reporter,* 13 (September 8, 1955), 27.

————, "The Supreme Court and its Critics." *Minnesota Law Review,* 45 (January, 1961), 305.

Lindley, Ernest K., "Of Harry Cain." *Newsweek,* 47 (May 28, 1956), 41.

Lipset, Harold K., "The Wiretapping-Eavesdropping Problem: A Private Investigator's View." *Minnesota Law Review,* 44 (April, 1960), 873.

Livingston, M. Stanley, "Science and Security." *Annals of the American Academy of Political and Social Science,* 300 (July, 1955), 4.

Long, Edward V., "Tom Hennings—The Man from Missouri." *Missouri Law Review,* 26 (November, 1961), 408.

Lucas, Scott W., "Congressional Hearings: A Plea for Reform." *New York Times Magazine* (March 19, 1950), 13.

Lyons, Eugene, "Is Freedom of Expression Really Threatened?" *American Mercury,* 76 (January, 1953), 22.

McCloskey, Robert G., "The Supreme Court Finds a Role: Civil Liberties in the 1955 Term." *Virginia Law Review,* 42 (October, 1956), 735.

————, "Useful Toil or the Paths of Glory? Civil Liberties in the 1956 Term of the Supreme Court." *Virginia Law Review,* 43 (October, 1957), 803.

————, "Tools, Stumbling Blocks, and Stepping Stones: Civil Liberties in the 1957 Term of the Supreme Court." *Virginia Law Review,* 44 (November, 1958), 1029.

MacDuffie, Marshall, "The Khrushchev I Know." *Collier's,* 135 (April 15, 1955), 96.

McKay, Robert B., "The Supreme Court and its Lawyer Critics." *Fordham Law Review,* 28 (Winter, 1959-60), 615.

McNamara, Francis J., "Witch-Hunting with the Left." *National Review,* 1 (January 4, 1956), 4.

McWilliams, Carey, "Bungling in California." *Nation,* 171 (November 4, 1950), 411.

————, "Wisconsin Previewed." *Nation,* 174 (March 22, 1952), 269.

Marks, Herbert S., and George F. Trowbridge, "Control of Information Under the Atomic Energy Act of 1954." *Bulletin of the Atomic Scientists,* 11 (April, 1955), 128.

Merson, Martin, "My Education in Government." *Reporter,* 11 (October 7, 1954), 15.

Milburn, George, "Monroney of Oklahoma." *Nation,* 177 (August 8, 1953), 110.

Mollenhoff, Clark R., *Des Moines Register,* December, 1954, and January, 1955.

————, "Senator Thomas C. Hennings, Jr., and the 'Right to Know.'" *Missouri Law Review,* 26 (November, 1961), 441.

Morgenthau, Hans J., "The Impact of the Loyalty-Security Measures on the State Department." *Bulletin of the Atomic Scientists,* 11 (April, 1955), 134.

Morris, A. T., "A Trap for Labor," *Nation,* 181 (December 3, 1955), 471.

Morse, Wayne, "Senator Thomas C. Hennings, Jr., and Civil Rights." *Missouri Law Review,* 26 (November, 1961), 420.

Nordheim, L. W., "Fear and Information." *Bulletin of the Atomic Scientists,* 10 (1954), 342.

Oakes, John B., "Report on McCarthy and McCarthyism." *New York Times Magazine* (November 2, 1952), 12.

O'Gara, James, "McCarthy: The Case Against Him." *Commonweal,* 57 (October 31, 1952), 91.

Palfrey, John G., "The AEC Security Program: Past and Present." *Bulletin of the Atomic Scientists,* 11 (April, 1955), 131.

Parker, Reginald, "The Right to go Abroad." *Virginia Law Review,* 40 (November, 1954), 853.

Pearson, Drew, "Washington Merry-Go-Round." *St. Louis Post-Dispatch,* January 7, 1953.

Phelps, John B., Ralph S. Brown, and S. A. Goudsmit, "Toward a Positive Security Program." *Bulletin of the Atomic Scientists,* 11 (April, 1955), 165.

Pollak, Louis H., "Proposals to Curtail Federal Habeas Corpus for State Prisoners: Collateral Attack on the Great Writ." *Yale Law Journal,* 66 (November, 1956), 50.

Prina, L. Edgar, "The Harry Cain 'Mutiny.'" *Collier's,* 136 (September 2, 1955), 32.

Rauh, Joseph L., Jr., *U. S. News and World Report,* 39 (August 26, 1955), 68.

————, "The Truth about Congress and the Court." *Progressive,* 22 (November, 1958), 30.

———, "Nonconfrontation in Security Cases: The Greene Decision." *Virginia Law Review,* 45 (November, 1959), 1175.

Rehnquist, William H., "The Bar Admission Cases: A Strange Judicial Aberration." *American Bar Association Journal,* 44 (March, 1958), 229.

Reston, James, *New York Times,* February 23, 1954; December 25, 1955.

Rodell, Fred, "Conflict over the Court." *Progressive,* 22 (December, 1958), 11.

Rosten, Leo, "Is Fear Destroying our Freedom?" *Look,* 18 (September 7, 1954), 21.

Rovere, Richard H., "Letter from Washington." *New Yorker,* 26 (May 13, 1950), 96.

———, "The Kept Witnesses." *Harper's,* 210 (May, 1955), 25.

———, "Letter from Washington." *New Yorker,* 33 (August 31, 1957), 72.

Schmandt, Henry J., "The Personnel of the 1943–1944 Missouri Constitutional Convention." *Missouri Historical Review,* 45 (April, 1951), 235.

Scientists' Committee on Loyalty and Security, "Fort Monmouth One Year Later." *Bulletin of the Atomic Scientists,* 11 (April, 1955), 148.

Segal, Benjamin D., and Joyce L. Kornbluh, "Government Security and Private Industry." *Reporter,* 16 (May 2, 1957), 25.

Shannon, William V., "The Administration and Civil Liberties." *Commonweal,* 59 (February 19, 1954), 490.

———, "Hubert Humphrey in Mid-Passage." *Progressive,* 22 (December, 1958), 19.

Shelton, Willard, "The Shame of the Senate." *Progressive,* 17 (February, 1953), 7.

Shils, Edward, "Security and Science Sacrificed to Loyalty." *Bulletin of the Atomic Scientists,* 11 (April, 1955), 106.

Silver, Edward S., "The Wiretapping-Eavesdropping Problem: A Prosecutor's View." *Minnesota Law Review,* 44 (April, 1960), 835.

Slotnick, Michael C., "The Anathema of the Security Risk: Arbitrary Dismissals of Federal Government Civilian Employees and Civilian Employees of Private Contractors Doing Business with the Federal Government." *University of Miami Law Review,* 17 (Fall, 1962), 10.

Smith, J. Malcolm, and Cornelius P. Cotter, "Freedom and Authority in the Amphibial State." *Midwest Journal of Political Science,* 1 (May, 1957), 40.

Speiser, Lawrence, "The Constitutional Rights Subcommittee: The Lengthened Shadow of One Man." *Missouri Law Review,* 26 (November, 1961), 449.

Stein, Jacob K., "The Defense of Army Security Risk Cases." *St. Louis University Law Journal,* 4 (Spring, 1956), 34.

Stephenson, Gilbert T., "The Story of a Trust Man." *Trusts and Estates,* 68 (April, 1939), 459.

Thompson, Dorothy, "Is There a Climate of Fear in America?" *Ladies' Home Journal,* 70 (September, 1953), 11.

Trussell, C. P., *New York Times,* December 28, 1951.

Warren, Earl, "The Law and the Future." *Fortune,* 52 (November, 1955), 106.

Westin, Alan F., "Wiretapping: The Quiet Revolution." *Commentary,* 29 (April, 1960), 333.

Whelan, Charles M., "Passports and Freedom of Travel: The Conflict of a Right and a Privilege." *Georgetown Law Journal,* 41 (November, 1952), 63.

White, Leonard D., "The Loyalty Program of the United States Government." *Bulletin of the Atomic Scientists,* 7 (December, 1951), 363.

White, William S., *New York Times,* September 29, 1951, and January 19 and 27, 1952.

———, "Democrats' Board of Directors." *New York Times Magazine* (July 10, 1955), 10.

Williams, Edward Bennett, "The Final Irony of Joe McCarthy." *Saturday Evening Post,* 235 (June 9, 1962), 21.

Wilson, H. H., "Why They Voted for McCarthy." *Nation,* 175 (September 20, 1952), 225.

———, "The Senate Sellout." *Nation,* 176 (January 24, 1953), 64.

Worthy, William, "Reporting in Communist China." *New Republic,* 136 (March 25, 1957), 9.

STAFF ARTICLES

Alabama Law Review, "Case Notes," 2 (Spring, 1950), 357.

America, 93 (August 27, 1955), 503; 94 (October 15, 1955), 60.

American Bar Association Journal, 37 (September, 1951), 673.

American Mercury, 78 (June, 1954), 109; 80 (June, 1955), 71.

Bulletin of the Atomic Scientists, "Government Loyalty Program," 9 (March, 1953), 63; "U.S. Security and Loyalty Programs," 9 (December, 1953), 387; 12 (March, 1956), 94; (May, 1956), 182; (June, 1956), 229; (September, 1956), 274; (December, 1956), 379.

Case and Comment, 60 (September–October, 1955), 3.

Christian Century, 67 (November 22, 1950), 1382; "Benton Invades Wisconsin," 69 (July 16, 1952), 821; "The Easy Road to Fame," 70 (January 21, 1953), 71; (September 23, 1953), 1068; 71 (June 9, 1954), 692; 72 (August 17, 1955), 940; (September 7, 1955), 1014; (October 12, 1955), 1163; 73 (June 27, 1956), 765.

Commonweal, "McCarthyism and the Campaign," 56 (September 12, 1952), 547; "Report on McCarthy," 57 (January 23, 1953), 393; 63 (December 2, 1955), 211; (December 16, 1955), 273; (January 20, 1956), 391; (February 24, 1956), 531; 66 (July 19, 1957), 412.

Congressional Digest, 29 (April, 1950), 97; "The Congressional Investigation—Its Authority, Record, Procedures, Future," 31 (May, 1952), 131; "Congress Acts on Supreme Court Decisions," 38 (October, 1959), 225.

Congressional Quarterly, 1 (1945), 79; 3 (1947), 85, 479; 4 (1948), 274; 5 (1949), 34; 6 (1950), 444.

Congressional Quarterly Almanac, 9 (1953), 70, 316, 334, 354; 10 (1954), 362, 366, 370, 375, 378, 456, 712–14; 11 (1955), 16, 27, 40, 383; 12 (1956), 579; 13 (1957), 34, 649, 659; 14 (1958), 297, 672, 716; 15 (1959), 47, 52, 54; 16 (1960), 232, 281, 322.

DePaul Law Review, "Criminal Procedure—Admissibility of Wiretap Evidence in State Courts," 12 (Autumn–Winter, 1962), 159.

Economist, "Return to Sanity" (July 2, 1955); "American Survey" (March 19, 1960).

Federal Bar Journal, "A Symposium on Congressional Hearings and Investigations," 14:1 and 2 (1954), entire issues; 19 (January, 1959), entire issue.

Harvard Law Review, "The Supreme Court, 1958 Term," 73 (November, 1959), 159, 196; "The Supreme Court, 1959 Term," 74 (November, 1960), 1.

Marquette Law Review, "Problems of Communications in a Pluralistic Society: A Symposium," 40 (Summer, 1956), entire issue.

Mirror, 10 (February 7, 1901), 4.

Missouri Law Review, 15 (January, 1950), 111.

Nation, 167 (November 13, 1948), 540; 171 (October 28, 1950), 385; (November 4, 1950), 405; "The Elections" (November 18, 1950), 451; "This Terrible Business," 173 (August 25, 1951), 142; "Joe Stubs His Toe" (October 6, 1951), 271; "The Shape of Things" (December 22, 1951), 537; 174 (April 5, 1952), 309; "Wisconsin: Wave of the Future," 175 (September 20, 1952), 223;

"Why They Voted for McCarthy" (September 20, 1952), 225; "Revolt Against McCarthy," 176 (March 7, 1953), 198; 178 (June 5, 1954), 474; 180 (April 9, 1955), 298; "That Man Lattimore," 181 (July 16, 1955), 45; "The Army Security Program" (August 20, 1955), 147; (November 26, 1955), 450; 182 (January 14, 1956), 21; (September 22, 1956), 250; 187 (October 11, 1958), 202.

Nation's Business, "Industry Goal: Simple Employee Loyalty Check," 43 (December, 1955), 40.

National Review, 1 (November 19, 1955), 12; (December 14, 1955), 12; (January 4, 1956), 4; (January 11, 1956), 15.

New Republic, 117 (August 11, 1947), 10; 119 (November 15, 1948), 6; 121 (August 1, 1949), 8; (November 11, 1949), 9; 122 (April 3, 1950), 12; 123 (October 9, 1950), 9; (October 30, 1950), 7; (November 20, 1950), 7; "Benton v. McCarthy," 125 (September 17, 1951), 8; "McCarthy Inquiry" (October 22, 1951), 6; "Ten Grand for Joe" (November 26, 1951), 7; 128 (January 12, 1953), 3; "The Financial Affairs of McCarthy" (March 30, 1953), 12; 130 (June 7, 1954), 6; 132 (January 31, 1955), 6; "Follow that Mother!" 133 (August 15, 1955), 4; (October 3, 1955), 18; "Senator Sourwine Investigates the Press," 134 (January 16, 1956), 3; (February 13, 1956), 9; "Cain's Conscience," 135 (November 5, 1956), 2.

New Yorker, 35 (May 16, 1959), 92.

Newsweek, 36 (October 23, 1950), 36; (November 13, 1950), 23; "Democrats Fume at McCarthy, But He Has Them Terrorized," 38 (August 20, 1951), 19; "Vote on McCarthy," 39 (March 17, 1952), 26; "Slicing the Bundle" (June 9, 1952), 28; "McCarthy on Benton," 40 (July 14, 1952), 32; "A Hunter Hunted," 41 (January 12, 1953), 17; "Why Langer's Outburst," 43 (March 1, 1954), 19; 45 (March 28, 1955), 24; 46 (October 17, 1955), 78.

Northwestern University Law Review, 51 (January–February, 1957), 788.

Progressive, 18 (April, 1954), entire issue on McCarthy; "Is This the End of McCarthy?" (November, 1954), 3.

Reporter, "The Road to Damascus," 12 (February 10, 1955), 4; (May 5, 1955), 4; 13 (October 20, 1955), 4; 14 (January 12, 1956), 4; 22 (February 18, 1960), 6.

Saturday Evening Post, 224 (February 16, 1952), 10; 226 (May 1, 1954), 10; 228 (July 23, 1955), 10; 230 (April 19, 1958), 10.

Saturday Review, 38 (May 14, 1955), 14.

Science, 124 (August 3, 1956), 201, 210; (October 26, 1956), 821.

Stanford Law Review, "The Role of Employer Practices in the Federal Industrial Personnel Security Program—A Field Study," 8 (March, 1956), 234.

Time, 42 (August 16, 1943), 22; 56 (November 13, 1950), 19; "The Wisconsin Primary," 60 (September 22, 1952), 23; 65 (June 27, 1955), 18; 67 (January 16, 1956), 56; "Digger on Capitol Hill," 73 (March 16, 1959), 74.

U.S. News and World Report, 25 (November 12, 1948), 26; "Candidates Explain Outcome," 29 (November 17, 1950), 14, 34; "The McCarthy Issue," 31 (September 7, 1951), 24; "McCarthyism: Is It a Trend?" 33 (September 19, 1952), 21; 35 (October 30, 1953), 99; 39 (August 26, 1955), 40; (September 9, 1955), 128; 40 (February 24, 1956), 56; 41 (July 13, 1956), 118; 43 (July 5, 1957), 86.

NEWSPAPERS

Baltimore *Sun.* November, 1955; July, 1957.

Cape Girardeau *Southeast Missourian.* September–November, 1950.

Chicago Tribune. September, 1951; October, 1955; February, 1958.

Christian Advocate. October 20 and 21, 1955.

Christian Science Monitor. September, 1951; November, 1955; February, 1960.

Columbia Missourian. May, 1950.

Columbia Tribune. September–November, 1950.

Des Moines Register. December, 1954; January, 1955.

Detroit News. March, 1960.

Dubuque *Witness.* September, 1955.

Hannibal Courier-Post. July, 1950.

I. F. Stone's Weekly. March 3 and 17, 1958.

Jefferson City *Daily Capital News.* October, 1950.

Jefferson City Post-Tribune. July, 1949; September, October, November, 1950.

Jefferson City Sunday News and Tribune. October, 1950.

Joplin Globe. September–November, 1950.

Kansas City Star (Times). July, December, 1949; April, July, October, November, 1950; August, 1951; September, November, 1955; April, 1958; April, 1959.

Kirksville Daily Express. September–November, 1950.

Labor's Daily. July, 1953; March, 1958.

Los Angeles Examiner. October, 1950; November, 1955.

Los Angeles Times. November, 1959.
Louisville Courier-Journal. September, 1951; May, 1954.
Macon Chronicle-Herald. September–November, 1950.
Madison Capital Times. January, 1953.
Manchester Guardian. September, 1951.
Mexico Evening Ledger. October, 1950.
Miami Daily News. September, 1951.
Minneapolis Star. July, 1957.
El Mundo (San Juan, Puerto Rico). May, 1942.
Our Sunday Visitor. October 2, 1955.
Nevada Daily Mail. September–November, 1950.
New York Daily News. September, 1955; July, 1957.
New York *Daily Worker.* July–December, 1955.
New York Herald-Tribune. September, November, December, 1955.
New York Journal-American. November, 1955.
New York Post. October, 1955; January, 1956; February, 1960.
New York Times. May, 1942; 1950–1960.
Poplar Bluff *Daily American Republic.* September–November, 1950.
St. Joseph News-Press. May, September, October, November, 1950; November, 1955.
St. Louis American. October, 1936.
St. Louis Argus. October, 1938.
St. Louis Call. September, 1940.
St. Louis Globe-Democrat. March, April, 1927; April, 1928; October, 1934; November, 1938; June, 1940; April, September, 1943; July, 1949–1960.
St. Louis Post-Dispatch. April, 1927; April, 1934; September, 1940; August, 1941; September, 1942; April, May, June, August, September, 1943; November, 1945; July, 1949–1960.
St. Louis Star-Times. August, 1938; June, 1942; April, May, June, September, 1943; January, 1944; January, July, October, December, 1941–December, 1950.
Sedalia Democrat. September–November, 1950.
Sikeston Daily Standard. September–November, 1950.
Springfield Leader-Press. September–November, 1950.
Tampa Tribune. February, 1959.
Wall Street Journal. March, 1958.
Washington Daily News. January, 1953; September, October, November, 1955; April, 1958; January, 1959.
Washington Post (and *Times-Herald*). July, 1951; March, November, 1952; January, June, August, October, November, December, 1955;

February, 1956; February, April, October, 1958; February, March, 1960.
Washington *Evening Star.* July, 1949; September, 1951; March, 1952; January, August, September, November, December, 1955; January, 1956; February, 1958; March, 1958.
Washington Times-Herald. July, 1949; July, 1951.

COURT CASES

Bailey v. Richardson, 182 F. 2d 46 (1950), 341 U.S. 918 (1951).
Barenblatt v. United States, 360 U.S. 109 (1959).
Bauer v. Acheson, 106 F. Supp. 445 (D.D.C. 1952).
Benanti v. United States, 355 U.S. 96 (1957).
Boudin v. Dulles, 136 F. Supp. 218 (D.D.C. 1955), 235 F. 2d 532 (D.C.Cir. 1956).
Bridges v. United States, 346 U.S. 209 (1953).
Briehl v. Dulles (Kent v. Dulles), 357 U.S. 116 (1958).
Brown v. Topeka, 347 U.S. 483 (1954), 349 U.S. 294 (1955).
Cole v. Young, 351 U.S. 536 (1956).
Dayton v. Dulles, 357 U.S. 144 (1958).
Dennis v. United States, 341 U.S. 494 (1951).
Elkins v. United States, 346 U.S. 206 (1960).
Emspak v. United States, 349 U.S. 190 (1955).
Ex parte McCardle, 7 Wall. 566 (1869).
Goldman v. United States, 316 U.S. 129 (1942).
Greene v. McElroy, 360 U.S. 474 (1959).
Harmon v. Brucker (Abramowitz v. Brucker), 355 U.S. 579 (1958).
Jencks v. United States, 353 U.S. 657 (1957).
Knauff v. Shaughnessey, 338 U.S. 537 (1950).
Lopez v. United States, 373 U.S. 427 (1963).
Mallory v. United States, 354 U.S. 449 (1957).
Mapp v. United States, 367 U.S. 643 (1961).
Olmstead v. United States, 277 U.S. 438 (1928).
On Lee v. United States, 343 U.S. 747 (1952).
Parker v. Lester, 227 F. 2d 708 (9th Cir. 1955).
Pennsylvania v. Nelson, 350 U.S. 497 (1956).
Peters v. Hobby, 349 U.S. 331 (1955).
Pugach v. Dollinger, 365 U.S. 458 (1961).
Railway Employees v. Hanson, 351 U.S. 225 (1956).
Schactman v. Dulles, 225 F. 2d 938 (D.C.Cir. 1955).
Schustack v. Herren, 234 F. 2d 134 (2d Cir. 1956).
Schware v. New Mexico, 353 U.S. 232 (1957).

Silverman v. United States, 365 U.S. 505 (1961).
Slochower v. Board, 350 U.S. 551 (1956).
Sweezy v. New Hampshire, 354 U.S. 234 (1957).
United States v. Flynn, 130 F. Supp. 412 (1955), 131 F. Supp. 742 (1955).
United States v. Lattimore, 112 F. Supp. 507 (D.D.C. 1953), 215 F. 2d 847 (D.C.Cir. 1954), 127 F. Supp. 405 (D.D.C. 1955), 232 F. 2d 334 (D.C.Cir. 1955).
Uphaus v. Wyman, 360 U.S. 72 (1959).
Vitarelli v. Seaton, 359 U.S. 535 (1959).
Watkins v. United States, 354 U.S. 178 (1957).
Yates v. United States, 354 U.S. 298 (1957).

PUBLIC DOCUMENTS

State of Missouri, *Official Manual of the State of Missouri, 1913-1914; 1933-1934; 1947-1948; 1951-1952; 1957-1958.* Jefferson City.
U. S. Commission on Government Security. *Report pursuant to Public Law 304, 84th Cong., as amended.* Washington, 1957.
U. S. Congress. Commission on Organization of the Executive Branch of the Government. *Legal Services and Procedure.* March, 1955.
U. S. *Congressional Record.* Relevant issues.
U. S. Department of Defense. *Industrial Personnel Security Review Program, First Annual Report.* 1956.
U. S. House of Representatives. Committee on Foreign Affairs. Report No. 2684, 85th Cong., 2d Sess., 1958.
U. S. House of Representatives. Committee on Government Operations. Report No. 2947, 84th Cong., 2d Sess., 1956. Reports No. 157 and No. 1619, 85th Cong., 1st Sess., 1957. Reports No. 1884 and No. 2578, 85th Cong., 2d Sess., 1958. Reports No. 234 and No. 1137, 86th Cong., 1st Sess., 1959. Reports No. 1224, No. 2084, and No. 2207, 86th Cong., 2d Sess., 1960.
U. S. House of Representatives. Committee on Government Operations, Special Subcommittee on Government Information. *Hearings,* Parts 1-17, 84th Cong., 1st Sess., 1955.
U. S. House of Representatives. Judiciary Committee. Reports No. 1815, No. 1878, and No. 2495, 85th Cong., 2d Sess., 1958.
U. S. House of Representatives. Judiciary Committee, Special Subcommittee to Study Decisions of the Supreme Court. *Hearings,* Part 1, 85th Cong., 2d Sess., 1958.
U. S. House of Representatives. Post Office and Civil Service Committee. Report No. 1201, 85th Cong., 1st Sess., 1957. Report No. 2687, 85th Cong., 2d Sess., 1958.

U. S. Senate. Committee on Government Operations, Subcommittee on Reorganization. *Hearings,* 84th Cong., 1st Sess., 1955.

U. S. Senate. Judiciary Committee. Reports No. 1586, No. 1621, No. 2228, No. 2230, and No. 2252, 85th Cong., 2d Sess., 1958. Report No. 1811, Parts 1 and 2, 86th Cong., 2d Sess., 1960.

U. S. Senate. Judiciary Committee, Subcommittee on Constitutional Rights. *Hearings,* Part 1; Citizens' Petition for the Redress of Grievances, *Hearings,* 84th Cong., 1st Sess., 1955. *Hearings,* Parts 1 and 2, 85th Cong., 2d Sess., 1958. *Hearings,* Parts 1, 2, 3, and 4, 86th Cong., 1st Sess., 1959. *Memorandum of Instructions to Staff of the Subcommittee on Constitutional Rights of the Committee on the Judiciary,* Committee Print, 84th Cong., 1st Sess., July 30, 1955. *Background Materials on a Comprehensive Federal Public Records Law—State Public Records Statutes and Notes on Related Court Decisions Compiled by the Constitutional Rights Subcommittee,* Committee Print, 86th Cong., 2d Sess., 1960.

U. S. Senate. Judiciary Committee, Subcommittee on Internal Security. *Hearings,* Parts 1–12, 84th Cong., 1st Sess., 1955. *Hearings,* Parts 1 and 2, 85th Cong., 1st Sess., 1957. *Hearings,* 86th Cong., 1st Sess., 1959.

U. S. Senate. Judiciary Committee, Subcommittee on Juvenile Delinquency. *Hearings,* 83rd Cong., 2d Sess., 1954. *Hearings,* 84th Cong., 1st Sess., 1955. Report No. 137, 86th Cong., 1st Sess., 1959.

U. S. Senate. Committee on Post Office and Civil Service. Report No. 2750, 84th Cong., 2d Sess., 1956.

U. S. Senate. Committee on Post Office and Civil Service, Subcommittee to Investigate the Government Employee Security Program. *Hearings,* Parts 1 and 2, 84th Cong., 1st Sess., 1955.

U. S. Senate. Committee on Rules and Administration. Report No. 647, 81st Cong., 2d Sess., 1950. Report No. 647, 82nd Cong., 1st Sess., 1951. Report No. 1081, 83d Cong., 2d Sess., 1954. Report No. 236, 84th Cong., 1st Sess., 1955. Report No. 23, 85th Cong., 1st Sess., 1957. Report No. 1203, 85th Cong., 2d Sess., 1958. Reports No. 31 and No. 429, 86th Cong., 1st Sess., 1959.

U. S. Senate. Committee on Rules and Administration, Subcommittee on Privileges and Elections. Report on S. Res. 187 and S. Res. 304, Committee Print, 82nd Cong., 2d Sess., 1952. *Hearings,* Part 1, 82nd Cong., 1st Sess., 1952.

U. S. Senate. *Rules and Manual of the United States Senate.* 1955.

U. S. Senate. Select Committee to Study Censure Charges. Report No. 2508, 83d Cong., 2d Sess., 1954. *Hearings,* Parts 1 and 2, 83d Cong., 2d Sess., 1954.

U. S. Senate. Special Committee on Investigation of Cover on Mail of Senators. Report No. 2510, 83d Cong., 2d Sess., 1954.

UNPUBLISHED WORKS

Beck, Carl, "Contempt of Congress: A Study of the Prosecutions Initiated by the House Committee on Un-American Activities." Doctoral dissertation, Duke University, 1959.

Brown, William H., "Judicial Review of Congressional Investigative Powers with Special Reference to the Period 1945–1957." Doctoral dissertation, American University, 1959.

Cooper, Joseph, "Congress and Its Committees: A Historical and Theoretical Approach to the Proper Role of Committees in the Legislative Process." Doctoral dissertation, Harvard University, 1960–1961.

Frye, Robert J., "Deportation of Aliens: A Study in Civil Liberties." Doctoral dissertation, University of Florida, 1959.

Goodsell, Charles T., "Congressional Access to Executive Information: A Problem of Legislative-Executive Relations in American National Government." Doctoral dissertation, Harvard University, 1960-1961.

Harris, Morron D., "Political Trends in Missouri." Master's thesis, University of Missouri, 1953.

Heubel, Edward J., "Reorganization and Reform of Congressional Investigations, 1945–1955." Doctoral dissertation, University of Minnesota, 1955.

Hobbe, Donald, "The Role of the Security Officer in Federal Administration." Master's thesis, University of Wisconsin, 1954.

Keele, Robert L., "The Supreme Court, Totalitarianism, and the National Security of Democratic America, 1941–1960." Doctoral dissertation, Emory University, 1960.

Koehler, H. James, "Total Security: A Critique of the Eisenhower Security Program." Senior thesis, Princeton University, 1956.

Meyer, Karl Ernest, "The Politics of Loyalty, from LaFollette to McCarthy in Wisconsin: 1918–1952." Doctoral dissertation, Princeton University, 1956.

Palamiotis, Alexander A., "The Citizen and Alien in American Constitutional Law." Doctoral dissertation, University of Utah, 1959.

Schmidtlein, Eugene F., "Truman the Senator." Doctoral dissertation, University of Missouri, 1962.

Shapiro, Martin Matthew, "The Supreme Court and the First Amendment." Doctoral dissertation, Harvard University, 1960–1961.

Straus, Melvin Potter, "The Control of Subversive Activities in Canada." Doctoral dissertation, University of Illinois, 1959.

Vestal, Theodore M., "The Warren Court and Civil Liberties." Doctoral dissertation, Stanford University, 1962.

Worth, Stephen W., "The Congressional Investigating Committee as an Instrument of Subversive Control: An Analysis of the Nature of the Committee, Its Procedures, and Its Scope of Inquiry." Doctoral dissertation, University of Washington, 1957.

COLLECTIONS

John T. Barker. Western Historical Manuscripts Collection, University of Missouri, Columbia.

Jesse W. Barrett. Western Historical Manuscripts Collection, University of Missouri, Columbia.

John Raeburn Green. Personal papers, St. Louis, Missouri.

Thomas C. Hennings, Jr. Western Historical Manuscripts Collection, University of Missouri, Columbia.

Thomas C. Hennings, Jr. Missouri Historical Society, St. Louis.

Thomas C. Hennings, Sr. Missouri Historical Society, St. Louis.

Stratford Lee Morton. Western Historical Manuscripts Collection, University of Missouri, Columbia.

Guy B. Park. Western Historical Manuscripts Collection, University of Missouri, Columbia.

V. E. Phillips. Western Historical Manuscripts Collection, University of Missouri, Columbia.

Franklin D. Roosevelt. Roosevelt Library, Hyde Park, New York.

Senate Subcommittee on Constitutional Rights. Senate Office Building, Washington, D. C.

Kimbrough Stone. Western Historical Manuscripts Collection, University of Missouri, Columbia.

Harry S Truman. Truman Library, Independence, Missouri.

INTERVIEWS

Robert L. Bevan, administrative assistant to Hennings. May, 1962.

Richard L. Carp, assistant counsel, Subcommittee on Constitutional Rights. May, 1962.

John R. Cauley, Washington correspondent, *Kansas City Star.* May, 1962.

Irving Dilliard, editor of editorial page, *St. Louis Post-Dispatch.* June, 1962.

John F. Doherty, first assistant to Assistant Attorney General, Department of Justice, Internal Security Division. May, 1962.

Bernard Fensterwald, Jr., administrative assistant to Hennings. May, 1962.

Benjamin Ginzburg, research director, Subcommittee on Constitutional Rights. May, 1962.

John Raeburn Green, Hennings' law partner. June, 1962.

Thomas J. Guilfoil, attorney. June, 1962.

Mrs. Thomas C. Hennings, Jr. May, 1962.

Mrs. Thomas C. Hennings, Sr. June, 1963.

Lon Hocker, chief counsel, Subcommittee on Constitutional Rights. June, 1962.

Marcia MacNaughton, research assistant, Subcommittee on Constitutional Rights. May, 1962.

Sadi J. Masé, adviser to Subcommittee on Constitutional Rights. May, 1962.

Joseph C. O'Mahoney, member, Subcommittee on Constitutional Rights. May, 1962.

John G. Scott, secretary to Representative Hennings. June and July, 1962 (by letter).

Belva T. Simmons, research assistant, Subcommittee on Constitutional Rights. May, 1962.

Charles H. Slayman, chief counsel, Subcommittee on Constitutional Rights. May, 1962.

Lawrence Speiser, director, Washington office of American Civil Liberties Union. May, 1962 (by telephone).

Harry S Truman, October, 1963.

Langdon C. West, administrative assistant to Hennings. May, 1962.

Thomas Yarbrough, *St. Louis Post-Dispatch*. June, 1962 (by telephone).

Index

Abolitionists: Supreme Court attacked by, 143

Abramowitz v. Brucker, 123*n*

Acheson, Dean: McCarthy's attack on, 28

Adams, John: McCarthy's conflict with, 190

Administrative Criminal Law: individual rights under, 100; Hennings' concern with, 109–13, 115, 125

Advisory Council of the Democratic National Committee, 171

Alien Registration Act of 1940 (Smith Act). *See* Subversives, legislation against

Aliens: antisubversive legislation on, 6, 8, 9, 9*n*; and Bill of Rights, 8

Allen, A. Leonard, 9

Allison, Emery W.: and 1950 primary, 18–19, 19*n*, 20, 20*n*, 21, 22*n*

Anglo-Saxon law, 111

American Bar Association: and the Court fight, 166, 178, 179, 185*n*

American Bar Association Journal, 45

American Civil Liberties Union, 12, 33, 196, 205

American Farm Bureau Federation, 144

American Jewish Congress, 104

American Legion, 42

American Political Science Association, 104

American University, 104

Americans for Democratic Action, 73, 130

Anderson, Jack, 55

Anti-Defamation League of B'nai B'rith, 106*n*

Association of the Bar of the City of New York: Special Committee on the Federal Loyalty-Security Program of, 126, 127, 140, 141

Attorney General's list: and loyalty-security procedures, 75, 75*n*; origin of, 78; proposed abolition of, 99, 108, 111; expansion of, 116–17; use of, 119, 136

Bailey v. Richardson: explanation of, 77*n*; significance of, 114*n*

Baker, Tom F., 41

Baptist Joint Committee on Public Affairs, 106*n*

Barenblatt v. United States: decision in, 183

Barrett, Frank A., 89

Bauer v. Acheson: significance of, 120*n*, 162*n*

Becker, William H., 20*n*
Benanti v. United States: decision in, 199; significance of, 201, 204
Benesch, Aaron, 132*n*
Bennett, Wallace, 62, 62*n*
Benson, Ezra Taft: and Ladejinsky case, 94, 95, 128
Bentley, Elizabeth: and Subcommittee on Constitutional Rights, 107, 108
Benton, William: anti-McCarthy proposals of, 40–47, 40*n*, 49-50, 52, 53*n*, 55–57, 67, 68*n*, 72; proposed expulsion of, 54, 54*n*, 55, 67; Hennings' report on, 58
Bethesda Naval Hospital, 53
Bevan, Robert, 153*n*, 183*n*, 196*n*, 202*n*, 205*n*, 212*n*
Big Brothers, 3
Bill of Rights: and Senator Hennings' career, 3; Hennings' eulogy of, 8; and rights of aliens, 8; and Bridges bill, 9; impact on Hennings of, 22; Hennings' defense of, 23; and Cold War, 24; erosion of, 100–102; Hennings' study of, 102; and the Eisenhower security program, 113; Hennings' defense of, 131, 150, 207; and internal security, 155; Warren's speech on, 184; dangers to, 205; Hennings' devotion to, 210; mention of, xi, 168
—First Amendment: and Smith Act, 6; threats to, 6; Hennings' concern for, 103; religion clause of, 103–4; extent of, 115; and security program, 115; abandonment of, 117; and freedom of information, 191; mention of, 100, 215
—Fourth Amendment: and wire tapping, 201–3
—Fifth Amendment: Hennings' concern for, 84; due process demands of, 119–20; and passport issue, 160–63; mention of, 97, 100, 144, 156
Billington, Ray A., 104*n*
Biltmore Hotel, 96
Binaggio, Charles: and the 1950 primary, 17, 19–20, 20*n*
Black, Hugo, 183

Blair, James T., Jr., 20*n*, 146*n*
Blanshard, Paul, 105*n*
Block, Herb, 30*n*
Bolling, Richard, 31*n*
Bontecou, Eleanor, 135*n*, 136
Boudin v. Dulles, 113*n*
Bower, Robert T., 105*n*
Bowers, Claude, 4, 4*n*
Boyle, William M., 40
Bozell, Brent, 166–67
Bradley, Edwin J., 201
Brannon, John, 196*n*, 205*n*
Brenkworth, Robert A., 129*n*
Brennan, William, 183
Bricker, John W., 88, 183*n*
Bricker Amendment: Hennings' opposition to, 88–90; Hennings' concern with, 211, 212; mention of, 170
Bridges, Harry R.: attempted deportation of, 9, 9*n*
Briehl v. Dulles, 162
Briggs, Frank P., 15
Browder, Earl, 39
Brown, Constantine, 48
Brown, Richard, 105*n*, 106*n*, 212*n*
Brown v. Board of Education of Topeka: and Court fight, 143, 151, 173–75
Brownell, Herbert, Jr.: and the Eisenhower security program, 79, 80, 99, 127–28, 128*n*; Hennings' conflict with, 136–40; and the Court fight, 155
Brucker, Wilbur M., 122*n*
Buckley, Daniel: and McCarthy investigation, 56, 66, 69
Buckley, William, Jr., 129
Bureau of Social Science Research, 104
Burkhart, James A., 33*n*
Butler, John M.: and the 1950 Maryland election, 36–40, 37*n*; and the industrial security program, 116, 116*n*; and the Court fight, 149–51; anti-Court proposals of, 166–71, 170*n*, 173–75, 179; amendment by, 185*n*
Butler, Paul M., 199*n*, 214

Cain, Harry P.: attack on Eisenhower security programs by, 94, 98–99;

G